THE COMPLETE BOOK OF
PAINT

Liz Wagstaff   Richard Lowther   Lynne Robinson

THE COMPLETE BOOK OF
PAINT

70 Techniques, Finishes and Designs for Your Home

CHRONICLE BOOKS
SAN FRANCISCO

p. 1: *Tones of a hue are created by adding white or umber (see pp. 30–2)*

pp. 2–3: *Chequerboard table tops with asymmetrical sections (see pp. 212–15)*

p. 5: *Stamped oak-leaf borders in three colourways (see pp. 142–3)*

First published in the United States in 2005 by Chronicle Books LLC.

Portions of this book were previously published in *Paint Recipes* and *Decorative Paint Recipes.*

Library of Congress Cataloging-in-Publication Data available.

ISBN 0-8118-4947-3

Manufactured in China

Art Director: Mary Evans

Editorial Director: Jane O'Shea

Design: Sarah Emery

Production Manager: Rachel Wells

Cover design: Tim Belonax

Distributed in Canada by Raincoast Books

9050 Shaughnessy Street

Vancouver, British Columbia V6P 6E5

10 9 8 7 6 5 4 3 2 1

Chronicle Books LLC

85 Second Street

San Francisco, California 94105

www.chroniclebooks.com

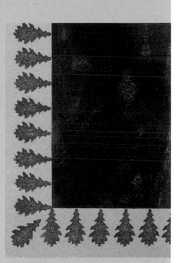

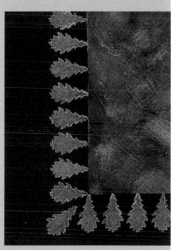

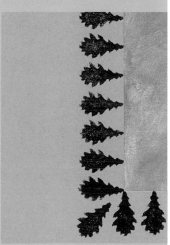

CONTENTS

PART ONE

GETTING STARTED

Everything you need to know about materials, equipment, techniques, and preparing the surface before you begin, plus special guidance on planning, choosing, and changing color and how to use the recipes

A checkerboard table top (see pp. 212–15) in sage green and red relies on a steady hand to paint the checks on the sponged-on base coat. Artists' brushes, screw-top jars for mixing the paint, and some saucers to use as palettes are the only equipment you will need for this stage.

THE PAINT

Most of our techniques and projects have been carried out with modern, water-based paints. They are safe to work with, usually odorless, and quick to dry. If you prefer to adapt any recipe to use oil-based media or traditional water-based paints such as milk paints, you must adjust the coloring material to suit (see chart) and make allowances for the differences in the way the paint behaves.

At the heart of many of our recipes is white latex flat paint. Do choose a good-quality one. Paints offered at bargain prices may be tempting, but in our experience they are loaded with so much chalky pigment that the resulting finish is not only lamentable, it is also too absorbent. High-quality latex paints perform well and make an excellent base for the addition of color. When we want a dark tone, we start with a base closer to our goal—black or red, for example.

To color the latex paint, we rely heavily on artists' acrylic colors. Although expensive compared to ordinary household paint, the quality of the pigment is high, and you need only a little to bring about a color change. Occasionally we make use of powder pigments. Unfortunately, many are toxic, especially if inhaled or handled. If you are using these, refer carefully to the manufacturers' instructions. If you decide to use latex semigloss or decorators' acrylic paint instead of latex flat, the color can also be modified with artists' acrylic colors.

A few of our recipes require oil-based materials. Chosen often for their superior durability or appearance, these paints have slower drying times. This means they can be worked for longer—an advantage when creating some textural effects. As the chart indicates, oil-based eggshell and floor paint can be colored with artists' oil colors or powder pigment. Gloss paint is less accommodating—coarse pigment reduces its reflective quality, turning the gloss to a satin finish—and therefore we would use only tiny amounts of artists' oils to color them.

PAINT TYPE	COLOR WITH	THIN WITH
WATER-BASED		
• Acrylic "milk" paint • Decorators' acrylic • "Eggshell" paint • Floor paint • Masonry paint • Latex flat • Latex semigloss	Artists' acrylic color or powder pigment	Water
• Casein/milk paint	Powder pigment	Water
OIL-BASED		
• Alkyd eggshell/satin • Floor paint • Masonry paint	Artists' oil color or powder pigment	Mineral spirits
• Gloss paint	Artists' oil color	Mineral spirits

LATEX PAINTS
Besides being widely available, latex paints readily mix with artists' acrylic colors. Four of these swatches began life as brilliant white. The fifth has black as its base. Each has had one or more colors added to produce the hues (see p. 30) found here.

POWDER PIGMENTS
These are a way to color paint. Their advantage is that they can be mixed with any type of paint. This can be handy if you are using a mix of media—for example latex flat for walls and oil-based paint for door and window frames. The color range is smaller than that of artists' acrylics— you will not find neutral gray, for instance—but it does include metallic finishes (see p. 19), which the artists' acrylics do not. Once the only option for coloring paint, powder pigments are still considered the quality color by some.

ARTISTS' COLORS
Acrylic colors (left) are used to color water-based materials, while oil colors are used for oil-based materials. Both are available in more hues than is strictly necessary. Buy top-quality products for the strongest pigments. Acrylics are normally sold as a thick paste, useful for stenciling, but are also available in a more fluid consistency. The color is just as powerful, but it is easier to apply, and it mixes more readily.

SPECIALIST PAINTS

Latex paint provides a fairly tough finish and, in conjunction with varnish, can be used for a surprising range of applications. Some of our floor and table top projects have latex paint as their base. Latex can also be turned into a more specialist paint by the simple addition of glazing liquid or white glue (see pp. 13 and 15).

Occasionally we have used a specialist paint to satisfy a particular need. Many of those on the market, such as colorwash, can be made at home, but one we do like is an acrylic-based paint formulated to look like traditional milk paint. It dries to a matte finish and, if you wish, can be rubbed back to imitate the wear and patina of an old piece of painted furniture. However, such treatment, popular though it is, belies one of milk paint's most notable characteristics—the fact that it is hardwearing and extremely durable.

Other specialist paints are sometimes needed for fitness of purpose rather than for their looks. For a well-sealed, durable, painted surface on a concrete floor, we would use an oil-based floor paint. It is specified for use on garage and car-showroom floors, so it should be capable of standing up to normal domestic wear and tear. Some of the simple wall finishes in Part Two are suitable for exterior use, and for these we suggest substituting a hardwearing, smooth masonry paint for the standard latex base coat. To emulate a decorative iron finish (see p. 18), we co-opt the opaque black of chalkboard paint.

Artists' suppliers stock a wealth of other specialist products. Among these are glass paints, one of which is used to create stained-glass effects, while another is a frosting varnish that is an alternative to etching your windows with etching cream or having them sand-blasted. You are unlikely to fool anyone with these products, so just treat them as decorative paints in the same way as we do.

MILK PAINTS
These are not always widely available, but they can be made at home from casein, borax, and powder pigments. The result will be a breathing, non-toxic traditional paint. Modern versions—also non-toxic—are bound with acrylic.

FLOOR PAINTS
These come in a wide variety of media but not always in a wide range of colors. Here we show one bound with an alkyd resin—the most common binder for all kinds of modern house-hold paints—reinforced with polyurethane for extra hardness. Choose a satin finish: a gloss finish will highlight any imperfections. Alternative treat-ments for floors include water- or spirit-based stains or colored varnishes.

GLASS PAINTS

GLASS PAINTS
Those we use are cellulose-based. They are quick-drying, almost impossible to brush out smoothly, highly flammable, and cannot take a second coat since the solvent in the paint softens the layer of paint below. If you are prepared for all that, you can get some colorful results with them.

FROSTING VARNISHES
Acrylic-based, these are more user-friendly than other glass paints. They produce a convin-cing frosted finish when sponged on, and can be tinted or, as here, colored with metallic and irides-cent powders. For an etched-glass look, use them with stencils or masking tape, but don't be afraid to brush or stamp them on, too.

SOLVENTS & GLAZES

Most of the glaze recipes include a glazing liquid and/or a solvent. Glazing liquid is a transparent medium which extends the working time of paint, giving it permanent translucency for decorative effect. It is available in water-based and oil-based form. Solvents also lengthen the working time; one is suitable for water-based materials, the others for oil-based. The right solvent for the job is also the right cleaner, and that applies to your brushes *and* your mistakes. Other useful thinner/cleaners include cellulose and isopropyl alcohol (see pp. 26–7).

SOLVENTS OR THINNERS

TYPE	USES	MIX WITH	TOXICITY
Water	Cleans and thins all water-based products. Also use to disperse water-based glazes for decorative effect.	Transparent acrylic glazing liquid and latex paint to create glazes, or with acrylic varnish	Toxic when mixed
Mineral spirits	Cleans and thins many oil-based products. Alternative: turpentine.	Transparent oil-based glazing liquid and eggshell paint to create glazes, or with gloss paint and some varnishes	High
Denatured alcohol	Cleans and thins many oil-based products. Also use to disperse water-based glazes for decorative effect.	Shellac or French enamel varnish	High

WATER-ON-OIL RESIST
Water sprayed onto an oil glaze and left to evaporate leaves distinctive circles— a useful texturing technique.

DISTRESSING PAINT WITH DENATURED ALCOHOL
Solvent rubbed into a dry coat of latex flat paint will create an aged look.

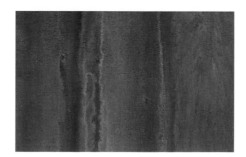

DISPERSING GLAZE WITH DENATURED ALCOHOL
Although normally used with oil-based products, denatured alcohol can be used to "weather" a water-based glaze.

INCREASING TRANSLUCENCY
Colorwashing is a good example of the effects of glazing liquid (here the water-based form) on a glaze-mix. Parts of the base color remain visible.

INCREASING THE WORKING TIME
Dragging requires long, continuous brushstrokes. Adding oil-based glazing liquid to the glaze-mix gives you more time to work the paint before it dries.

GLAZES

TYPE	USES	MIX WITH	TINT WITH	THINNER / CLEANER	TOXICITY
Acrylic or water-based glazing liquid (transparent)	Makes paint appear translucent and lengthens the time it can be worked. Use with water-based paint and varnish.	Latex paint or acrylic varnish	Artists' acrylic color or powder pigment	Water	Medium
Patina (also called antiquing patina)	Ages a variety of decorative paint finishes — in particular, water-based crackle.		Artists' acrylic color	Water	Medium
Linseed oil	An ingredient of oil-based glazing liquid (see below), but also used separately to thin or extend the working time of oil color.	Artists' oil color	Artists' oil color	Mineral spirits	High when mixed
Oil-based glazing liquid (transparent)	Makes paint appear translucent and lengthens the time it can be worked. Use with oil-based paint and varnish.	Eggshell or gloss paint, or matte polyurethane varnish	Artists' oil color or powder pigment	Mineral spirits	High

PATINA
Available in umbers and siennas for aging water-based finishes on wood.

ACRYLIC GLAZING LIQUID *left*
Thinned with water and used in water-based finishes.

OIL-BASED GLAZING LIQUID
Thinned with mineral spirits and used in oil-based finishes.

WAXES, POWDERS & PASTES

Waxes, powders, and pastes are important, versatile ingredients in many paint recipes. Mixed with paint, oil color, or other ingredients, they are used to produce a variety of effects. Waxes also often form an essential part of the protective stage of paint finishes. Always check the chart for the appropriate solvents and thinners, as some pastes, in particular, can be difficult to remove from brushes. Some of these materials can be obtained from hardware and art-supply stores; for others you will need to go to a specialist supplier. Store carefully and make sure all lids are secure.

WAXES

TYPE	USES	TINT WITH	THINNER / CLEANER	TOXICITY
Artists' beeswax	Soft, bleached alternative to beeswax, ideal for decorative resist work.		Mineral spirits	High
Beeswax or furniture wax	Use for resist technique when aging or distressing painted wood. Also polishes and seals wood. Available in pellet form.		Mineral spirits	High
Black polish	Mix with silver metallic powder to create an iron finish. Black shoe polish (but not shoe cream) is a good alternative.		Mineral spirits	High
Clear wax	Polishes and seals wood. Can also be tinted to darken wood.	Artists' oil color, powder pigment, or shoe polish	Mineral spirits	High
Liming wax	Mix with whiting (see opposite) to age decorative finishes. Also polishes and seals wood.	As above	Mineral spirits	High
White polish	Seals and polishes wood.	As above	Mineral spirits	High
White wax	Seals and enhances wood.	As above	Mineral spirits	High

BEESWAX PELLETS
Melt in a double boiler before using. Artists' beeswax is also melted but flows on more smoothly.

BLACK POLISH
Mix with metallic powder for an iron effect (see p. 18).

FURNITURE WAX
Use, like beeswax pellets (above), as a resist when aging paint. Aerosol beeswax is a useful alternative, but avoid silicone polishes.

LIMING WAX *right*
Use for a limed effect on wood or mix with whiting to age wall finishes.

CLEAR WAX *below*
Use by itself to enhance wood or tinted to suggest the darkening that comes with age.

WHITE WAX *below*
Mix with oil color for a tinted polish or use alone for a rich effect on wood.

WHITE POLISH *left*
Seals and reveals wood beneath light rubbed-back glazes. Also in liquid form.

POWDERS

TYPE	USES	MIX WITH	TINT WITH	TOXICITY
Powdered chalk	See whiting.			
Sand	Gives texture and/or interest to decorative finishes; usually added to base coat and frequently rubbed back to add aging. Available in various grades from fine to coarse, the latter usually used only with exterior paint.	Eggshell, latex, or exterior paint	Artists' acrylic color or powder pigment	Medium when mixed
Whiting or powdered chalk	Combines with paint, white glue, or liming wax for aged or dusty effects on simple finishes. Also a useful, non-waxy alternative for resist work.	Latex paint, white glue, liming wax, or water	Powder pigment and, when mixed, artists' acrylic color	Medium when mixed

USING LIMING WAX
Wax plays a vital part in the process of distressing the surface to create an impression of age for the simple fresco effect. After the glaze has been sanded, a layer is applied to retain the whiting, which is rubbed in to create a dusty look.

USING WHITING
Here whiting was applied to areas of detail when the paint was almost dry to suggest the crusty, weathered look of aged lead.

SAND
Sand of various grades can be used to give paints and glazes extra texture.

WHITING
Used for resist work or to add texture to simple finishes.

WHITE GLUE
Mixed with pigment, it stains or seals plaster, metal, and wood finishes.

PASTES

TYPE	USES	MIX WITH	TINT WITH	THINNER / CLEANER	TOXICITY
White glue, or PVA adhesive	Seals porous and flaky surfaces, such as plaster; used before water-based paints. Or use with powder pigment to stain wood.	Latex paint to create glaze (alternative to glazing liquid)	Artists' acrylic color or powder pigment	Water	Medium
Waterproof adhesive bond	The water-resistant version of white glue (see above).		As above	As above	Medium

VARNISHES & SEALANTS

These are often needed for the final stage of a simple finish, so keep a variety in stock. However, besides sealing and protecting your effects against hard wear or weathering, they can play a part in the finishes themselves—either mixed with color for the darkening that comes with age or to provide an aging crackle effect on paint. Most varnishes and sealants are highly toxic and must be handled with care and stored with the lids well secured. Always check the drying times, and follow the manufacturers' instructions for applying additional coats.

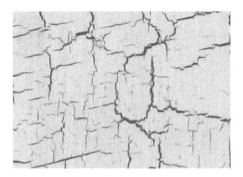

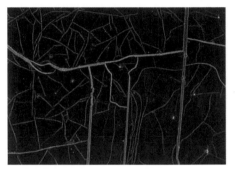

WATER-BASED CRACKLE
Used with latex paint. The cracks are short and jagged. This is the varnish to choose for a stylized effect.

OIL-BASED CRACKLE
Used with oil-based eggshell paint. With wide-spaced cracks overlying a network of hairline cracks, this is the varnish for an antique effect.

ACRYLIC VARNISH
Water-based itself, acrylic varnish is an ideal sealant for water-based finishes, as it is quick-drying and durable. A matte or semigloss finish is specified in the recipes to enhance the various effects.

CRACKLE VARNISH
Both water-based (top) and oil-based (bottom) crackle varnish are used for aged effects on wood (see above). Follow the manufacturers' instructions carefully because the method can vary from make to make.

MATTE VARNISH
This produces a flat sheen for a tough sealant on oil-based finishes.

FRENCH ENAMEL VARNISH
A decorative sealant used for ornamental finishes; available in a range of colors.

SHELLAC *left*
Use amber shellac to seal gilded finishes.

POLYURETHANE VARNISH (TINTED)
Primarily for exterior use; satin and matte are most sympathetic over paint finishes.

MARINE VARNISH
A tough exterior-quality varnish: for use over water- and oil-based finishes.

VARNISHES & SEALANTS

TYPE	USES	MIX WITH	TINT WITH	THINNER / CLEANER	TOXICITY	INTERIOR OR EXTERIOR USE
Acrylic varnish: clear matte or satin	Seals and protects water-based paint finishes. Quick to dry and durable.		Artists' acrylic color or powder pigment	Water	Medium	Interior
Crackle varnish	**Water based** Creates cracked-paint effect if applied between water-based base and top coats.			Water	Medium	Interior
	Oil based Creates wider-spaced cracking if two coats are applied over oil-based base coat.			Water (unusually)	High	Interior
Matte varnish	A traditional product which seals and protects oil-based paint finishes.	Transparent oil-based glazing liquid	Artists' oil color or powder pigment	Mineral spirits	High	Interior
French enamel varnish	Seals and colors bronzed and gilded surfaces. Available in a wide range of colors.			Denatured alcohol	High	Interior
Oil fixative	Seals cold patination effects on metal. Also seals wood.			Mineral spirits	High	Interior
Polyurethane varnish: clear gloss, satin, or matte	Protects water- and oil-based finishes. Slow-drying and durable; gloss is the most long lasting.	Transparent oil-based glazing liquid	Artists' oil color	Mineral spirits	High	Exterior
Shellac (amber)	Seals and ages gilded surfaces. Also used on wood for French polishing.		Artists' oil color or powder pigment	Denatured alcohol	High	Interior
Marine or exterior varnish: clear gloss or satin	Protects oil- and water-based paint finishes. Extremely tough and durable.	Transparent oil-based glazing liquid	Artists' oil color	Mineral spirits	High	Exterior

See also Clear wax and White wax (p. 14).

METALLIC FINISHES

Imitation metal leaf and metallic powders and paints, today's cheaper alternatives to real gold and precious metal leaf, have made gilding and its related finishes affordable possibilities. In many ways, these modern materials are some of the most rewarding to work with, as they provide such stunning results. They are also available in many different colors and tones, giving you great scope for experiment. Take time to learn the techniques of distressing and aging described in the recipes—they can transform sometimes harsh, tinny effects into opulence and beauty.

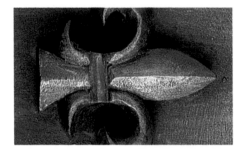

METALLIC POWDER AND WAX
Silver metallic powder mixed with black polish and rubbed in over a base coat of chalkboard paint creates a convincing iron effect.

SPATTERING WITH GOLD PAINT
The least expensive form of gold finish is used for a jewel-like fantasy finish.

OIL-BASED *below*
The traditional size, this takes a long time to dry.

WATER-BASED *above*
A modern form: fast-drying.

SIZES

TYPE	USES	MIX WITH	TINT WITH	THINNER / CLEANER	TOXICITY
Water-based size	Provides an adhesive, quick-to-dry base for metallic powders and leaf. Also use as a sealant on some paint finishes.		Artists' acrylic color	Water	Medium
Oil-based gold size	Provides an adhesive, slow-to-dry base for bronze and metallic powders and real gold leaf.	Transparent oil-based glazing liquid to make size more visible, or with oil-based paint for a good base color.	Artists' oil color or powder pigment	Mineral spirits	High

PAINTS, POWDERS & LEAF

TYPE	USES	SEALANT COAT	TO THIN SEALANT	TOXICITY
Bronze powders	Brush onto oil- or water-based size to create a metallic finish on any surface. Available in tones of bronze, gold, silver, and copper. Cheaper than imitation metal leaf and more effective than paint.	French enamel varnish	Denatured alcohol	High
Imitation metal leaf: copper, gold, and aluminum	Lay down on oil- or water-based size to create a metallic finish on any surface; aluminum makes an effective silver finish. Cheaper than real gold leaf. Available in whole leaves or fragments.	Amber shellac/ French enamel varnish. (See also p.119.)	Denatured alcohol	High
Gold paint or paste	Creates a gold finish on any surface. Simpler to use and cheaper than gold imitation metal leaf and bronze powders, but not recommended for gilding.			High
Metallic powders and graphite	Brush onto oil- or water-based size to create a wide variety of colored metallic finishes for realistic or fantasy effects on any surface.	French enamel varnish	Denatured alcohol	High
Silver paint	Creates a silver finish on any surface. Simpler to use and cheaper than aluminum imitation metal leaf, but not recommended for gilding.			High

BRONZE POWDERS
Available in a range of gold, silver, copper, and bronze tones. Brush onto size.

GOLD PAINT
Quick and easy to apply, this is an oil-based material.

GOLD PASTE
Rub or paint onto a red iron oxide primer.

SILVER PAINT
Like gold paint, this is best reserved for stamped decoration.

GRAPHITE POWDER
Add to paints and waxes to create a dark, "metallic" look.

METALLIC POWDERS
Available in a great range of colors, they can be brushed onto partly dry size or mixed with wax (see opposite) to create a variety of realistic and fantasy metal finishes.

IMITATION METAL LEAF
This composite leaf offers a cheaper but satisfactory alternative to real metal leaf. It is available in many gold tones, as well as aluminum (for a silver effect) and copper. Made in sheets 6in. (15cm.) square, it is also obtainable in broken form. The traditional gilding tools shown are a knife for cutting leaf and a burnisher with an agate set at its tip.

PAINTERS' TOOLS

Most of the techniques in Parts Three and Four can be accomplished with a basic collection of paintbrushes and artists' brushes of varying sizes and qualities. In Part Two, some of the techniques call for specialist brushes; the chart on p. 23 details these, along with less expensive alternatives.

A well-stocked hardware store or home center will offer paintbrushes in a huge range of types, sizes, and prices. Some, called latex brushes, have synthetic bristles and are intended for use with water-based paints; most brushes intended for oil-based paints have natural bristles, although some synthetic brushes can be used for either water- or oil-based paints.

We specify a different brush for each color. This is convenient but expensive; and you can manage with fewer if you clean and reuse them. Very cheap brushes, sometimes called tossaway brushes, can be used for materials such as glazes and crackle varnish that are difficult to remove.

PAINTBRUSHES
Some of ours are worn old favorites that still perform well. Shown at bottom right is a varnish brush, reserved only for varnish. Water-based paint dries quickly, so always rinse paint out and wash with mild soap and water as soon as you finish. Use two jars of mineral spirits to remove oil-based paint, pouring enough to cover. Work off the paint in jar 1 and rinse in jar 2, removing clogged paint with a scrubbing brush. Then wash in soapy water and rinse.

ROLLERS AND ROCKERS

Rollers are an excellent way of applying latex paint. For small areas we sometimes apply the paint with a brush, then roller out the brush marks. We find the most convenient rollers are the fairly small ones with push-on covers which allow for quick clean-ups and changes of color or texture as the job demands. Rollers will last as long as brushes if you care for them in the same way. Loaded rollers and brushes can be wrapped in plastic wrap for short periods. The picture also shows a rubber graining rocker. It can be rolled over a surface to create a wood-grain effect.

OTHER ESSENTIALS

Fanned out on the plate, which we use as a palette, are just a few artists' brushes—bristle flats and fitches on the right, soft-haired natural or nylon on the left. The tile is an ideal surface for rolling paint out when you are stamping. Sitting on it are two steel decorators' combs and a bunch of sponges. Combs are available in a range of different-sized teeth and widths and are used to create ridge patterns in wet paint. Some of our sponges have had their corners trimmed, some have been cut into small balls. Where a natural, random look is important over larger areas—in some of the simple finishes in Part Two, for example—we recommend the use of more expensive natural sponge. The tiny natural sponge is reserved for the finest of decorative effects.

CONTAINERS AND PALETTES

You will need all sorts of containers and palettes. Jars are for cleaning brushes; lidded ones are for mixing and storing paint. Paint kettles are for mixing large quantities of paint for immediate use. Plastic ones are fine for water-based paints and glazes, but a metal kettle is essential for oil-based materials. We like to mix the small amounts used in decorative painting by first stirring in a screw-top jar, then putting the lid on and shaking furiously. For mixing very large quantities you should consider upgrading to an electric drill fitted with a paint-mixing whisk. For palettes we use saucers, plates, and ceramic tiles. When using these with acrylic colors, do not wash unused paint down the drain. Let it dry on the plate, then soak off the paint film in hot water and throw it in a trash can. Clean the measuring spoons and plastic pitchers in the same way.

BASIC PROTECTIVE WEAR

Rubber household gloves are ideal for general tasks. For more delicate work, switch to thin latex ones. A paper mask will cut down on the inhalation of powder pigments or of dust thrown up when cleaning or sanding, but it will not protect you from inhaling the harmful poisonous vapors given off by some solvents. For these you need special masks.

SPECIALIST BRUSHES

Some home centers and paint stores are now selling specialist brushes. The shape and feel of many of these make them desirable, let alone the implicit promise that here are tools that will, at a stroke, turn messy old paint into any number of fine finishes. You could, of course, tackle all our recipes with ordinary paintbrushes, but for some of the broken-color techniques in Part Two you may wish to move up a level and use a brush designed for the job in hand. Some are expensive, but you can be confident that they have proved their worth over many years, are an absolute pleasure to use, and, if cared for, will last a lifetime. But note too, that there are inexpensive brushes, such as the dusting and block brushes, which can do excellent work beyond their allotted task.

SPECIALIST BRUSHES

TYPE	FILLING	FUNCTION	ALTERNATIVE
Badger blender	Very expensive, originally made from badger hair; cheaper versions now usually made from fine hog hair	Used for softening water- and oil-based glazes on walls and wood. Available in various sizes.	Dusting brush or large paintbrush
Block brush	Inexpensive; synthetic or coarse-fibered pure bristle	Good for painting roughly textured interior and exterior surfaces; can also serve as a cheap alternative to a stippling brush.	
Dragging brush	Flat, long, pure bristle or horse hair	Used for bold, uniform strokes on glazes and for wood-graining techniques.	Standard paintbrush (see p. 20): choose one with long bristles
Dusting brush	Long, soft hog hair or cheaper filling, designed to splay out	Used for dusting surfaces after sanding. Also as a cheaper alternative to a badger blender.	
Glider	Pure bristle or thin, light squirrel hair	Used to apply oil-based glazes.	Standard flat paintbrush
Stippling brush	Expensive; long, fine pure bristle, set in a wooden stock with a curved grip	Used for taking off dots of glaze for decorative effect.	Block brush
Striping brush	Extremely long, tapered squirrel hair; needs careful storage	Used for painting thin decorative lines on furniture. Also to create veins in marbling. Available in many sizes.	Fine artists' brush

PREPARING THE SURFACE

For your paintwork to look good and perform well, the surface on which it lies must be clean, free of grease, smooth, without holes or cracks, and properly primed. The chart on pp. 26–7 is a guide to the treatment of both new and old materials commonly found in the home. If the surface you are working on is not listed there, seek advice in a specialist manual or at your local hardware store.

Firstly you must clean off any dust or grubbiness. Detergent is often sufficient but must be properly rinsed off. De-greaser also etches the surface and provides a tooth for the new paint. Do not swamp bare wood, fresh plaster, or ferrous metals with water, as they will be damaged. Marks such as grease can be removed with a solvent such as mineral spirits, acetone, or denatured alcohol.

Holes, cracks, or dents must now be filled. Choose a filler to suit the surface and the size of the problem. Next, smooth the surface as flat as possible. Electric sanders produce a lot of dust and do not get into the corners. Using waterproof sandpaper with water gets around the dust problem, but it cannot be used with an electric sander. Some surfaces, such as wallpaper and some gypsum plasters, cannot be sanded at all.

Finally, most surfaces must be primed to seal and stabilize them and to ensure that they will accept the paint.

BASIC CLEANING EQUIPMENT
If you are painting over previously decorated surfaces, you will need a bowl, sponge, rubber gloves, and de-greaser. Alternatives to de-greaser are washing soda or detergent powders. All will remove grease, but you should rinse off their residue well with plenty of clean water. Rough-textured surfaces or tough grime may also need a scrubbing brush to bring them up to scratch.

SANDING
Graded by number, abrasive papers range from 120 (coarse) to 600 (fine). Ordinary sandpaper is cheap but clogs readily. It is good for general use. Aluminum oxide paper, the yellow paper above, is superior. It clogs less readily and is less scratchy. Emery cloth is a tough abrasive for metals. All types are used dry and create dust, so take precautions and never dry-sand lead-based paint. Silicon carbide, also shown, can be used with water and is the most versatile. Used wet, it does not clog or cause dust. For flaky or rusty surfaces, use emery cloth, a wire brush, steel wool, or a pan scourer.

MECHANICAL SANDING
This will make short work of large, flat areas. The small sander is easy to use, with its speed controls and disks attached by hook-and-loop tape. It produces an excellent finish but will not deal with curves and corners. And despite the bag, it kicks up dust.

PREPARING THE SURFACE

MATERIAL	CLEAN/ DE-GREASE	REPAIR/ FILL	RUB DOWN/ SAND	PRIMER*	SAFETY
Wood including plywood	Can be washed, but as a general rule do not wet lumber—it will raise the grain and may even cause warping.	• Spackling paste • Wood filler • Cellulose filler	• Dry-sand. Machines can speed things up. • Smooth with fine sandpaper after primer.	Stain-blocking sealer, if needed, plus: • Acrylic primer undercoat (w) • Wood primer (o)	• Dust mask • Goggles
Waxed wood	Very difficult to strip but essential or paint will not adhere. Try: • mineral spirits • liquid-stripping • heat-stripping • proprietary wax remover	As wood	As wood plus steel wool	As wood	
MDF, chipboard, and particleboard	Wipe clean of dust and grime, but avoid getting too wet or will swell and distort.	As above. Chipboard does not have a smooth texture so spot-filling shows. Skimming the whole surface with spackling paste is an option if it is not a floor.	• Can be lightly abraded to give tooth for paint, but cannot be made smoother with sandpaper— only rougher. • Smooth with fine sandpaper after primer.	• Latex flat (w) • As wood	Dust mask
Ferrous metal e.g. steel tables	• De-grease with mineral spirits and steel wool or rag. • Brush down loose rust.	Plastic filler for car-body repair	• Steel wool • Waterproof sandpaper used with mineral spirits • Emery cloth	• Zinc phosphate (o) • Red iron oxide Essential to prevent corrosion	• Dust mask • Rubber gloves • Goggles
Non-ferrous metal e.g. aluminum window frames	• De-grease with mineral spirits and steel wool or rag. • Wash with detergent.	As above	Waterproof sandpaper with water	• Etching primers (o) • Zinc phosphate (o)	Dust mask
Plaster	• Brush down. • Can be washed, but allow to dry out completely before painting, especially if using oil-based paint.	• Spackling paste • Cellulose filler • Plaster	• Dry-sand • Waterproof sandpaper. Take care. Some plasters, e.g. gypsum, can be damaged when sanded.	• Acrylic primer undercoat (w) • Thinned white glue (w) • Primer-sealer • Alkali-resisting primer (o)	• Dust mask • Rubber gloves
Wallboard	Usually new so should be clean	• Spackling paste • Cellulose filler • Plaster	Dry-sand. Use very fine abrasives and sand only the filler, not paper coating on board.	• As plaster • Thinned latex flat (w)	

* Some of the wood finishes in Part Two—specifically Aging Wood, Rubbing off on Wood, and Woodwashing—depend partly for their effect on revealing the grain of the wood itself. For them no primer (or undercoat) is needed.

• Choose from the listed options. See also pp. 24–5 (cleaning/repair/rubbing down) and 28–9 (priming).

MATERIAL	CLEAN/ DEGREASE	REPAIR/ FILL	RUB DOWN/ SAND	PRIMER*	SAFETY
Cement skim coat on walls	• Stiff brush • De-greaser • Detergent	• Spackling paste • Mortar	Not possible	• Primer-sealer (o) • Acrylic primer undercoat (w) • Primer-sealer (o)	
on floors	As walls	• Mortar	Not needed		
Previously painted surfaces	• De-greaser • Detergent • Mineral spirits Paint may be stripped with liquid paint remover or burned off.	Depends on what lies below. Spackling paste suits most circumstances, or use filler specific to plaster, wood, metal, etc.	• Dry-sand • Waterproof sandpaper on sound paint and where support is non-absorbent	Unnecessary on many sound surfaces. In doubt, use acrylic primer undercoat (w) or all-purpose primer (o) Spot-prime bare patches as appropriate.	• Dust mask • Rubber gloves, mask and goggles
Papered walls	If unsound, strip off completely and treat support accordingly. It will probably be plaster. If sound, wipe clean. Vinyl paper must be stripped: it is hard to paint.	• Spackling paste • Cellulose filler	No—except dry-sand filler	• Acrylic primer undercoat (w)	
Varnished surfaces	Treat as previously painted surfaces.	Treat as previously painted surfaces.	Treat as previously painted surfaces.	Treat as previously painted surfaces.	
Laminates and plastics	• De-greaser • Detergent • Mineral spirits	Plastic fillers for car-body repair	• Waterproof sandpaper • Coarse emery cloth	• Metal primer, followed by acrylic primer undercoat if using water-based paint	• Rubber gloves
Fiberglass	As plastics/ laminates	As plastics/ laminates	As plastics/ laminates	As plastics/ laminates	Dust mask
Glass and glazed ware	• Detergent • Denatured alcohol			Glazed titles can be primed with tile primer (w)	
Terracotta	• Stiff brush • Detergent	Spackling paste	Dry-sand	• Acrylic primer undercoat (w) • All-purpose primer (o)	Dust mask
Cork tiles unvarnished varnished	• Detergent • De-greaser		• Sand lightly • Steel wool	None None	

(w) = water-based (o) = oil-based

PRIMERS & UNDERCOATS

A primer will be needed on most bare materials or on surfaces that are unsound. It provides the right foundation for subsequent coatings and prevents the paint from peeling or becoming blemished. Choosing the right one is clearly essential to the success of any paintwork, and the choice will depend on the underlying surface: a rust inhibitor for metal, for example, or a primer-sealer for dusty plaster. In general most primers will accept any subsequent coating. As for the paint you use afterward, there is certainly no problem in applying oil-based paints over water-based primers, and in most cases you can put a water-based paint over an oil-based primer. What makes paint stick is a good tooth with no grease or dust. Our chart lists choices, but it is always wise to follow manufacturers' guidelines. One other consideration is the decorative effect you are after. If this involves transparency or rubbing back to reveal what is underneath, color your primer appropriately.

Undercoats may be needed with traditional gloss paint. This can be quite transparent, and the undercoat is there to hide all unevenness of color as well as to provide the perfect surface for a single top coat of gloss. It may serve as a primer, too, so check the can before buying.

WOOD PRIMER
The ideal foundation for oil-based paints on wood, wood primer is available in several colors.

ALL-PURPOSE PRIMER
A good sealant for a variety of surfaces, including those in doubtful condition, this is a useful item to have on hand.

METAL PRIMER
This primer prevents corrosion under oil- and water-based finishes. Also available in gray or red.

RED IRON OXIDE
The classic metal primer, it also gives a good base for gilding and bronzing effects.

PRIMER-SEALER
A useful primer for less than perfect walls, this binds flaky and porous surfaces.

PRIMERS & UNDERCOATS

TYPE	USES	THINNER / CLEANER	TOXICITY	INTERIOR OR EXTERIOR USE
PRIMERS All suitable for use under water- or oil-based paints unless otherwise stated				
GENERAL				
Acrylic primer undercoat, or universal acrylic primer	Seals any unpainted porous surface and patches broken areas on painted surfaces.	Water	Low	Both
All-purpose primer, or universal oil primer	See acrylic primer undercoat for function. This is the primer to use when in doubt about a surface or its condition.	Mineral spirits	High	Both
METAL				
Etching primer	For ferrous and, particularly, non-ferrous metal. Some types can be painted over at once; others need an appropriate metal primer (see below). Both contain acid to create a suitable tooth for paint.	Isopropyl alcohol (available from pharmacies)	High	Both
Metal primer	Provides a stable base for painting metal and prevents corrosion. Lot of options, depending on type of metal (steel, iron, aluminum, copper, zinc, tin, or bronze), its finish (galvanized or anodized), and its condition (clean or rusty). See also red iron oxide and zinc phosphate metal primers.	Varies according to type: see manufacturers' instructions.		Both
Red iron oxide primer	Prevents metal corrosion; the better option when using dark colors. Also a good base color for gilding and bronzing.	Mineral spirits	High	Both
Zinc phosphate metal primer	Superior rust-inhibitor, developed as an alternative to the traditional highly toxic red lead primer. Suitable for all ferrous and non-ferrous metal surfaces.	Mineral spirits	High	Both
WALLS				
Alkali-resisting wall primer	Designed for chemically unstable old plaster or cement walls showing effects of alkali attack.	Mineral spirits	High	Both
White glue	General-purpose adhesive mixed with water or latex paint for a resilient primer and sealer on unpainted plaster and other porous surfaces.	Water	Low	Interior
Primer-sealer	Binds highly porous, powder, old surfaces, such as cement and plaster.	Mineral spirits	High	Both
WOOD				
Stain-blocking sealer	Seals knots and sap streaks in bare wood, especially pine. Dries quickly.	Denatured alcohol	High	Both
Wood primer	Seals wood.	Mineral spirits	High	Both
GLAZED WARE				
Tile primer	Formulated to provide a base for painting on glazed tiles, glass, and melamine. Not recommended for floors.	Water	Low	Interior
UNDERCOAT				
Oil undercoat	Heavily pigmented paint which dries to matte finish. Designed for use under gloss paint to provide body and color. Use a lighter tone than finish coat. Normally applied over suitable primer, although some are dual purpose.	Mineral spirits	High	Both

COLOR INSPIRATION

If, as we suggest, you are to sidestep the impositions of the paint manufacturers and blend your own colors, you need to be able to predict what might happen. It is encouraging to know that color can be changed in only three ways.

Wishing something paler is wanting a change of *tone*, and is most commonly achieved by the addition of white. To go darker, we may add black, but often raw umber is a better choice, giving softer, more natural tones. To reduce a color's brightness means changing its *intensity* or *chroma* without changing its tone. Adding gray will achieve this, but match the gray to the color—a dark one for dark colors and a pale one for light colors. To change red to orange—in other words to change the red's *hue*—add yellow. Attempting to change to a particular hue may not be possible, though. For instance, changing red to purple by adding blue is particularly problematic.

When choosing colors to use in combination, it is useful to limit yourself to a single hue and vary only the tone within the design. Or color a design with only three or four hues, all of the same grayness or intensity. Working within disciplines such as these will prevent you from creating visual pandemonium, while you won't fall into the trap of being too timid and painting your walls antique white.

HUES
Reds, blues, yellows, and greens are all different hues. In theory you can mix two primary hues together to make oranges, greens, and purples, but in practice it is better to buy these colors if you want pure, intense pigment. This applies to the earth colors, too.

TONES

Tones or tints are achieved through the addition of white to a hue. To make a shade, you can add black, as we did to this blue, but with some colors this may also result in a change of hue. Here, besides being made paler with white, the ocher has been gradually toned down with raw umber, and the red with burnt umber.

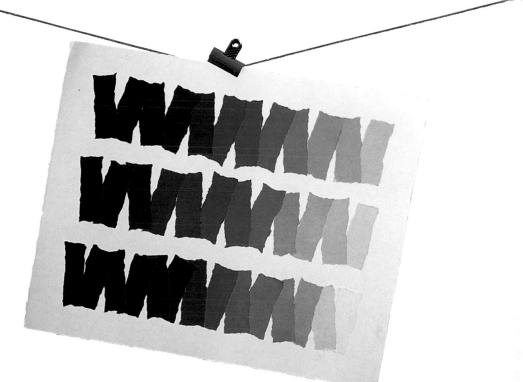

INTENSITY

When you want to subdue a color without changing its tone, add gray. The gray may be bought in, or mixed from black and white. Intensity will always be reduced, too, when you add other hues, especially the earth colors. Colors that contain gray or an earth color form the basis of many of the recipes given in Part Three and Part Four.

COLOR INSPIRATION

WHITE BASE
This group of recipes all start with white latex flat. Some of them include grays, some earth colors, some both. The swatch on top has had yellow ocher and ultramarine added, while the next is the white with yellow ocher and Payne's gray. The third mix is with dioxazine purple and Payne's gray, the fourth with raw sienna and magenta, and the last is the white plus cadmium yellow.

GREEN BASE
These swatches show how powerful a pigment phthalocyanine green is. You need only a little in any mixture, and even then the color may be too garish. On the right of this trio, the green has been subdued with raw umber, while on the left it has been darkened with Payne's gray. In the center, it has been made paler with white.

YELLOW BASE
If you try to darken cadmium yellow with, say, Payne's gray, it will turn toward green, as shown on the left of this trio. Instead, try one of the earth colors such as raw umber, as seen on the right.

BLUE BASE
Cobalt blue mixed with yellow ocher and white produces a subdued gray-blue, which may be surprising, as you might expect a green to be the result. However, the ocher is close to orange, while the cobalt blue leans toward violet. Mixing these almost complementary colors will always result in a gray. The pure cobalt on the right is modified with increasing amounts of ocher.

Adding colors to one another will bring about a change of hue, tone, or intensity, and possibly all three (see pp. 30–1 and opposite). Follow the instructions in Parts Two to Four carefully for successful mixing with the minimum of wastage. In Parts Three and Four, where color-matching is especially important, we have ensured that our color-mixing is as predictable as possible by using mainly artists' acrylic colors made from a single classifiable pigment. Each pigment has a reference number, and high-grade paints should give details of the pigments they contain. Thus Mars red is, in fact, PR101, a single pigment sometimes called red oxide or Venetian red.

The order of mixing is important when creating a glaze. Always add the thinner (water for water-based paint and mineral spirits for oil-based paint) last and slowly. It is easier and less wasteful to add more thinner than to correct a runny mix with more paint or glazing liquid.

Always test for color and consistency before applying paint or glaze to a surface. It is much easier to adjust tone, intensity, or mix at this early stage. Old pieces of wood, wallboard, or thick cardboard make ideal test boards; keep some primed with white paint for the purpose. To test the effect of a glaze coat accurately you must first apply a coat of the appropriate base color and any previous glaze specified. When checking wood washes, try to test on wood of a similar type and grain.

Color correction is simple if you follow the instructions on mixing. Add all colors slowly, checking the effect as you work, but take particular care with dark hues (maybe adding them last) and with all pigment colors (they are particularly intense), or you will waste a lot of white paint or color adjusting to the tone you want.

If a glaze does not move well when tested or lacks the characteristic translucent appearance, try gradually adding more of the appropriate glazing liquid.

Correcting mistakes of technique is always difficult. Oil-based paints and glazes dry slowly and can, with care, be wiped off with a lint-free cloth soaked in mineral spirits. Remember to wear gloves and disturb as little of the surface as possible. With water-based paints and glazes you have to act quickly, wielding a water-soaked sponge or cloth, but be prepared to paint another base coat and begin again.

Do not forget, especially if you are using powder pigments, oil-based paints, or solvents, that these are very toxic substances. Wear gloves and dust masks, and do not smoke, eat, or drink while working.

Apart from health risks, paint can mess up the environment. Protect the immediate one by spreading newspaper and drop cloths, but when disposing of solvents and unused paint, don't forget the wider one. If you wipe and scrape as much paint as possible off equipment when cleaning up, you will need less solvent and so create less damage to the environment. Dispose properly of solvents, and remember that oil-based paint and solvent-soaked rags are flammable.

PLANNING A DESIGN

A little forethought will enable you to carry through your ideas effectively. If you are working on a large wall or floor, take a good look at it and note the position of any architectural details, such as doors and windows, that will have to be included in your design. Consider such things as the height of your planned border in relation to the windows in the room, the position of light fittings and outlets if you are contemplating stripes on your wall, or how to fit a repeat pattern above a mantelpiece without ending up with incomplete motifs at either side.

It may help to sketch your design out on graph paper. If you work in standard measurements you should use a scale of 1:12, with 1 inch equaling 1 foot. If you use metric measurements, use a scale of 1:10, so that 10 centimeters represent 1 meter. With a scale of 1:10, a wall 3.2 x 2.7m. (10 x 9ft.) would be drawn to 32 x 27cm. (12³/₅ x 10³/₅in.).

This same wall is 90ft.² (8.6m.²). A quart of latex flat can cover up to 161ft.² (15m.²), so if the wall includes a window or a door, you will be able to coat it twice, but it all depends on the thickness of the paint and the absorbency and texture of the wall. Cans of paint and primer usually carry information on coverage, so take a list of dimensions with you when you go shopping. Our recipes specify what area they will cover.

PLANNING
Once you have chosen your motif, you must plan your design. Plenty of graph paper, a long ruler, right-angled triangle, pencils, and a calculator are the basic items you will need. Once you have drawn a scale plan that fits, you will be ready to mark it out on the surface you are decorating.

MARKING OUT POSITIONS

As you work, you will need to mark your surface with center lines, horizontals, and registration marks. If these are not to be covered by paint, they must be temporary. Masking tape is useful for this, as it can be written on. Water-soluble markers are also handy, as the marks they make can be wiped off most non-absorbent surfaces. As a precaution, though, use a marker to match the paint you will be using.

To rule long, straight lines, stretch out a length of string, securing it with nails or masking tape. Or use a builders' chalk line. Stretch the chalky string tightly between two points and pluck it to snap a line on floor or wall. Horizontals and verticals can be ruled with a spirit level at least 3ft. (1m.) long. But there is also the school of thought that says you must line up designs with floors and ceilings even if these are not completely straight, and we would not disagree with that. If the layout looks right, go ahead and start painting.

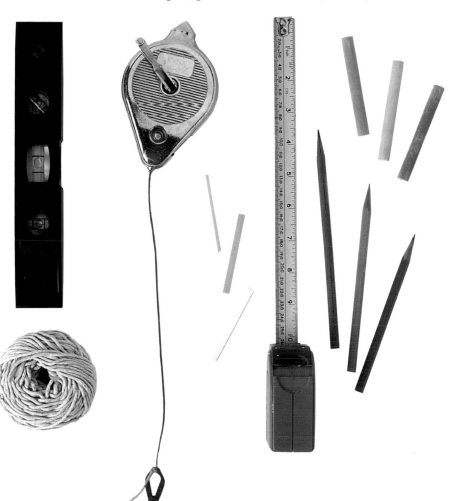

MARKING
Tautly stretched string makes an excellent guide which will not harm the surface, nor will the builders' chalk line which doubles as a plumb bob. If you have to draw on your surface, choose pencils for a wooden surface and artists' water-soluble markers for non-absorbent ones. Chalks are good for rough layouts and tracing down designs (see p. 216). All can be erased or wiped off.

SPIRIT LEVEL
Small spirit levels are useful in tight spots, but a longer one is best for ruling horizontals or verticals.

STENCILS

Essential equipment for making stencils are a craft knife or X-Acto knife and a cutting mat. Access to a photocopier will save your having to trace and transfer designs. Stencils can be cut from cardboard, paper, or plastic. If they are to be used repeatedly, we use oiled manila stencil board. The oil makes the board more durable and also easier to cut.

Photocopy the image you want at the size you want, then stick it to your board using repositionable spray adhesive. Repeat patterns will be a lot easier to line up and register if you place your image at the center of a square or rectangular piece of board. Cut through both photocopy and board with the knife. Be firm and try to cut in a single stroke. For a softer edge, tear the shape out instead of cutting it. We sometimes use acetate sheet. This has the advantage that you can photocopy a design directly onto it.

MATERIALS FOR STENCILS
Top left is a stencil torn from oiled manila board, and alongside it, one that has been cut with a knife. Images need be nothing more than photocopies of leaves, held in place on the board with repositionable spray adhesive, then cut through to make the stencil. Use masking tape to mark the positions of your stencils on the wall, and spray adhesive to hold them in place without damaging the surface while you stencil. Take great care when using spray adhesive. It is highly toxic.

2 With the stencil still in place, sponge in a second color along the bottom edge and partway up the side. Once most of the paint has left the sponge, start moving the sponge up the motif to form a shadow, its color fading gradually away. Add some of the same color to the stalk also.

1 Hold the stencil in place with spray adhesive, and have ready a spoonful of acrylic paint on a saucer and a piece of trimmed cellulose sponge. Dip the sponge into the paint, but do not overload it. Gently dab the color into the stencil. Aim for allover distribution of the paint, but do not be too concerned about achieving an even texture.

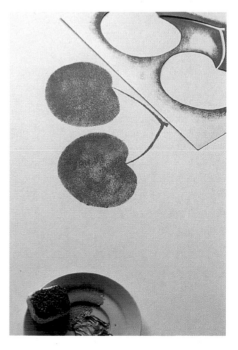

3 Once the stenciling is completed, peel away the stencil board and allow to dry.

4 You will be left with a pair of gently shaded cherries.

STAMPS

Stamps are a quicker way of applying designs than stencils and are ideal for small, uncomplicated motifs. Most of our stamps are made from thin, foam-rubber mat of the kind backpackers carry. This is very easy to cut and holds its shape well, while being elastic enough to print on top of uneven surfaces. You can also make stamps from sponge cleaning cloths or flocked draining mats used for wineglasses. Experiment with whatever is available.

Cut your design using an X-Acto knife. Work on a cutting mat to do this. The stamp must then be glued to a backing board, which should remain rigid and not warp when wet. Foamcore board, available from art-supply stores, is quick and easy to cut. You may also use offcuts of wood or balsa-core plywood. These are cheaper and have the advantage that you can screw handles or knobs to their backs, which makes the stamping a great deal easier.

Much smaller stamps can be carved from an eraser with an X-Acto knife. If you cannot find an eraser big enough, glue four together with extra-strong glue. These will not need a backing board.

When you are cutting your stamps, do not forget that you are making a mirror image. Getting the motif the wrong way around may not be too serious for many of the projects in this book, but if you intend to stamp any lettering, make sure you get it right.

MATERIALS FOR STAMPS
Foam rubber is cut to shape and glued to a backing board with contact cement. For complex shapes, trace the design onto paper, cut it out, and use as a template to draw around with a fine waterproof marker. For a mosaic effect, make stamps from small pieces of foam rubber glued to a backing board. For a two-color motif, use two interlocking stamps, as shown here.

1 To apply the paint to small stamps, use a roller to spread the paint onto a tile, then press the stamp into the paint. Reload the stamp with paint for each print.

2 Place the stamp in position along a guideline, which can be masking tape, as here, or a stretched-out string, then press down firmly. The wooden backing board is thick enough for you to grip comfortably with your fingers.

1 This larger stamp has the paint applied to it directly with a roller. This roller is made of sponge covered in flock and was originally designed for painting behind radiators.

2 Test your stamp on a piece of paper before you start work to ensure that you are applying pressure equally to all sections of the motif.

MASKING OUT

We find masking tape indispensable. Because it does not stick permanently to a surface, it can be used in all sorts of ways—holding stencils in place, attaching color swatches and sketches to a wall, marking height lines and center lines, and so on.

It is sold in a number of forms. The ordinary type is good for masking off windows, floors, and all those fixtures that you would otherwise have to paint around very carefully. Mostly though, we use it within a design to prevent paint from drifting into the wrong area, or to create stripes or smart finishes to the edge of a shape. However, ordinary tape can pull a paint film off if it is very fresh or has been applied to a poorly prepared surface. Manufacturers now make tapes for delicate or freshly painted surfaces, but you should test them out in an unobtrusive place before pressing them into service. Another specialist tape is one that will follow a curve, made from a type of crepe paper.

Some techniques and projects in Parts Three and Four require you to mask off well beyond the shape you are working on. This can be done by sticking cash register tape alongside thin tape, rather than by buying wide tape. If you use double-coated masking tape, this is very easy to do.

Cash register tape and paper can also be turned into masking with the aid of repositionable spray adhesive. And tape and paper can all be torn to give a softer edge to a design rather than the super-straight one that you usually get with tapes.

MASKING TAPES
This selection of masking materials includes masking tape that can follow a curve, as well as a blue tape, also called painter's tape, for use on delicate surfaces. The tape for delicate surfaces is very flat, allowing almost no seepage of paint underneath if it is well applied. Cash register tape and parcel paper can also be made into masks.

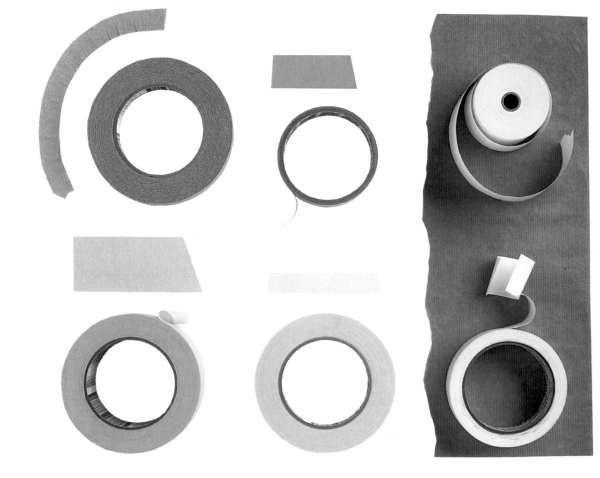

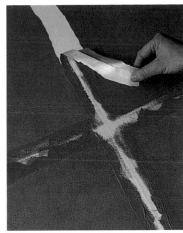

1 Tear cash register tape along its length, spray it with repositionable spray adhesive, and use to mask out a cross.

2 Apply the paint with a small roller, taking care not to press too hard and force paint underneath the masking.

3 Slowly peel the masking away. The uneven edges left by the torn tape leave a soft, natural look.

1 Lay out a grid of masking tape, pressing it down well, then sponge undiluted color evenly into the exposed squares.

2 With careful sponging, it is possible to color individual squares differently.

3 Once the paint is touch-dry, peel the tape away to reveal a crisp-edged motif.

1 Use a combination of cash register tape and masking tape to mask off alternate stripes on a colorwashed background, then apply a second color using a roller.

2 Wait until the paint is touch-dry, then carefully peel off the masking to reveal colorwashed stripes.

MORE MASKING OUT

Masking can also be used to draw and shade motifs. Ordinary masking tape can easily be torn along its length, and strips of torn tape can be built up into attractive, angular motifs. Flexible masking tape can be used for curvilinear designs. It may be difficult to find, and in some cases ⅛in. (3mm.)-wide Fineline tape can be substituted, in conjunction with regular masking tape. Use the Fineline tape to mask the curved edges. Secure it in place, to prevent paint from spilling over, with short pieces of regular masking tape; you can clip into these to get around the curves. Make sure both tapes are well stuck down.

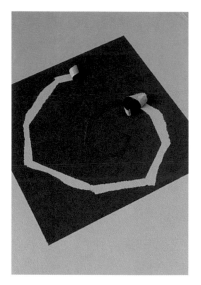

1 Tear small strips of tape along their length and stick them down in a spiral with their ragged edge facing outward.

2 Use more tape and cash register tape to mask off a square around the spiral. Apply the color with a roller.

3 Once the paint is touch-dry, carefully remove all the masking to leave behind an angular spiral on a square. You could "tile" a whole floor in this way.

1 Stick flexible masking tape firmly down on a line drawn with water-soluble marker. Mask off a square around the spiral. Sponge the color on lightly but evenly, using dryish paint.

2 When the paint is touch-dry, slowly remove the tape.

3 Remove the rest of the masking and you will be left with a spiral design on a square.

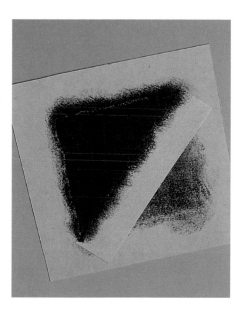

1 Mask off a square. Sponge lightly all over in red, then use a torn strip of stencil board to mask across the diagonal. Sponge again in red on one side of the diagonal.

2 Use a second torn strip of stencil board to mask across the other diagonal and sponge lightly in blue.

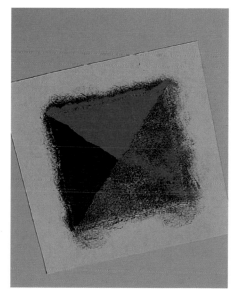

3 Using both strips together across the diagonals, sponge in the final section in a solid blue.

4 Your finished result will appear to be a pyramid with each face illuminated in a slightly different manner.

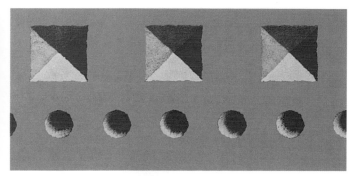

5 This technique was used to make the stenciled border on p. 159.

PART TWO

SIMPLE FINISHES

Traditional and contemporary finishes for walls, finishes to make all kinds of surfaces look like wood, stone and metal, plus ornamental finishes for that decorative final touch

A contemporary look for a paint finish with a past (see p. 85). Paint has been aged for centuries to lend stature to humbler pieces of furniture, but there is more than a hint of irony in the choice of brightly contrasting colors and the emphatic use of aging for this new table of doubtful parentage. The wall has been colorwashed and rubbed back in similar tones (see p. 48).

INTRODUCTION

Paint has been used for centuries to decorate all kinds of homes, and in that time many different finishes and effects have been employed beyond the flat coverage of a simple painted surface.

Many of what are now regarded as traditional paint effects have their origins in the great houses of the European aristocracy and were later adopted by the rising merchant classes, who wanted to share in those splendors themselves. In the Middle Ages in Italy, for example, it was the fashion for merchants to commission artists to paint "hangings" on their walls to simulate the opulence of fabrics they had seen abroad. And the skilled art of dragging was developed in eighteenth-century France by those with more taste than money who wished to enjoy the look of silk-lined walls.

Transformation, illusion, or, more frankly, deception, was usually the guiding principle. As early as the fourteenth century, for example, the art of gilding — applying thin layers of gold to surfaces such as wood or plaster — became an immensely popular way of imitating the real gold decoration that only the richest could afford. Similarly, a trend for simulating marble began during the Renaissance in Italy and France, though in time marbling techniques became enormously sophisticated, with some painters developing fantastical colors instead of realistic grays and pinks and yellows.

The opening of the silk route from China to Europe also had a profound effect on the history of paint finishes. Items decorated with inlaid shell were traded with Europe, and by the sixteenth century Italian craftsman had found a way to repeat the effect and were inlaying shell using pewter. The following two centuries saw French, Dutch, and German craftsmen using the same methods to produce fine objets d'art and furniture. Inlaid tortoiseshell, in particular, was highly prized, but demand outstripped supply, so a simulation technique was developed; this reached the height of its popularity in the late seventeenth century.

The eighteenth century also saw the development of other stone finishes with the fashion for simulating the look of exterior stonework inside the home. At first the finishes were used on large areas and architectural details. Later, they were scaled down for smaller rooms and less grand objects.

The need to transform or simulate materials continues to the present day in the techniques used to produce theatrical scenery and properties. With limited budgets and tight deadlines, these tend to be economical, simple, and quick-drying.

Today great houses may have the best-preserved examples of traditional paint finishes, but there are other good examples of wonderful effects in much simpler public buildings and in homes and apartment buildings all over the world, because alongside the grand tradition there has always been the vibrant legacy of folk and popular

style — demonstrated in this collection of recipes by, for example, the cool blue-gray color palette of the traditional Scandinavian interior and the sober tones of the Shaker community in the United States. These are styles and finishes firmly rooted in the often harsh climatic and economic and/or social realities of a particular region, perpetuated over centuries by people for whom the concept of style has often, for one good reason or another, been meaningless.

Many of the materials used in the past are still available, and experts working on great old buildings and antique funiture undertake restoration work using the same equipment and techniques. However, for less elevated interiors modern substitutes can work well. Since these materials offer quicker results and lower toxicity and in many cases are available in a wider range of colors, they are an attractive alternative.

You have in Part Two a battery of traditional and contemporary effects that will enable you to undertake projects in any number of different styles. Remember, too, that these simple paint finishes can do far more than change the color of a room. We all now recognize how cool blues and warm reds can transform a room's mood, but take that a stage further and you'll find that clever use of color can transport you to other countries and climates. What could be more Mediterranean than those sun-bleached blues? Paint finishes can also revive some favorite memory. For example, a room that reminds you of the sea on sunny summer mornings might be achieved with the translucent glazes of colorwashing.

We hope these recipes will also open up for you the possibilities of painting furniture and other objects. Old or commonplace furniture can so easily take on a new personality, and new, utilitarian pieces that lack life and interest can be fun to age and distress. The latter may seem like madness at first, but the right paint finishes can lift a piece that might otherwise have been simply commonplace into something unusual and genuinely individual.

Eventually you will feel able to adapt the recipes for yourself. Mixing your own colors also adds another dimension, for you can match almost anything from a dish of butter to a leaf picked up on a country walk. After all, if the results are not satisfactory, a surface can always be painted again with a different color or a different finish. Remember, too, that with a little hard work almost any surface, however poor, can be prepared for paint.

There really are no limits to what you can do. So have fun with texture and color as you experiment with the wide range of finishes open to you. Go wild with those sponges; spatter, stipple, and rub down to your heart's content. When you finally rest from your labors, you will have the satisfaction of having created something extraordinary from a simple can of paint.

COLORWASHING

Colorwashing is among the group of finishes that have their beginnings in fine art. Called the broken-color techniques, they all involve distressing a semi-translucent paint or glaze over a contrasting, opaque base coat to produce subtle variations of tone. Specifically, colorwashing involves the application of thin washes of glaze in which the brush marks are left apparent to give the finish texture and depth. It provides an interesting alternative to flat color and can be used to decorate period or modern, town or country interiors.

A terracotta color-wash was used to decorate this farmhouse. Traditionally painted in flat, pale colors or simply in white, such interiors respond well to a rubbed-in wash technique. For this effect, brush the glaze on and then rub it into the wall with a cloth, using a random action.

BASIC RECIPE—YELLOW OCHER ON STONE

INGREDIENTS

To cover approximately 12m² (129ft²)
Base coat ► 34 oz. (1 liter) white latex semigloss paint / 1tbsp. neutral gray artists' acrylic color / 2tbsp. yellow ocher artists' acrylic color / ¹/₂tbsp. raw umber artists' acrylic color
Glaze coat ► 17 oz. (500ml.) white latex flat paint / 17 oz. (500ml.) acrylic glazing liquid (transparent) / 3tbsp. yellow ocher artists' acrylic color / 2tsp. vermilion red artists' acrylic color / 1tsp. raw sienna artists' acrylic color / 14–17 oz. (400–500ml.) water
Optional protective coat ► 1 qt. (1 liter) clear matte acrylic varnish (one coat)

EQUIPMENT

2 containers / paint roller plus tray and 1 x 3in. (75mm.) paintbrush / large, hard-bristled latex brush / badger blender or 1 x 3in. (75mm.) soft-bristled paintbrush / 1 x 2in. (50mm.) varnish brush (optional)

INSTRUCTIONS
Base coat

1 Pour the latex semigloss paint into one of the containers. Add the neutral gray, yellow ocher, and raw umber; stir well.
2 Apply evenly to prepared surface (see pp. 24–7) with a roller. Allow to dry (2–4 hours).

❶ YELLOW OCHER ON STONE
The basic recipe described opposite: its subtle effect works well in traditional interiors.

❷ BLUE ON WHITE
White latex semigloss paint is used for the base coat, and the glaze is colored with 3tbsp. cobalt blue and 2tbsp. ultramarine acrylic color.

❸ TERRACOTTA ON STONE
The stone base follows the basic recipe, and the glaze is colored with 3tbsp. Venetian red and 1tbsp. yellow ocher. A large brushstroke was used.

❹ LILAC ON WHITE
This bold, modern colorway works well in traditional rooms too. The base is white latex semigloss paint, and just 3tbsp. brilliant purple to color the glaze coat.

❺ MINK ON WHITE
A soft, neutral look for a period home or modern interior: white latex semigloss paint for the base, and 2tbsp. neutral gray and 2tbsp. bronze ocher to color the glaze coat. Bold crosshatching was used to create the diamond effect.

❻ GREEN ON WHITE
The glaze is colored with 3tbsp. bright green over a base of white latex semigloss paint, and a bold random brush stroke was used.

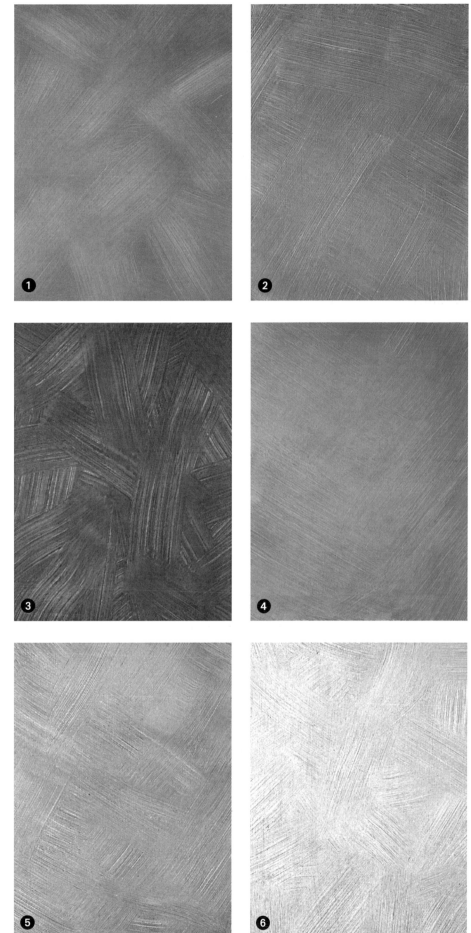

COLORWASHING

Glaze coat

1 Pour the latex flat paint into the other container. Add the acrylic glazing liquid, yellow ocher, vermilion red, raw sienna, and water (a little at a time), and stir well until you have a runny, but not too thin, glaze. The right consistency is important here—the base coat should show through the glaze in the final effect.

2 Apply the glaze coat, using a 3in. (75mm.) paintbrush. Work with random strokes, concentrating on an area of no more than 3ft.² (1m.²) at a time. If you want a more even effect, use arc-like brush strokes instead.

3 Using the dry, hard-bristled brush, go quickly over the surface again, working with random strokes in all directions.

4 Holding the badger blender (or soft-bristled brush), skim the surface lightly, just touching it with the brush. This softens the brushstrokes; but take care—overdo it and you will drag the glaze. Leave to dry (2 hours).

Notes You can repeat the glaze stage if you want a greater depth of color. Latex paint and glazing liquid together dry to a tough finish, but if you are colorwashing an area that will receive a lot of wear, such as a hallway, it is best to protect it with one or two coats of varnish, according to the manufacturers' instructions.

When colorwashing on wood, make sure you apply both base and glaze coats in the direction of the grain. Brush on the base coat, and when it is dry, rub on the glaze using a cloth. Soften the glaze coat as in step 4 above. Again, apply one or two coats of varnish if required.

Exterior use Substitute smooth masonry paint in the base coat, and finish with two coats of matte polyurethane varnish.

Soft blue tones have been used to colorwash this hallway. An ideal use of a simple color effect, it has brightened a narrow, slightly gloomy passageway, and the small amount of ocher used in the glaze mix has taken the coldness out of the end effect.

This simple MDF magazine rack has had an ocher colorwash applied over a stone base coat, following the ingredients given in the basic recipe. The freehand and stenciled decoration are inspired by the Bloomsbury style.

SPONGING OFF AND ON

Sponging is a modern broken-color technique. Natural sponge, moistened with water or soaked in glaze, is used over a contrasting glaze or opaque base coat to produce a softly mottled effect—either by removing or adding color. We like to combine the two methods in a versatile finish which produces both subtle and striking results: pastel hues create an airy lightness, while stronger, related colors give rich, deep tones. Use natural sponges if you can—they create more interesting textures than the uniform marks made by synthetic ones.

BASIC RECIPE—GRAY ON STONE

INGREDIENTS

To cover approximately 12m² (129ft²)

Base coat ▶ 34 oz. (1 liter) white latex semigloss paint / 2tbsp. burnt umber artists' acrylic color / ¹/₂tsp. ultramarine artists' acrylic color / ¹/₂tbsp. Mars black artists' acrylic color

First glaze coat ▶ 17 oz. (500ml.) white latex flat paint / 8¹/₂ oz. (250ml.) acrylic glazing liquid (transparent) / 2tbsp. neutral gray artists' acrylic color / 1tbsp. burnt umber artists' acrylic color / ¹/₄tbsp. Mars black artists' acrylic color / 6¹/₂ oz. (200ml.) water

Second glaze coat ▶ 17 oz. (500ml.) white latex flat paint / 8¹/₂ oz. (250ml.) acrylic glazing liquid / 2tbsp. Mars black artists' acrylic color / ¹/₂tbsp. burnt umber artists' acrylic color / 8¹/₂ oz. (250ml.) water

Optional protective coat ▶ 1 qt. (1 liter) clear matte acrylic varnish (one coat)

EQUIPMENT

3 containers for mixing paint and glaze / 2 x 3in. (75mm.) paintbrushes or 1 paint roller / roller tray / natural sponges in various sizes / water for dampening and rinsing sponges / disposable gloves / 1 x 2in (50mm) varnish brush (optional)

INSTRUCTIONS

Base coat

1 Pour the latex semigloss paint into one of the containers. Add the burnt umber, ultramarine, and Mars black, and stir well.

2 Apply evenly to prepared surface (see pp. 24–7) with a 3in. (75mm.) paintbrush (or roller). Allow to dry (2–4 hours).

First glaze coat

1 Pour the latex flat paint into a second container. Add the acrylic glazing liquid, neutral gray, burnt umber, Mars black, and water (a little at a time); stir well.

2 Apply an even coat of glaze using a 3in. (75mm.) paintbrush and covering the base coat completely. (You can use a roller if you prefer, but only for large areas.)

3 Immerse one of the sponges in water and wring out until almost dry. Put on the gloves and apply it to the surface, partially removing the glaze with soft dabbing movements. Vary your wrist position to create a variety of effects and strokes. You can also create varied effects with sponges of different sizes. Allow to dry (1–2 hours).

Second glaze coat

1 Pour the latex flat paint into a third container. Add the acrylic glazing liquid, Mars black, burnt umber, and water (a little at a time—this glaze must be more watery than the first). Stir well.

2 Pour a little of the glaze into the clean roller tray, refilling as required. (Small quantities reduce the risk of overloading the sponge.)

3 Put on the gloves, and, using another slightly damp sponge, apply the glaze to the wall in light dabbing movements, turning the sponge to vary the pattern. Again, sponges of varying size will help. Rinse them in water regularly to prevent them from clogging. Allow to dry (2 hours).

Notes Apply one or two coats of varnish for a hardwearing surface, according to the manufacturers' instructions. The combination of these techniques gives greater depth to the color and finish, but you can use either of them alone.

❶ GRAY ON STONE
The basic recipe: an ideal treatment for a traditional interior. Above the chair rail the gray glaze has simply been sponged off; below it the same glaze has been sponged off and then on.

❷ DUSKY PINK ON CORAL
The coral base coat is colored with 2tbsp. cadmium red and 1tbsp. raw umber, and the glaze with 2tbsp. cadmium red, 1tbsp. raw umber, and 1/2tbsp. neutral gray. These rich hues work well in traditional or modern interiors.

❸ OCHER ON SAND
A neutral look to complement natural fabrics: color the base coat with 2tbsp. yellow ocher and 1tbsp. raw umber, and the glaze with 3tbsp. yellow ocher.

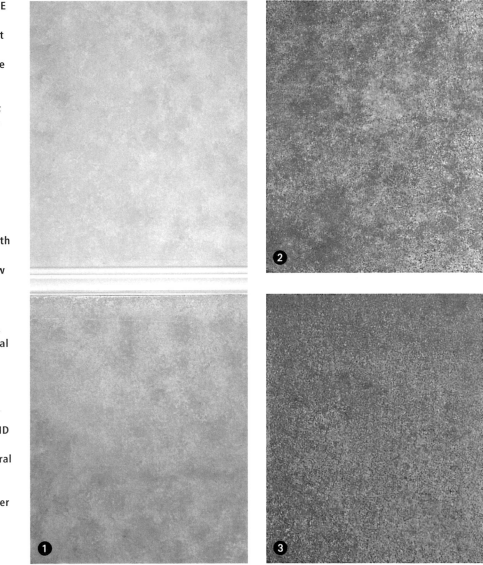

DRAGGING

Developed in the eighteenth century, dragging derives from the techniques of wood graining. Translucent glaze is brushed onto a base coat, and a clean, long-haired brush is drawn from top to bottom to reveal the base color in a series of fine lines. Traditionally a dark, oil-based glaze was used, and oil-based paints remain the more satisfactory medium because they dry more slowly than water-based ones, allowing for longer working; also, the intensity of oil color gives a better result. Attempt it only on smooth surfaces—lumps and bumps spoil the vertical lines.

BASIC RECIPE—OIL-BASED DEEP BLUE ON WHITE

INGREDIENTS

To cover approximately 16m² (172ft²)
Base coat ▶ 1 qt. (1 liter) white oil-based eggshell paint
Glaze coat ▶ 17 oz. (500ml.) oil-based glazing liquid (transparent) / 2tbsp. ultramarine artists' oil color / 1tbsp. Prussian blue artists' oil color / ¹/₂tsp. yellow ocher artists' oil color / 5 oz. (150ml.) mineral spirits
Protective coat ▶ 1 qt. (1 liter) oil-based clear matte varnish

EQUIPMENT

2 x 3in. (75mm.) tossaway brushes or 1 paint roller plus tray / container for mixing glaze / dragging brush or 1 x 3in. (75mm.) flat, long-bristled paintbrush / rags / disposable gloves / steel wool (optional) / 1 x 2in. (50mm.) tossaway brush

INSTRUCTIONS

ALWAYS WORK IN A WELL-VENTILATED AREA

Base coat

Stir the oil-based eggshell paint well, and apply an even coat to your prepared surface (see pp. 24–7) with a 3in. (75mm.) tossaway brush (or roller). Allow to dry (24 hours).

Glaze coat

1 Pour the oil-based glazing liquid into the container. Add the ultramarine, Prussian blue, and yellow ocher, and mix well.
2 Stir in the mineral spirits (a little at a time) until the glaze has a milky consistency.
3 Using a 3in. (75mm.) tossaway brush (or roller), apply to the base coat, working evenly with horizontal and vertical strokes
4 Put on the gloves and wear for the remainder of this stage. Starting at the top of the surface, use the dragging or long-bristled brush to draw or drag the glaze down to the bottom in one uninterrupted stroke. Wipe the brush clean on a rag. Keeping a check on the alignment, begin another stroke. For a rougher effect, repeat the action after each stroke or once the entire wall has been dragged. Or re-drag using steel wool instead of the brush. (Wipe the steel wool clean after each stroke.) Allow to dry (24 hours).

Protective coat

Apply one coat of matte varnish, using the 2in. (50mm.) tossaway brush, according to the manufacturers' instructions.

❶ DEEP BLUE ON WHITE and PALE BLUE ON ULTRAMARINE The upper section illustrates the colorway and method used in the basic recipe. The lower section appears as a mirror image of the other, but different colors are used to achieve the effect. The base coat is a premixed oil-based ultramarine eggshell paint, and the glaze tone is a mix of 2tbsp. titanium white and ¹/₄tsp. ultramarine. It has been dragged and then re-dragged three or four times with steel wool. The border was stenciled with tinted eggshell paint.

❷ OCHER ON STONE

A pale glaze dragged over a deeper base coat: a modern approach. The glaze is tinted with 2tbsp. yellow ocher and 1tbsp. raw umber and applied to a base coat that is colored simply with 2tbsp. yellow ocher.

❸ PALE PINK ON TERRACOTTA

The base coat is coloured with 2tbsp. yellow ocher and 1tbsp. red oxide, and the glaze coat uses 2tbsp. titanium white and ¹/₂tbsp. cadmium red and ¹/₂tsp. cobalt blue. The result: another pale-on-dark colorway.

❹ DEEP RED ON AQUA GREEN

The base coat is colored with 1tbsp. viridian green and 1tbsp. cobalt blue, the glaze with 1tbsp. cadmium red, ¹/₂tbsp. red iron oxide, and ¹/₂tbsp. burnt umber. This gives a sumptuous look.

❺ SEA GREEN ON WHITE

White eggshell was used for the base coat, and the glaze colors are 2tbsp. viridian green and 2tbsp. cobalt blue: a fresh colorway that works equally well in modern and period rooms.

STIPPLING

Traditionally stippling entails the reworking of newly applied paint to create a finely textured, matte finish. Glaze brushed over a different hue or tone and stippled (as here) will reveal glimpses of the color below. A well-prepared surface is essential—the technique emphasizes any imperfection—and oil-based paints are preferable over large areas. Stippling brushes give the best results; block brushes (or shoe brushes) are cheaper alternatives. An elegant effect which adds subtle aging to a room, it also looks good on wood paneling, furniture, and frames.

BASIC RECIPE—OIL-BASED RED ON RED

INGREDIENTS

To cover approximately 16m² (172ft²)
Base coat ▶ 1 qt. (1 liter) premixed deep red oil-based eggshell paint
Glaze coat ▶ 17 oz. (500ml.) oil-based glazing liquid (transparent) / 3tbsp. cadmium red artists' oil color / ¹/2tbsp. raw umber artists' oil color / 1tbsp. linseed oil / 5 oz. (150ml.) mineral spirits
Protective coat ▶ 1 qt. (1 liter) oil-based clear matte varnish

EQUIPMENT

2 x 3in. (75mm.) tossaway brushes or 1 paint roller plus tray / container for mixing glaze / disposable gloves / stippling or block brush / rags / 1 x 2in. (50mm.) paintbrush

INSTRUCTIONS

Base coat

ALWAYS WORK IN A WELL-VENTILATED AREA

Stir the oil-based eggshell paint well and apply an even coat to your prepared surface (see pp. 24–7) with a 3in. (75mm.) tossaway brush (or roller). Allow to dry (24 hours).

Glaze coat

1 Pour the oil-based glazing liquid into a container. Add the cadmium red and raw umber, and stir well.
2 Add the linseed oil and a little mineral spirits, and mix again. Stirring all the time, add more mineral spirits until you have a milky, but not too runny, consistency.
3 Apply to the base coat with a 3in. (75mm.) tossaway brush (or clean roller), using vertical and horizontal strokes for an even finish and covering the base coat completely. If you use a brush, quickly dab the end of it over the glazed surface to get rid of any brush marks.
4 Put on the gloves and wear for the remainder of this stage. Lightly dab the stippling or block brush over the surface, using a gentle tapping action. Clean any drips with a rag. Work with the wrist rather than the arm, as it is less tiring and gives a softer look. Vary the finish by changing the angle of the brush occasionally. Allow to dry completely (24 hours).

Protective coat

Apply one coat of matte varnish, using the 2in. (50mm.) tossaway brush, according to the manufacturer's instructions.

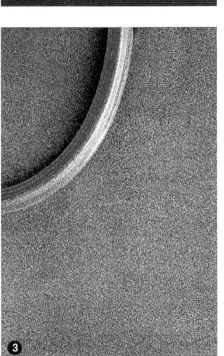

2

3

4

① RED ON RED
The basic recipe: in this classic scheme the deep red glaze appears even more intense alongside tiny flecks of the red base coat. The result is a subtle but dramatic way of executing the effect.

② GREEN ON GREEN
For the base coat, 34 oz. (1 liter) white oil-based eggshell paint is tinted with 1¹/₂tbsp. sap green. The glaze coat follows the basic recipe, but using 1¹/₂tbsp. sap green and 1tbsp. titanium white. This would be a lovely scheme for a bathroom.

③ DEEP GREEN ON STONE
The coloring in the base coat is 2tbsp. yellow ocher and ¹/₂tbsp. raw sienna (stirred into 34 oz. [1 liter] white oil-based eggshell paint). Again, the glaze follows the basic recipe, but using 2tbsp. sap green and ¹/₂tbsp. raw umber. These striking tones have the authority for a period setting.

④ YELLOW ON YELLOW OCHER
A bold colorway for a contemporary home: 34 oz. (1 liter) white oil-based eggshell paint is colored with 2tbsp. yellow ocher to create the base, while the glaze follows the basic recipe, but using 3tbsp. yellow ocher and ¹/₂tbsp. cadmium yellow.

WATER-BASED STIPPLING

Apply two coats of a premixed deep red latex paint. Allow to dry (2–4 hours). Then mix a glaze using the same quantities as for the basic recipe but substituting acrylic glazing liquid and artists' acrylic for the oil-based glazing liquid and oil colors, and water for the linseed oil and mineral spirits. Apply the glaze and stipple as described opposite. Allow to dry (2–4 hours) and apply one coat of a matte or semigloss acrylic varnish as required. It is important to work quickly, as water-based products dry faster than oil-based ones.

DRY BRUSHING

In this technique the brush is kept relatively dry as glaze is applied lightly over a base coat to create a cloudy effect. We have used a white base coat for all these examples, but the finish is just as successful on a tinted base or when the dry-brushed coat is the lighter. It can be subtle if applied in soft hues with soft strokes or bold if you use hard-bristled brushes and strong colors. An easy way to give texture to modern interiors, it is also used to create an aged finish for period settings—scene painters often use it to age scenery and props. It is ideal for highlighting architectural moldings and, because it is extremely resilient, for furniture.

BASIC RECIPE—DEEP BLUE ON WHITE

INGREDIENTS

To cover approximately 12m² (129ft²)
Base coat ▶ 1 qt. (1 liter) white latex flat paint
Glaze coat ▶ 8¹/₂ oz. (250ml.) white latex flat paint / 8¹/₂ oz. (250ml.) acrylic glazing liquid (transparent) / 3tbsp. ultramarine artists' acrylic color / 1tbsp. neutral gray artists' acrylic color / 4oz. (120ml.) water
Optional protective coat ▶ 1 qt. (1 liter) clear matte or semigloss acrylic varnish

EQUIPMENT

1 x 3in. (75mm.) paintbrush or paint roller plus tray / container for mixing glaze / 1 x 2in. (50mm.) hard-bristled brush / scrap wooden board / 1 x 2in. (50mm.) varnish brush (optional)

INSTRUCTIONS
Base coat

Stir the latex paint well and apply an even coat to your prepared surface (see pp. 24–7) with the 3in. (75mm.) brush (or roller). Allow to dry (2–4 hours).

Glaze coat

1 Pour the latex paint into the container. Add the acrylic glazing liquid, colors and water (a little at a time), stirring well. **2** Dip the tip of the hard-bristled brush into the glaze and remove excess paint on the wooden board. Working with random, short brushstrokes, apply to the base. Recharge the brush as the glaze becomes too light, still letting some of the base show through. Leave to dry (2 hours).

Notes For greater depth of color, repeat the glazing stage once the paint is dry. For a hardwearing finish, apply one coat of varnish, according to the manufacturers' instructions.
Exterior use Substitute smooth masonry paint for the base coat, and finish with two coats of polyurethane varnish.

Above left: This wall was dry-brushed in several hues to give interest and variety. The dramatic mix of three separate glaze coats—green, lilac, and purple applied in random patches and then blended together—has a modern feel that confirms an eclectic taste is at work here.

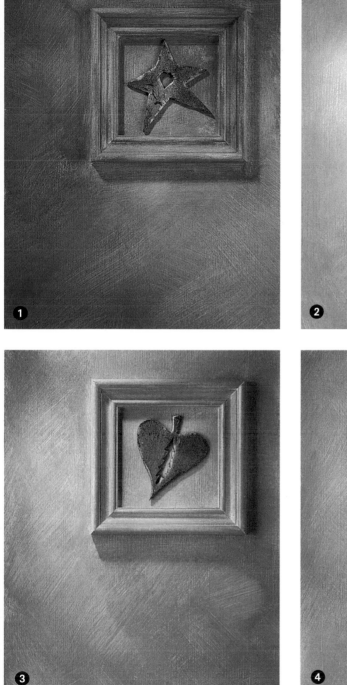

❶ DEEP BLUE ON WHITE
The basic recipe colorway: this delightful bathroom blue was dry-brushed only once.

❷ YELLOW ON WHITE
Here the bright glaze is tinted with 2tbsp. cadmium yellow and 1/2tbsp. vermilion red. This is a sunny, cheering scheme that would sit extremely well in the living or dining room of either a modern or more traditional home.

❸ PEACH PINK ON WHITE
The glaze color is a mix of 2tbsp. rose madder pink and 1tbsp. titanium white, spiked with 1/2tsp. cadmium yellow for a gentle, feminine look that would work in a bedroom.

❹ BRIGHT GREEN ON WHITE
This vibrant glaze is colored with 2tbsp. chromium green and 1tbsp. cadmium yellow. The resulting tone would be ideal in a kitchen or bathroom. Try it in a sunroom, too, where it is surprisingly effective.

LOOSE-GLAZE BRUSHING

Loose-glaze brushing is a softer, looser form of dragging which we developed from period finishes we studied in stately homes of the eighteenth and early nineteenth centuries. Because the effect uses water-based paints, it is simple to achieve, and it dries a great deal faster than conventional dragging (see p. 54) but gives much the same pleasing results. As the technique and materials require less effort to control than in oil-based dragging, you can brush the glaze horizontally or diagonally as well as vertically, which makes it a versatile finish. A

longhaired paintbrush is the only tool you will need, and this is far cheaper than a dragging brush. Another advantage of loose-glaze brushing is that it can be used on poor surfaces. The water-based glaze is thinner, and the effect you are aiming for less precise, so minor imperfections tend not to show up. However, do fill any large cracks or holes to stop paint from collecting there. As a resilient and hardwearing finish, loose-glaze brushing can also be used successfully on furniture.

This room has been loose-glaze brushed vertically in a soft green to give the same sense of height as vertical stripes. Although based upon period effects, the finish will adapt well to a variety of modern interiors.

BASIC RECIPE—DEEP GREEN ON MINT GREEN

INGREDIENTS

To cover approximately 12m² (129ft²)

Base coat ▸ 34 oz. (1 liter) white latex flat paint / 2tbsp. viridian green artists' acrylic color / 1tbsp. brilliant green artists' acrylic color

Glaze coat ▸ 17 oz. (500ml.) white latex flat paint / 8¹/₂ oz. (250ml.) acrylic glazing liquid (transparent) / 2tbsp. viridian green artists' acrylic color / 2tbsp. oxide of chromium green artists' acrylic color / 1tbsp. emerald green artists' acrylic color / 10 oz. (300ml.) water

Optional protective coat ▸ 1 qt. (1 liter) clear matte or semigloss acrylic varnish

EQUIPMENT

2 containers / 1 x 3in. (75mm.) paintbrush / 1 x 5in. (125mm.) long-bristled paintbrush / rags / 1 x 2in. (50mm.) varnish brush (optional)

INSTRUCTIONS

Base coat

1 Pour the latex paint into one of the containers. Add the viridian and brilliant greens, and stir well.

2 Apply evenly to your prepared surface (see pp. 24–7) with the 3in. (75mm.) brush. Allow to dry (2–4 hours).

Glaze coat

1 Pour the latex paint into the other container. Add the acrylic glazing liquid, viridian, oxide of chromium and emerald greens, and water (a little at a time), stirring well.

2 Load the 5in. (125mm.) brush with glaze and apply in a series of single, uninterrupted strokes, working from top to bottom of the surface and overlapping each stroke slightly.

3 Using the same brush, work over the surface again until faint brush lines appear on the glaze as you begin to drag it. Eradicate any drips with a rag. Allow to dry (2 hours).

Notes For a hardwearing finish, apply one coat of varnish, according to the manufacturers' instructions.

❶ DEEP GREEN ON MINT GREEN The basic, traditional colorway, but with diagonal brushstrokes to suggest an engaging alternative. The effect is loose and free without being sloppy.

❷ STONE ON BLUE Here a pale glaze has been applied to a premixed deep blue latex base. The strokes are horizontal. The glaze color-mix is 2tbsp. titanium white, 1/2tbsp. raw sienna, and 1/2tbsp. yellow ocher.

❸ PALE PINK ON RED This example, with vertical brushing, recalls the classic dragged look. The glaze is colored with 2tbsp. titanium white, 2tbsp. cadmium red, and 1/2tbsp. rose madder pink and applied to a base of premixed red latex paint.

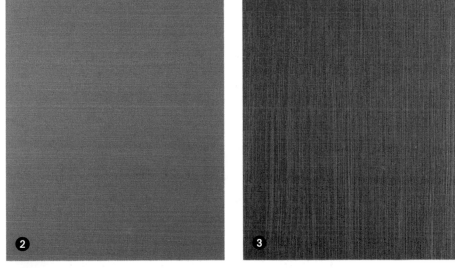

SIMPLE FRESCO

This finish gives the look often seen in old Italian frescos, where medieval painters perfected a technique that involved the application of water-based colors to wet plaster. Thankfully our recipe does not have to be applied to newly plastered walls—it just looks as if it does. Most authentic when undertaken in the colors of true fresco, this hardwearing effect is ideal for walls and ceilings and resilient enough for kitchens and bathrooms. A good way of aging new interiors, it is also an excellent backdrop for stenciling. Plaster moldings and other architectural details respond well to the technique too, and you can perform miracles with old furniture and frames.

BASIC RECIPE—TERRACOTTA ON CORAL

INGREDIENTS

To cover approximately 12m² (129ft²)

Base coat ▸ 34 oz. (1 liter) white latex flat paint / 2tbsp. Venetian red artists' acrylic color / ¹/₂tbsp. raw sienna artists' acrylic color

Glaze coat ▸ 17 oz. (500ml.) white latex flat paint / 8¹/₂ oz. (250ml.) acrylic glazing liquid (transparent) / 2tbsp. bronze ocher artists' acrylic color / 2tbsp. raw sienna artists' acrylic color / ¹/₂tbsp. Venetian red artists' acrylic color / 8¹/₂ oz. (250ml.) water

Distressing the surface ▸ 1 x 500ml can liming wax / 2 oz. (60g.) whiting

EQUIPMENT

2 containers for mixing paint and glaze / 1 x 3in. (75mm.) paintbrush / 1 x 2in. (50mm.) hard-bristled brush / disposable gloves / rags / water for soaking rags / medium-grade sandpaper

INSTRUCTIONS
Base coat

1 Pour the latex paint into one of the containers. Add the Venetian red and raw sienna, and stir well.

2 Apply to your prepared surface (see pp. 24–7) with the paintbrush, using random strokes. Allow to dry (2–4 hours).

Glaze coat

1 Pour the latex paint into the other container. Add the acrylic glazing liquid, bronze ocher, raw sienna, Venetian red, and water (a little at a time), and stir well.

2 Apply to the base coat, using the hard-bristled brush. Work in all directions, using rough, uneven brushstrokes.

3 Wear gloves for all the remaining stages. Quickly immerse a rag in water and wring it out until almost dry. Use the damp rag to rub the glaze into the base coat with a circular motion, varying the effect as much as possible. Allow to dry (1 hour).

Distressing the surface

1 Rub sandpaper over the surface in some areas to remove some of the paint.

Above left: Here the simple fresco technique has been applied to a plaster-cast head of Dante, using the archetypal terracotta on coral colorway of the basic recipe. Note how rubbing whiting into the surface has taken off some of the color.

2 Rub liming wax into other areas with a clean rag.

3 Again using a clean rag, quickly rub a little whiting into the waxed areas to create a dusty effect.

Notes If you want a greater depth of color, repeat the glazing and sandpapering sequences before you begin steps 2–3 of Distressing the surface.

Exterior use Substitute smooth masonry paint in the base coat, and finish with two coats of matte polyurethane varnish.

❶ TERRACOTTA ON CORAL
On a flat surface the basic color-way seems to gain intensity. This is a rich scheme for a grand neoclassical living room.

❷ COBALT BLUE ON STONE
The base coat is tinted with 1tbsp. raw sienna and 1tbsp. burnt umber, and the glaze with 3tbsp. cobalt blue and 1tbsp. Prussian blue for a color popular in medieval frescos.

❸ GREEN ON STONE
This bright variation is an experiment in modern colors. The base coat is made as for sample 2, while the glaze color-mix is 3tbsp. bright green with 1tbsp. yellow ocher.

❹ SALMON PINK ON STONE
Another fresco scheme, this would suit modern or period rooms. The stone base of sample 2 softens a glaze tinted with 2tbsp. rose madder pink, ¹/₂tbsp. titanium white, and ¹/₂tsp. yellow ocher.

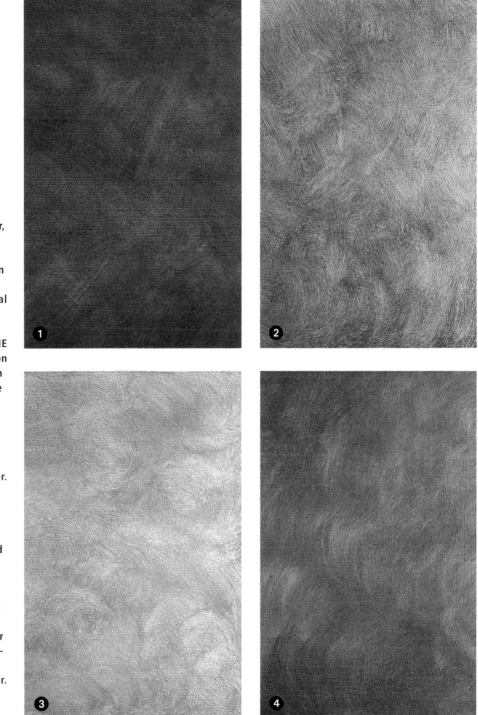

MOCK PLASTER

This *faux* finish, with its look of aged paint brushed onto rough plaster, was reputedly first used in French café-bars of the 1970s. In fact, the broken-color effect requires a conventional latex base, topped with a mix of whiting and powder pigment rubbed into a layer of wax. You can adapt this recipe to use subtle earth hues, but experimenting with bright colors is fun, and the real delight of working with pigment is the intensity of color you can achieve. Remember, though, that the strength of pigment color can be alarming on first view, so run several tests before you begin painting. Pigment colors also need thorough mixing; if you want to tone them down with more whiting, make sure you avoid streaking.

A mock-plaster finish can add interest to plaster moldings and other architectural details. We used cadmium green to highlight a standard ceiling rosette.

The finish works best on a white base, but tints can be used successfully: remember, it must be acrylic color for the water-based latex paint. Mock plaster will suit new or old interiors, and the waxed surface makes it easy to wipe clean. Try it on garden ornaments too, especially those made of plaster.

BASIC RECIPE—ULTRAMARINE ON WHITE

INGREDIENTS

To cover approximately 12m² (129ft²)
Base coats ▶ 2 qts. (2 liters) white latex flat paint
Top coat ▶ 1 x 1 pint (500ml.) tub white wax / 9 oz. (250g.) ultramarine powder pigment / 9 oz. (250g.) whiting or powdered chalk

EQUIPMENT

1 x 3in. (75mm.) paintbrush or paint roller plus tray / rags / protective mask / small container for mixing pigment / 1 x 2in. (50mm.) varnish brush (optional)

INSTRUCTIONS
Base coats

Stir the latex paint well, and apply two even coats to your prepared surface (see pp. 24-7), using the brush (or roller). Allow 2–4 hours for each coat to dry.

Top coat

1 Using a rag and a circular action, rub a thick but even layer of white wax into the base coat.
2 Put on the mask. Place the ultramarine and whiting (or powdered chalk) in the container, and stir well.
3 Using another rag, rub the whiting mixture quickly into the wax with a downward action to give a broken color finish very like real plaster. Allow to dry completely (2–3 hours).

Notes Repeat the top coat with a toner color (see pp. 30–31 to vary the effect.
Exterior use Add a coat of wax polish after the top coat, to protect the surface of your piece.

64

1 **ULTRAMARINE ON WHITE**
The basic recipe: this strong color is ideal for a bathroom, where mock plaster's wipe-clean qualities would be appreciated.

2 **PINK ON WHITE**
Three powder pigments are used to create a dramatic pink for the top coat: $4^2/5$oz. (125g.) alizarin crimson and $3^1/2$oz. (100g.) magenta, sharpened with $9/10$oz. (25g.) ultramarine. Follow the basic recipe for the base coats.

3 **OCHER ON WHITE**
A sample to demonstrate the use of pure yellow ocher pigment in the top coat (quantity as for the basic recipe). This stunning variation would look delightful in a traditional interior. Again, follow the basic recipe for the base coats.

RUBBED-BACK PLASTER

This technique is inspired by the rough-painted walls of unrestored artisan cottages of the late nineteenth and early twentieth centuries. Money and time were limited, so the inhabitants often painted straight over the previous color in a single coat, making the paint stretch farther by applying it sparingly or by diluting it with water. The effect is achieved by adding whiting to contrasting glazes to age them, by applying the paint roughly with hard-bristled brushes, and by rubbing down with sandpaper. The result is a finish similar to, but softer than, the limewashing often seen in English interiors.

BASIC RECIPE—AQUAMARINE ON PALE PINK

INGREDIENTS

To cover approximately 12m² (129ft²)
Base coat ▸ 1 qt. (1 liter) white latex flat paint
First color ▸ 8¹/₂ oz. (250ml.) white latex flat paint / 4¹/₄oz. (125ml.) rose madder pink artists' acrylic color / 3¹/₂oz. (100g.) whiting / 4¹/₄oz. (125ml.) water
Second color ▸ 8¹/₂ oz. (250ml.) white latex flat paint / 4tbsp. turquoise blue artists' acrylic color / 2tbsp. bright green artists' acrylic color / 1tbsp. cobalt blue artists' acrylic color / 3¹/₂oz. (100g.) whiting / 4¹/₄oz. (125ml.) water
Optional protective coat ▸ 1 qt. (1 liter) clear matte acrylic varnish

EQUIPMENT

1 x 3in. (75mm.) paintbrush or paint roller plus tray / 2 containers for mixing colors / 2 x 3in. (75mm.) hard-bristled brushes / disposable gloves / medium-grade sandpaper / 1 x 2in. (50mm.) varnish brush (optional)

INSTRUCTIONS
Base coat

Stir the latex paint well and apply an even coat to your prepared surface (see pp. 24–7), using the 3in. (75mm.) paintbrush (or roller). Allow to dry (2–4 hours).

First color

1 Pour the latex paint into one of the containers, and add rose madder pink, whiting, and water (a little at a time). Stir well.
2 Using one of the hard-bristled brushes, apply to the base coat in random strokes. Allow to dry (2–4 hours).
3 Put on the gloves and rub sandpaper gently over the surface to reveal some of the base coat.

Second color

1 Pour the latex paint into the other container. Add the turquoise, green, cobalt blue, and whiting (or powdered chalk), and mix. Then add the water (a little at a time), stirring well.
2 Using the other hard-bristled brush, apply to the first color in random strokes. Allow to dry (2–4 hours).
3 Sand vigorously to reveal some of the first color and base.

Notes For a hardwearing finish, apply one coat of varnish, according to the manufacturer's instructions.
Exterior use Substitute smooth masonry paint for the base coat and finish with two coats of matte polyurethane varnish.

RUBBED-BACK PLASTER

❶ AQUAMARINE ON PALE PINK
The basic recipe: this subtle finish has a cloudy, aged look which is extremely appealing. The colorway would suit a bath-room or bedroom.

❷ PALE GREEN ON OLIVE
The first color here is a deep, pre-mixed olive green, and the top color simply 8½oz. (250ml.) white latex flat paint, tinted with 1tbsp. viridian green. Follow the basic recipe for quantities of whiting and water.

❸ CREAMY WHITE ON YELLOW
A bright scheme for a kitchen or a living or dining room: 2tbsp. cadmium yellow is used to tint the first color coat, with a dash (½tbsp.) of raw umber for the top coat.

❹ WARM GRAY ON WHITE
This gentle color-way could be used in modern or period homes. The first color coat is pure white, while the second is tinted with 2tbsp. neutral gray and ½tbsp. yellow ocher.

TEXTURING

There are many different ways to texture paint. You can add sawdust for a coarse grain or whiting for subtlety—here we use fine sand in the base coat for a medium-grade finish. The way you apply your mix can give surface interest too. The obvious advantage of texturing is that it is a wonderful disguise for imperfect walls. But it can bring character to any surface, or a tough finish to a sunroom or exterior wall. Premixed textured paints are now available in a wider color range, although in most cases it is more satisfactory to mix your own using artists' acrylics, and the brighter hues make this simple technique remarkably versatile. The samples here use a white base, as it best illustrates the finish. But the latex paint can be tinted before sand is added. Try texturing garden ornaments: statues and pots take on an antique look when a textured base is used under a rust, verdigris, or lead finish (see pp. 106–11).

Textured finishes inside and out: a bold, contemporary use of color and surface interest have combined to make this an excellent choice for a minimalist home in Mexico.

BASIC RECIPE—YELLOW OCHER ON WHITE

INGREDIENTS

To cover approximately 12m² (129ft²)
Base coat ► 1 qt. (1 liter) white latex flat paint / 8 oz. (240g.) fine sand
Glaze coat ► 8¹/₂ oz. (250ml.) white latex flat paint / 8¹/₂ oz. (250ml.) acrylic glazing liquid / artists' acrylic colors: 2tbsp. yellow ocher and 1tbsp. raw sienna / 5 oz. (150ml.) water
Optional protective coat ► 1 qt. (1 liter) clear matte acrylic varnish

EQUIPMENT

2 containers for mixing paint and glaze / 2 x 3in. (75mm.) paintbrushes / 1 x 2in. (50mm.) varnish brush (optional)

❶ YELLOW OCHER ON WHITE
The basic recipe colorway, demonstrating two different textures above and below a chair rail colorwashed (see p. 48) in purple. More sand (13oz. [370g.]) was added to the base coat used on the lower panel to create a distinctly heavier texture.

❷ SOFT GRAY ON WHITE
This sample illustrates the potential subtlety of the finish. A little very fine sand (4oz. [115g.]) was used in the base coat to create the gentle texturing, and 2tbsp. neutral gray and ½tbsp. magenta colored the glaze.

❸ ROSE ON WHITE
A strong color for a modern interior: the glaze is tinted with 3tbsp. magenta and 1tbsp. cadmium red, mellowed with ½tbsp. burnt umber. Again 13oz. (370g.) sand was added to the base coat.

INSTRUCTIONS
Base coat

Pour the latex paint into a container. Add the sand, stirring well. Apply to the prepared surface (see pp. 24–7). Allow to dry (2–4 hours).

Glaze coat

1 Pour the latex paint into the other container. Add the acrylic glazing liquid, yellow ocher, raw sienna, and water (a little at a time) and stir well.
2 Apply to the base coat in random brushstrokes. Work over the glaze several times, still allowing some of the base coat to show through. Leave to dry (2–3 hours).

Notes For a hardwearing finish, apply one coat of varnish.
Exterior use Use textured masonry paint for the base coat (no sand needed), and finish with matte polyurethane varnish.

AGING WOOD

Wood ages naturally through general wear and tear. Furniture exposed to sunlight fades, and polished wood slowly darkens as it collects dust and grime. It is that sense of time past that gives any well-used and loved piece its appeal, and since the nineteenth century craftsmen have striven to simulate this look on new wood. Virtually any wood can be aged, and there are any number of reasons for wanting to do so. Perhaps you have a new pine chest that needs to be aged to fit alongside older pieces. Or maybe a move to a more traditional home has left modern pieces looking out of place. The distressing techniques may seem a little drastic, but it is up to you to decide how far to go.

BASIC RECIPE—AGING PINE

INGREDIENTS

For a small wooden chest
Antiquing glaze ▶ 17 oz. (500ml.) / white glue / 34 oz. (1 liter) water / 1¹/₃oz. (40g.) raw sienna powder pigment / 1¹/₃oz. (40g.) raw umber powder pigment (one coat)
Optional protective coat ▶ 1 pint (500ml.) clear matte acrylic varnish (one coat)

EQUIPMENT

Bradawl or 2in. (50mm.) nail and hammer / craft knife (optional) / container for mixing glaze / 1 x 3in. (75mm.) tossaway brush / lint-free cotton rags / 1 x 2in. (50mm.) varnish brush (optional)

This modern pine chest has been aged with a glaze that suggests something of the look of liming. You can still see the original color—just inside the open drawer. The white glue solution was colored with 1¹/₃oz. (40g.) burnt umber and 1oz. (30g.) white powder pigment. The modern knobs were replaced with others more in keeping with its aged look.

INSTRUCTIONS
Distressing the wood

Use the bradawl (or nail and hammer) to make the small clusters of holes typical of woodworm. You can also, if you like, add occasional scratches, using a craft knife, and small indentations with the hammer.

Antiquing glaze

1 Pour the white glue into the container. Add the water (a little at a time), and stir well.

2 Add the raw sienna and raw umber, and again stir well, making sure that no lumps remain.

3 Brush the glaze onto your prepared surface (see pp. 24–7) in random strokes.

4 Make a flat pad of cotton rag and use it to rub the glaze into the surface, paying particular attention to the distressed areas. (This process will also help remove any excess glaze.) Change the rag frequently, as it will quickly become clogged with glaze. On small areas the drying time is approx. 1 hour; if you are aging a large surface, such as a floor, work on an area no larger than 6ft.^{2} (2m.^{2}) at a time.

Notes Repeat the glaze stage for a greater depth of color. For a more hardwearing finish apply one or two coats of varnish, following the manufacturers' instructions.

❶ AGING PINE Here the basic recipe colorway is applied to a new pine drawer. The resulting dark color represents the look pine wood might acquire after some years in a hard-working area such as a kitchen.

❷ OCHER ON ASH This paler hue is made by coloring the glaze with 2oz. (60g.) yellow ocher and ^{3}/4oz. (20g.) raw umber. The resulting effect works well with old pine. The original wood was ash, which has a grayish hue.

❸ GRAY ON LIMED WOOD Two antiquing glazes are used to create a gray tone on limed wood. The first glaze is tinted with 1oz. (30g.) white and ^{3}/4oz. (20g.) black, while the second one is colored with ^{3}/4oz. (20g.) burnt umber and ^{1}/3oz. (10g.) ultramarine blue.

SPATTER

Spatter is a useful technique which forms the basis of a variety of paint finishes (see, for example, granite on p. 100), but it is also fun to use the technique alone. It works well on architectural features, such as pillars, molding, and paneling, and on small items of furniture. But avoid the temptation to spatter walls: over a large area those tiny dots can create weird optical effects. Spattering looks easy, but achieving a pleasing, even result takes practice; so use a test board to try out the effect before you begin. It is also a difficult finish to control—careful masking and protection are essential.

❶ GOLD
The basic recipe: for moldings.

❷ RED
Base color: premixed deep red. Spatter colors (all 1tbsp.): 1st, raw umber; 2nd, alizarin crimson; 3rd, yellow ocher; 4th, white.

❸ OYSTER
Base color: 2tbsp. neutral gray and 1tbsp. burnt umber. Spatter colors: 1st, 1tbsp. raw umber; 2nd, 1tbsp. neutral gray; 3rd, 1/2tbsp. neutral gray and 1/2tbsp. titanium white; 4th, 1tbsp. titanium white.

❹ BLUE
Base color: 1tbsp. cobalt blue and 2tbsp. permanent light blue. Spatter colors: 1st, 1tbsp. ultramarine; 2nd, 1tbsp. neutral gray; 3rd, 1/2tbsp. cobalt blue and 1/2tbsp. titanium white; 4th, 1tbsp. titanium white.

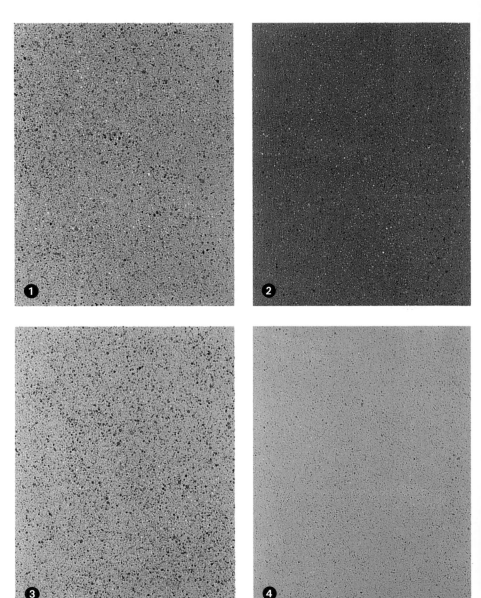

BASIC RECIPE—GOLD IN FOUR COLORS

INGREDIENTS

To cover approximately 6m² (65ft²)
Base coat ▶ 17 oz. (500ml.) white latex flat paint / 1tbsp. Venetian red artists' acrylic color / 1tbsp. raw umber artists' acrylic color / 1/2tbsp. yellow ocher artists' acrylic color

First spatter ▶ 1tbsp. burnt umber artists' acrylic color / 1tbsp. water
Second spatter ▶ 1tbsp. raw sienna artists' acrylic color / 1tbsp. water
Third spatter ▶ 1tbsp. yellow ocher artists' acrylic color / 1tbsp. water
Fourth spatter ▶ 1tbsp. titanium white artists' acrylic color / 1tbsp. water
Optional protective coat ▶ 1 pint (500ml.) clear matte or satin acrylic varnish
(one coat)

EQUIPMENT

Container for paint / 1 x 2in (50mm.) paintbrush / drop cloths / masking tape / rag / 4 small jars for glaze / disposable gloves / 4 x 1in. (25mm.) fitches / 1 x 2in. (50mm.) varnish brush (optional)

INSTRUCTIONS
Base coat

1 Pour the latex paint into the container. Add the Venetian red, raw umber, and yellow ocher, and stir well.

2 Apply an even coat to your prepared surface (see pp. 24–7) with the paintbrush, and allow to dry (2–4 hours).

Spatter coats

1 Lay down the drop cloths to protect the surrounding areas and use masking tape to cover any parts of the surface you do not wish to spatter—the spray will go everywhere. (It is wise to remove most of the tackiness on a rag before sticking the tape onto the surface.)

2 Place each of the four acrylic colors into a separate small jar. Add the water to each and stir well.

3 Put on the gloves and load the first fitch with the darkest glaze. Tap it firmly against another clean, dry fitch held about 6–10in. (15–25cm.) away from the surface. Your aim is to create a "mist" of large, close-spaced paint dots. It is important to determine the correct loading of paint on the brush before you begin: consistency is one of the greatest problems with this technique. Work from top to bottom of the surface, concentrating on a wide area to avoid creating a "column" effect and taking care not to leave any bald patches. Finer, well-spaced spatter is created by standing closer to the surface.

4 Repeat step 3 with the other spatter coats, using a clean brush for each and applying the darkest glaze first and finishing with the white. You can vary each coat by changing the distance from the wall at which you hold the brush. Allow all coats to dry (2 hours).

Notes Apply one or two coats of matte or satin varnish if a hardwearing finish is required, following the manufacturers' instructions. You can also spatter by loading a toothbrush or similar flat, hard-bristled brush with paint and flicking back the bristles with your fingers, but determine the correct loading of paint on the brush before you begin.

Spatter adds individuality to this simple stool. A premixed deep ultramarine blue base coat was used, and the spatter colors were: 1st, 1/2tbsp. cobalt blue and 1/2tbsp. white; 2nd, 1/2tbsp. ultramarine blue and 1/2tbsp. black; 3rd, 1tbsp. yellow ocher; and 4th, 1tbsp. titanium white.

WATER-BASED CRACKLE

The simulation of the crazing that appears on painted or varnished furniture when the underlying wood expands and contracts as a result of changes in temperature was first undertaken in France as early as the eighteenth century. Today, with the help of proprietary preparations, this aging technique seems almost magical in its simplicity. One or two coats of a transparent crackle varnish are applied over a colored base coat which has been allowed to dry. As the crackle varnish itself dries, it begins to work against the base coat, and cracks appear in its surface. Then, when the contrasting topcoat is applied and left to dry, the base-coat color is thrown into relief and the cracks become even more apparent. Tinted glazes can also be rubbed into the surface to enhance and antique the finish. The effect can be traditional or contemporary, depending on the color combination you choose. A natural for wood and plaster—it captures something of the aging often seen on Italian Renaissance frescos and painted panels—crackle can also give even the ugliest plastic laminate a new dimension.

BASIC RECIPE—STONE ON BLUE

INGREDIENTS

To cover approximately 6m² (65ft²)
Base coat ▶ 1 pint (500ml.) premixed sky blue latex flat paint
Crackle coat ▶ 8¹/₂ oz. (250ml.) acrylic crackle varnish (transparent)
Top coat ▶ 1 pint (500ml.) premixed stone-colored latex flat paint
Optional antiquing coat ▶ 8¹/₂ oz. (250ml.) pale antiquing patina
Protective coat ▶ 1 pint (500ml.) clear satin acrylic varnish (one coat)

EQUIPMENT

2 x 2in. (50mm.) paintbrushes / 1 x 1in. (25mm.) tossaway brush / 1 x 2in. (50mm.) varnish brush / rags (optional)

INSTRUCTIONS
Base coat

Stir the latex paint well, and apply one coat to your prepared surface (see pp. 24–7), using one of the paintbrushes. Allow to dry (2–4 hours). A premixed latex paint reacts more effectively against the crackle varnish, so don't mix a color.

Crackle coat

Using the tossaway brush, apply one coat of crackle varnish to the entire surface, working horizontally if you want horizontal cracks and vertically if you want vertical ones. As it dries, the varnish begins to crack or craze. The thicker this coat is, the fewer and larger the cracks will be; the more it is worked the finer and more numerous. Allow to dry (2 hours).

Above left: The horizontal crazing on this simple MDF box was created by brushing a single coat of water-based crackle varnish in one direction over a base of premixed stone-colored latex paint. The topcoat is a premixed deep blue latex paint.

❶ STONE ON BLUE
The basic color-way: two coats of crackle varnish are applied in opposite directions for an attractive, heavily crazed effect. The final two coats of protective varnish will make this an extremely durable surface.

❷ PEA ON STRAW
Two coats of crackle varnish, again cross-brushed, over a base coat of straw-colored latex paint: the pea green of the top coat was widely used in Victorian times, so this scheme would suit a nineteenth-century interior.

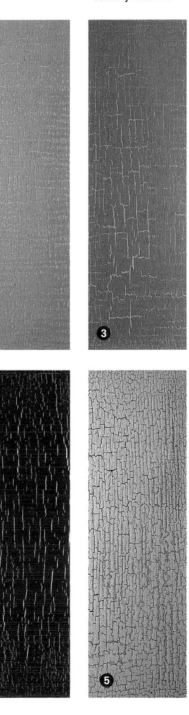

❸ SOFT LILAC ON ICE-CREAM YELLOW
This colorway works well in a modern setting. Here again two coats of cross-brushed crackle varnish are used.

❹ DEEP RED ON STONE
For a color combination popular in the Victorian era: a stone latex base coat under a deep red top coat. Only one coat of crackle was applied in vertical strokes.

❺ WARM GRAY ON BRICK
The deep red base under warm gray is typical of the Georgian period, and the two coats of crackle varnish are cross-brushed and well worked to create fine crazing.

WATER-BASED CRACKLE

Top coat

Stir the latex paint well, brush an even coat onto the crazed surface using the other latex brush, and leave to dry (2–4 hours). As the topcoat dries, the cracks will become apparent once more, revealing the blue of the base coat. (You can speed the drying process with a hairdryer.)

The palest green water-based crackle on a paneled wall could work wonderfully well in a period setting.

Protective coat

Using the varnish brush, apply one coat of varnish, according to the manufacturers' instructions. Repeat if a particularly hardwearing finish is required.

Notes If you want an even more pronounced effect, repeat the crackle stage before applying the top coat, brushing the varnish on in the opposite direction. For a more antique finish, use a rag to rub in a layer of antiquing patina after the topcoat has dried and leave to dry (1 hour) before applying the protective coat.

OIL-BASED CRACKLE

Oil-based crackle produces an effect of greater age than its water-based counterpart (see p. 74), and cracks tend to be more widely spaced and varied. Here two layers of transparent crackle varnish are standard, and they work against each other while drying. A tinted glaze brushed on and rubbed off to remain only in the cracks completes the effect. The look can be subtle or bold, depending on the color contrast. Oil-based crackle varnish is an unpredictable material. Experience has taught us three things: follow the manufacturers' instructions, use premixed paint for the base coat, and work in an evenly heated, dry area. It is also best confined to small, flat surfaces. But do not be put off. Crackle is a remarkable finish which can produce wonderful results.

BASIC RECIPE—RED ON BLACK

INGREDIENTS	***To cover approximately 7m² (75ft²)*** Base coat ► 1 pint (500ml.) premixed black gloss paint Crackle coats ► 1 qt. (1 liter) premixed oil-based crackle varnish (transparent) Top coat ► 2tbsp. cadmium red artists' oil color / 1tbsp. oil-based glazing liquid / 1tbsp. mineral spirits Optional protective coats ► 1 qt. (1 liter) clear satin or gloss polyurethane varnish
EQUIPMENT	2–3 x 2in. (50mm.) tossaway brushes / 1 x 1in. (25mm.) varnish brush / container for mixing glaze / rags
INSTRUCTIONS **Base coat**	ALWAYS WORK IN A WELL-VENTILATED AREA Stir the gloss paint well; apply two coats to your prepared surface (see pp. 24–7), allowing 24 hours for each coat to dry.
Crackle coats	**1** Apply an even coat of crackle varnish to the surface, using the varnish brush, and leave until tacky (approx. 30 minutes). **2** Brush on a second coat, and allow both coats to dry completely (1 hour). As the second coat dries, it pulls against the first, creating fine cracks in the surface of the varnish.

Two variations on the basic recipe: (left) a dark green gloss base coat and a top coat tinted with 2tbsp. jaune brillant; (right) a deep red gloss base coat and a top coat color-mix of 1tbsp. titanium white, 1/2tbsp. cadmium red, and 1/2tbsp. jaune brillant.

OIL-BASED CRACKLE

❶ RED ON BLACK
The classic color-way of the basic recipe: a striking combination which works well with Chinese antiques.

❷ BLUE ON OCHER
This modern look can find a place in a traditional home. A deep antique yellow is used for the gloss base coat, and the top coat is colored with 2½tbsp. cobalt blue and ½tbsp. titanium white.

❸ RED ON ANTIQUE YELLOW
An authentic look: cracks in the stone gloss base coat are revealed with a top-coat color-mix of 1tbsp. yellow ocher, ½tbsp. red iron oxide, and ½tbsp. raw umber.

❹ PALE GRAY ON BURGUNDY
Another bold colorway in the oriental style. The crazing over the burgundy gloss base coat is tinted with a top coat colored with 1tbsp. neutral gray and 1tbsp. titanium white.

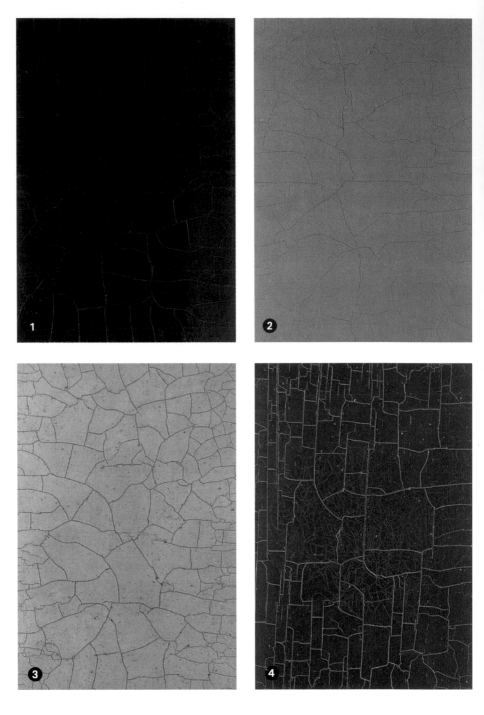

Top coat

1 Place the cadmium red in the container. Add the oil-based glazing liquid and mineral spirits, and stir well.

2 Apply an even coat to the entire surface, using a second tossaway brush.

3 Wipe most of the glaze off with clean rags—when you have finished, red glaze should remain only in the cracks. It is important to keep changing rags, or you will begin recoating the surface with glaze. Allow to dry (24 hours).

Notes For a more hardwearing finish, apply two coats of varnish with a third tossaway brush, following the manufacturers' instructions.

RUBBING OFF ON WOOD

We developed this technique to color and age wood simultaneously in a subtle and stylish way. It is an immensely satisfying method of giving old wood a new lease on life and an equally effective route to creating furniture that blends with your decor. Searching secondhand shops for old pieces to transform is fun—simple, uncluttered lines are often the most successful. The effect is soft, as some of the wood's color remains visible, and the detail and graining are still apparent, but dark varnish works against it, so have wood stripped, if necessary, before sealing it. If you decide to work with a new piece, you can age it first; and, of course, there is no need to limit yourself to one color. You could choose one for the legs and back of a chair and another for the seat. Seal the entire surface and use masking tape to protect areas you do not want to color with your first glaze. Then apply and rub off; remask and repeat for your second color.

BASIC RECIPE—MOSS GREEN ON BLOND WOOD

INGREDIENTS

To cover approximately 6m² (65ft²)
Sealant coat ▶ 1 x 17 oz. (500ml.) white polish
Rubbed-off glaze ▶ 17 oz. (500ml.) white latex flat paint / 2tbsp. acrylic glazing liquid (transparent) / 1tbsp. Hooker's green artists' acrylic color / $\frac{1}{2}$tbsp. pale olive green artists' acrylic color / $\frac{1}{2}$tbsp. yellow ocher artists' acrylic color / 1tbsp. water (one coat)
Optional protective coat ▶ 1 pint (500ml.) clear matte or satin acrylic varnish

EQUIPMENT

Bradawl or 2in. (50mm.) nail and hammer (optional) / craft knife (optional) / lint-free cloths / medium-grade sandpaper / container for mixing glaze / 1 x 2in. (50mm.) tossaway brush / 1 x 2in. (50mm.) varnish brush (optional)

INSTRUCTIONS
Aging (optional)

Use the bradawl (or 2in. [50mm.] nail and hammer) to make the small clusters of holes typical of woodworm in your prepared surface. You can also add occasional scratches, using a craft knife, and small indentations with a hammer.

Above and p. 80: These chairs were stripped and left to dry for 7 days before work began. Colors as follows. Green: basic recipe. Lilac:

Sealant coat

1 Form a pad of lint-free cloth and apply a thin, even coat of white polish. Allow to dry (1 hour) and buff with clean cloth.
2 Using the sandpaper, rub lightly over the entire surface. Your aim is to create a slightly rougher surface to which the glaze coat will adhere, but it is important that you not take off too much of the polish.

$1\frac{1}{2}$tbsp. pale violet and $\frac{1}{2}$tbsp. titanium white. Blue: $1\frac{1}{2}$tbsp. ultramarine and $\frac{1}{2}$tbsp. burnt umber. Sand: $1\frac{1}{2}$tbsp. yellow ocher and $\frac{1}{2}$tbsp. raw umber.

❶ MOSS GREEN ON BLOND WOOD The colors of the basic recipe give a natural look for a country home. A durable, hardwearing finish, it would do especially well in a kitchen. In all four examples rubbing off in the direction of the grain has produced an effect almost like dragging.

❷ RICH UMBER A versatile colorway that brings a natural, deep tone to the wood: 2tbsp. raw umber color the glaze mix.

❸ VIOLET This contemporary look is created by tinting the glaze with 2tbsp. brilliant purple.

❹ TURQUOISE Another bright, modern look, its seaside tones would be fun in a bathroom. The glaze is colored with 1¹/₂tbsp. turquoise blue and ¹/₂tbsp. cobalt blue.

Rubbed-off glaze

1 Pour the latex paint into the container. Add the acrylic glazing liquid, Hooker's and pale olive greens, yellow ocher, and water (a little at a time), stirring well.

2 Apply the glaze thickly onto the entire surface with the tossaway brush and leave until it becomes tacky (approx. 5 minutes).

3 Using another cloth, wipe most of the glaze off—your aim is to leave a fine haze of color on the flat surfaces and a buildup of glaze in any detail. Allow to dry (2 hours).

Notes Repeat the rubbing-off stage if you want a greater depth of color. For a more hardwearing finish, apply a coat of varnish, according to the manufacturers' instructions.

Exterior use Finish with two coats of satin polyurethane varnish, again according to the manufacturers' instructions.

WOODWASHING

This simple way to color wood creates a pale, washed effect. It is ideal for kitchens and for pieces of furniture that you wish to fit into a new scheme or setting. Like the previous finish but even easier to handle, the look is soft, with the graining and detail of the wood still visible. It is also an ideal way to improve cheaper soft woods, making them an attractive option for the budget conscious. Premixed wood washes are now available, but the color range is limited and mixing your own is cheaper. Varnish surfaces you plan to use in kitchen and bathroom.

❶ DEEP BLUE
The basic recipe: this subtle look, showing plenty of the wood's graining through the glaze, would work well in a kitchen or bathroom.

❷ DUSKY PINK
Another soft colorway with the beauty of the wood still apparent: 1tbsp. alizarin crimson, 1tbsp. titanium white, ¹/₂tbsp. raw sienna and ¹/₂tbsp. lilac make the delicate tones.

❸ PALE GREEN
A subtle color, versatile in kitchens and sunrooms, it was created by coloring the wash with 2tbsp. sap green, 1tbsp. raw sienna, and ¹/₂tbsp. titanium white.

❹ RAW SIENNA
A versatile color to enhance most new woods: the color-mix is 2tbsp. raw sienna and 1tbsp. raw umber.

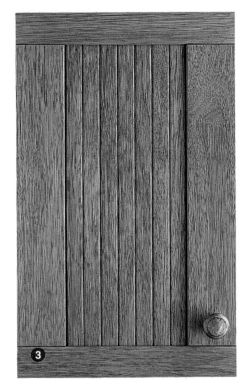

BASIC RECIPE—DEEP BLUE

INGREDIENTS

To cover approximately 6m² (65ft²)
17 oz. (500ml.) white latex flat paint / 2tbsp. ultramarine artists' acrylic color / 1tbsp. cobalt blue artists' acrylic color / ¹/₂tbsp. burnt umber artists' acrylic color / 5–7 oz. (150–200ml.) water
Optional protective coat ▶ 1 pint (500ml.) matte or satin acrylic varnish (one coat)

EQUIPMENT

Container for mixing wash coat / 1 x 3in. (75mm.) paintbrush / lint-free cloth / 1 x 2in. (50mm.) varnish brush (optional)

INSTRUCTIONS

1 Pour the latex paint into the container. Add the ultramarine, cobalt blue, burnt umber, and water (a little at a time), stirring continuously—you are aiming for a milky consistency.
2 Using the paintbrush, apply the wash to the wood, working in the direction of the grain—you should be able to see it through the wash. Allow to dry a little (15–20 minutes).
3 Make a pad with a lint-free cloth, and wipe the surface to reveal further grain and texture. Leave to dry (1 hour).

Notes If you want a hardwearing finish, seal with one or two coats of varnish, according to the manufacturers' instructions.

Above: Door and baseboard have been woodwashed in a lovely blue. This is an ideal finish to complement the stained-plaster look of the walls.

AGING PAINT

We devised this effective technique to give furniture and woodwork the appearance of many layers of paint slowly peeling off after decades of wear and tear. The art of simulating aging paint, like crackle (see pp. 74–8), dates back to eighteenth-century France, and it is still an excellent way to make cheaper, new wood look as though it has been in your home for years. The finish can have a period look, through the use of dark reds and greens, or a more contemporary one, with bright, contrasting hues; and peeling can be subtle or emphatic, depending on the degree of aging. To create an authentic look, study genuine old pieces before you begin, and discover where natural aging occurs.

BASIC RECIPE—DEEP YELLOW ON BURNT UMBER

INGREDIENTS

To cover approximately 6m² (65ft²)
Wax coat ▶ 1 x ¹/₂ pint (250ml.) can furniture wax (clear) or beeswax
Wash coat ▶ 2tbsp. burnt umber artists' acrylic color / 1tbsp. water
Latex coat ▶ 17 oz. (500ml.) white latex flat paint / 2tbsp. cadmium yellow artists' acrylic color / 1tbsp. bronze ocher artists' acrylic color / ¹/₂tbsp. Venetian red artists' acrylic color
Glaze coat ▶ 17 oz. (500ml.) white latex flat paint / 1tbsp. cadmium yellow artists' acrylic color / ¹/₂tbsp. bronze ocher artists' acrylic color / 4tbsp. water
Optional protective coat ▶ ¹/₂ pint (250ml.) furniture polish (clear) or 1 pint (500ml.) clear satin acrylic varnish

EQUIPMENT

1 x 1in. (25mm.) tossaway brush / pencil / paper (for sketch plan) / 3 containers for mixing wash, latex paint, and glaze / 1 x 1in. (25mm.) paintbrush / 2 x 2in. (50mm.) latex brushes / scraper or spatula / rags / medium-grade sandpaper / 1 x 2in. (50mm.) varnish brush (optional)

INSTRUCTIONS
Wax coat

Using the tossaway brush, dab wax onto those areas of the prepared wooden surface (see pp. 24–7) you wish to reveal. It is best to apply the wax evenly in a series of lines rather than random strokes, but vary the size and spacing as much as possible. This is essentially a resist technique—paint will not adhere permanently to the waxed areas—so you must visualize the final effect and sketch it as a reminder when you begin to distress the paint later. Leave to dry (24 hours).

Wash coat

1 Place the burnt umber in one of the containers, and add the water (a little at a time), stirring well.
2 Use the 1in. (25mm.) paintbrush to apply the wash to the wood in the direction of the grain. Allow to dry (1 hour).

Latex coat

1 Pour the latex paint into a second container. Add the cadmium yellow, bronze ocher, and Venetian red, and stir well.

Opposite: This new occasional table was aged using a shortened version of the aging paint technique. The bright yellow was created by using 3tbsp. cadmium yellow in the wash, the latex coat was omitted, and the glaze was colored with 2tbsp. bright green.

❶ DEEP YELLOW ON BURNT UMBER
The basic recipe: this natural mix is typical of French country furniture and would be good in a kitchen, where it makes a hard-wearing finish.

❷ BURGUNDY ON CORAL
There is a country feel to this rich colorway too, another variation on the basic recipe. Here a wash coat is not used. The latex coat is tinted with 2tbsp. cadmium red, 1/2tbsp. titanium white, and 1/2tbsp. raw sienna. The glaze-coat mix uses 2tbsp. raw sienna and 1tbsp. red oxide.

❸ PALE BLUE ON ULTRAMARINE
Again the wash coat is omitted. The latex coat is colored with 3tbsp. ultramarine blue, and the glaze with 1tbsp. cobalt blue, 1tbsp. light ultramarine blue, and 1tbsp. titanium white.

❹ PURPLE ON STONE
This contemporary version tints the wash coat with 1³/₄oz. (50g.) yellow ocher powder pigment. The other coats revert to acrylic color: for the latex, 3tbsp. yellow ocher; for the glaze, 2tbsp. brilliant purple and 1tbsp. cobalt blue.

2 Using one of the 2in. (50mm.) paintbrushes, apply an even coat of paint to the surface in the direction of the grain. Allow to dry (2–4 hours).

Glaze coat

1 Pour the latex paint into a third container. Add the cadmium yellow, bronze ocher, and water (gradually), stirring well.

2 Apply an even coat in the direction of the grain, using the other 2in. (50mm.) paintbrush. Allow to dry a little (30–40 minutes).

Distressing the paint

1 Referring to your sketch plan, use the scraper (or spatula) and rags to remove as many layers of paint as you can in the waxed areas.

2 Smooth the rough edges of the paint with sandpaper.

Notes If you want a more hardwearing finish, seal the surface with a layer of furniture polish or with a coat of varnish, according to the manufacturers' instructions.

SCANDINAVIAN

This door has been painted in colors typical of the Scandinavian palette, using an aging paint technique (see p. 85), and the wall painting is a characteristic floral design.

In recent years the Scandinavian color palette has become increasingly popular. It is a look that derives largely from nature. The misty, cool blues and greens of those northern landscapes predominate, spiked with a variety of earth tones in the highly decorated detailing of plants and flowers. It was in the long winter months, when the elements prevented work on the land, that peasant men and women spent many hours carving and painting the cabinets, dressers, and chests that are now so much admired. A characteristic simplicity of form and airy lightness of effect make this an ideal look for kitchens and bathrooms.

In this recipe we have devised a simple, undecorated, aged finish which works well with the Scandinavian color palette. As a broken-color technique—that is, as a glaze applied on a contrasting flat base coat and then rubbed back—it has authenticity, as well as plenty of texture and body. It is ideal for furniture that receives heavy wear and, because it uses water-based products, is easy to apply to most wooden surfaces. This is a charming way of rejuvenating old kitchen cabinets.

BASIC RECIPE—BLUE-GRAY ON IVY GREEN

INGREDIENTS

To cover approximately 6m² (65ft²)
Latex coat ▶ 17 oz. (500ml.) white latex flat paint / 3tbsp. Hooker's green artists' acrylic color / 2tbsp. pale olive green artists' acrylic color
Glaze coat ▶ 17 oz. (500ml.) white latex flat paint / 3tbsp. monestial blue artists' acrylic color / 1tbsp. cobalt blue artists' acrylic color / 1tbsp. Payne's gray artists' acrylic color / 2tbsp. water (one coat)
Optional protective coat ▶ 1 pint. (500ml.) clear satin acrylic varnish

EQUIPMENT

2 x 2in. (50mm.) paintbrushes / 2 containers for mixing paint / rags / 1 x 2in. (50mm.) varnish brush (optional)

 87

INSTRUCTIONS

Latex coat

1 Pour the latex paint into one of the containers. Add the Hooker's and pale olive greens, and stir well.

2 Apply to your prepared surface (see pp. 24–7), working in the direction of the grain, and allow to dry (2–4 hours).

Glaze coat

1 Pour the latex paint into the other container. Add the monestial blue, cobalt blue, Payne's gray, and water (a little at a time), stirring well

2 Apply to the entire surface in the direction of the grain.

3 When this coat is set but not dry (approx. 30 minutes), wipe off gently with a rag, working again in the direction of the grain to reveal some of the latex coat. Allow to dry (2–3 hours).

Notes For a deeper tone, repeat the glaze coat or leave the water out of that stage. If you decide to use no water, the glaze will dry more quickly, so do not wait for it to set before wiping off. If you want a more hardwearing finish,

❶ BLUE-GRAY ON IVY GREEN
The classic tones and an ideal base for decoration: the glaze coat was left to set for approx. 10 minutes.

❷ GREEN ON STONE
This is made by coloring the latex coat with 2tbsp. yellow ocher, and the glaze with 3tbsp. forest green and 1tbsp. monestial green.

❸ GRAY ON PALE BLUE
The latex coat is tinted with 3tbsp. cobalt blue, and the glaze with 3tbsp. neutral gray and 2tbsp. burnt umber.

❹ CORAL ON UMBER
A modern alternative: color the latex coat with 4tbsp. burnt umber, the glaze with 2tbsp. raw sienna.

apply one coat of varnish, according to the manufacturers' instructions.

Exterior use It is best to follow Scandinavian custom and use wood stain for exterior surfaces. Oil-based and water-based wood stains are available in a range of colors. Finish with a polyurethane varnish, following the manufacturers' instructions: satin is better for looks, but gloss will last longer. For exterior woodwork, such as window frames and shutters, oil-based stains can be used, but again remember to finish with polyurethane varnish for durability.

The trompe l'oeil windows contribute to this unusually flamboyant Scandinavian interior. Much more traditional in feel are the handsome paneling and beautifully decorated chair backs.

S H A K E R

The Shaker look seems to speak to many people today. Perhaps it is the simplicity and sheer coherence of the Shaker way of life that appeal. Every aspect of Shaker life was organized, and this is reflected in their simple architecture, home decoration, and furnishings.

They painted the exteriors of their work buildings in tans and yellows; more expensive white paint was restricted to meeting houses. Their communal homes were often painted cream, with dark brown, bottle green, or deep red woodwork inside. The believers liked bold, solid colors, and although their furnishings were characteristically free of ornamentation, the shapes and colors are extremely attractive.

This deep brown paneling is typical of Shaker coloring. Their unpainted woods were often maple and pine.

In their frugal, self-supporting communities, paint was often hard to come by and had to be made from available materials. Whole milk was the usual medium, mixed with costly powder pigments and a little lime,

and the resulting milk (or casein) paints were cheap, durable, and easy to apply, drying to a flat, smooth finish with a depth of color seldom found in synthetic paints. Milk paints can still be bought today, in a wide range of Shaker colors, although now they are sold either premixed with buttermilk or skimmed-milk powders or simply as pigment with instructions for mixing. They are certainly the best way of creating the authentic colors of a Shaker home. We recommend that you use them for this recipe, which depends for its aged effect on an extremely simple resist technique.

BASIC RECIPE—DEEP COLONIAL RED ON YELLOW OCHER

INGREDIENTS

To cover approximately 11m² (118ft²)
Base coat ▶ 1 pint (500ml.) yellow ocher milk (casein) paint (one coat)
Wax coat ▶ 1 pint (500ml.) beeswax or furniture wax (clear)
Top coat ▶ 1 pint (500ml.) deep red milk (casein) paint

EQUIPMENT

2–3 x 2in. (50mm.) tossaway brushes / 1 x 1in. (25mm.) tossaway brush / steel wool / disposable gloves

INSTRUCTIONS

Base coat

ALWAYS WORK IN A WELL-VENTILATED AREA

Stir the yellow ocher milk (casein) paint thoroughly. Using one of the 2in. (50mm.) tossaway brushes, apply an even coat to your prepared surface (see pp. 24–7) and allow to dry

1 DEEP COLONIAL RED ON OCHER
The basic recipe: deep tones and density of color are common on Shaker woodwork. The pale base gives a wonderfully aged effect.

2 ANTIQUE YELLOW ON SOLDIER BLUE
Another popular colorway: the main area of wear is the doorknob, but the aging can be more pronounced if you wish.

3 OCHER ON DEEP RED
This reverses the colors of the basic recipe for a less imposing effect.

4 SOLDIER BLUE ON OCHER
A lovely color-mix and typical of the Shakers' pure hues, this would be good in a kitchen or in a bathroom.

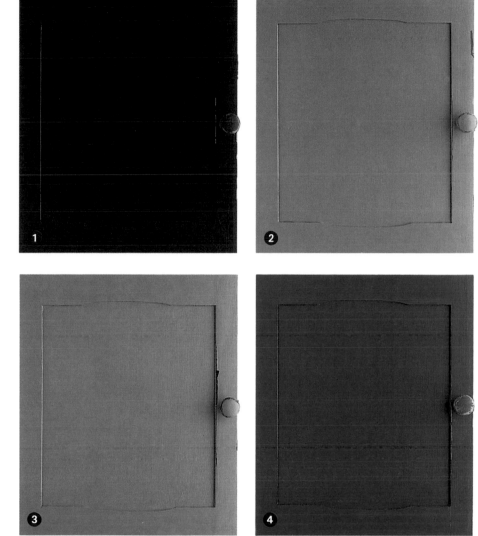

(24 hours). Milk paints create such a flat, smooth finish that you often do not need to add a second coat.

Wax coat

Brush a liberal coat of the beeswax onto the areas you wish to distress, using the 1in. (25mm.) tossaway brush. (The top-coat will not adhere permanently wherever there is a wax coating.) Allow to dry (1 hour).

Top coat

1 Stir the deep red milk paint thoroughly and apply a good, even coat with a second 2in. (50mm.) tossaway brush. Allow to dry (24 hours).
2 Put on the gloves and rub the steel wool gently over the surface, concentrating on the areas where you applied the wax, until you reveal the ocher paint beneath.

These trugs were all painted with water-based materials. This gives more scope for color variation, but do check picture references to maintain the correct feel. Almost all the colors described here are artists' acrylics and were added to 17 oz. (500ml.) latex semigloss paint.

The stone base coat for the brown and dusky pink trugs was colored with 2tbsp. yellow ocher. The brown top coat tint was 3tbsp. raw umber, 1tbsp. yellow ocher, and 1tbsp. burnt umber. The dusky pink was made by mixing 2tbsp. cadmium red, 1tbsp. raw umber, and 1/4tbsp. cobalt blue.

The green was created with 3tbsp. sap green and 1tbsp. raw umber and applied to the dusky pink described above. The blue was a premixed latex semigloss paint and was applied to a base coat colored with 2tbsp. cobalt blue.

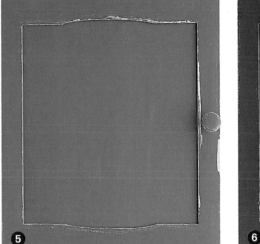

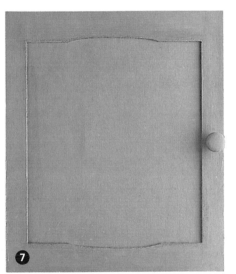

❺ SEA GREEN ON WHITE
The green is made by adding 3tbsp. chromium green and 1tbsp. cobalt blue to 17 oz. (500ml.) white latex semigloss paint: a clean colorway with a different feel but still in the Shaker tradition.

❻ TERRACOTTA ON GRAY
This rich combination would make a good choice for a kitchen or bathroom. The terracotta is a premixed latex semigloss paint, but the base coat adds 2tbsp. neutral gray to 17 oz. (500ml.) white latex semigloss paint.

❼ CREAM ON PALE BLUE
A light color-mix but again typical of Shaker taste: the base coat is made by adding 2tbsp. cobalt blue to 17 oz. (500ml.) white latex semigloss paint; the cream by adding 2tbsp. yellow ocher to 17 oz. (500ml.) white latex semigloss paint.

❽ PALE BLUE ON TERRACOTTA
Another lively alternative: the base coat is the premixed terracotta used in sample 6, and the top coat adds 3tbsp. cobalt blue to 17 oz. (500ml.) white latex semigloss paint.

WATER-BASED SHAKER

Milk paints take a long time to dry, so you may prefer to use water-based latex semigloss paint instead. These are now available in the deep colors of the Shaker palette, and may be more appealing in a small, dark room, which could appear claustrophobic with surfaces given the dense, flat look of milk paint. Because of their low toxicity, latex paints are also preferable for furnishings in a child's room.

Follow the quantities given in the basic recipe, using premixed paints or coloring 17 oz. (500ml.) latex semigloss paint with artists' acrylic colors. You may need two top coats for a finish to equal that of milk paint. Allow 2–4 hours for each coat to dry. Use the beeswax and steel wool as indicated. For a hardwearing finish, seal with acrylic varnish, using a 2in. (50mm.) varnish brush, according to the manufacturers' instructions, but it is vital to remove all the wax first.

A convincing range of acrylic "milk" paints is also available.

STONE FINISHES

Stone comes in many colors and textures, and reproducing it in paint can be complicated. Nevertheless a reasonable resemblance to some of the less exotic stones is possible. The main pieces of equipment you need are nothing more than a cellulose sponge and a bowl of water.

LIMESTONE

INGREDIENTS

To cover approximately 4m² (43ft²)
See swatch captions.

EQUIPMENT

3 or 4 containers / coarse-textured paint roller plus tray / 3 or 4 cellulose sponges / scissors / bowl of water / 2 x 3in. (75mm.) paintbrushes / masking tape / 1 or 2 spray bottles / denatured alcohol / large plate / short-haired fitch / stick

INSTRUCTIONS

❶ PINK LIMESTONE
The joint color is 6tbsp. white latex flat and 2tsp. raw umber. For each of the following, begin with 6tbsp. white latex flat. For the base color, add ½tsp. each yellow ocher and raw umber. For the first color, 1tsp. raw umber and 2tsp. yellow ocher, and for the second color, 2tsp. neutral gray and ½tsp. yellow ocher. Add dabs of yellow ocher, gray, and white.

1 Prepare the surface thoroughly (see pp. 24–7). If you do not want joint lines, go straight to step 3. Otherwise, mix the joint color and brush it on in an uneven layer. Allow to dry completely (4 hours).

2 Using torn masking tape, mask out a pattern of ragged-edged joint lines over the painted surface.

3 Mix the base color and use the roller to apply one coat. Allow to dry (1 hour).

4 Trim two or three cellulose sponges (see pp. 20–1).

5 Using the first colour, follow steps 3–5 on p. 132.

6 If you want a finer texture, reduce the amount of water and use a spray bottle to apply some of it. You can also work with a finer sponge.

7 Another variation is to splash or spray on denatured alcohol. The water and color will flow away from the denatured alcohol, forming different shapes.

8 For color variation, sponge on dabs of other suitable colors, but resist the temptation to overdo it. Once you have achieved the desired effect, allow to dry (1–2 hours), then remove any masking tape.

❷ GRAY LIMESTONE
For the joints, mix 4tbsp. white and 2tbsp. black latex flat. The base coat is 6tbsp. white latex flat and 2tsp. neutral gray. The first color is 4tbsp. Payne's gray, 2tbsp. white, and 4tsp. burnt umber, while the second color is white. For a more granular effect, we spattered on ¼tsp. each of black and white, softened with a spray of denatured alcohol.

9 Mix the second color and apply it in the same way as before, adding dabs of color if you wish. Leave to dry thoroughly.

10 To create stone with a more granular appearance, spatter on black and white paint. Load a short-haired fitch with diluted paint and tap it hard against a stick held 12–16in. (30–40cm.) from your work. A longhaired brush will spatter everything around. The consistency of the paint is important. Too thin and you will splash, not spatter; too thick and the paint will not leave your brush.

SLATE

INGREDIENTS

To cover approximately 4m² (43ft²)
See swatch captions.

EQUIPMENT

1 or 2 containers / cellulose sponge / masking tape / 1 x 3in. (75mm.) paintbrush / spatula / wax

INSTRUCTIONS

1 Follow steps 1 and 2 above, but sponge on the joint color instead of brushing it on.

2 Use the paintbrush to apply one coat of the base color and allow to dry (4 hours).

3 Mix the slate color, and use the spatula to apply it in a not-too-thick layer to a small area. Smooth out the paint, using small circular movements. As it begins to dry, add a little wax and rub it in along with the paint. This burnishing action will give a hard, polished, slatelike finish. You will soon see when to add the wax, and will discover how to make slight changes to the patina by varying your timing.

4 While still working on the first area, you can start to spread and burnish fresh paint alongside. You can work on two or three areas at the same time. Work across the whole surface without stopping to prevent any joints from showing. Allow to dry for a day.

❸ **SLATE**
The joint color is the same medium-gray as gray limestone, while the slate base color is 3½oz. (100ml.) black latex flat. The slate color consists of 5tbsp. Payne's gray, 1tbsp. white, 1tbsp. phthalocyanine green, and 2tsp. burnt umber.

MARBLING

Marbling is perhaps the most well used of the stone finishes. It is possible, with careful study and practice, to make accurate copies of specific types of marble, but in these recipes we show you how to create two *faux* or fantasy marbles. The method is less complicated, and there is more room for artistic license. However, even here a successful result depends on not overdoing the technique. And for "authenticity," use picture references of real marble as a guide. Before you begin, decide on a basic pattern for the veining and other markings—it may be governed by the surface on which you are working—and keep the colors of your glazes close. Too much contrast gives unconvincing results.

BASIC RECIPE—GRAY FANTASY MARBLE

INGREDIENTS

To cover approximately 6m² (65ft²)

Base coat ► 17 oz. (500ml.) white oil-based eggshell paint / 2tbsp. neutral gray artists' oil color

First glaze coat ► 12¹/₂ oz. (370ml.) oil-based glazing liquid (transparent) / 3tbsp. zinc white artists' oil color / 7 oz. (200ml.) mineral spirits (approx.)

Second glaze coat ► 12¹/₂ oz. (370ml.) oil-based glazing liquid / 2tbsp. neutral gray artists' oil color / 1tbsp. zinc white artists' oil color / 7oz. (200ml.) mineral spirits (approx.)

First veining ► 1tbsp. black artists' oil color / ¹/₂tbsp. mineral spirits

Second veining ► 1tbsp. yellow ocher artists' oil color / ¹/₂tbsp. mineral spirits

Sealant ► 1 pint (500ml.) clear satin polyurethane varnish / 1³/₄ oz. (50g.) powdered chalk

EQUIPMENT

3 large and 2 small containers for mixing paint and glaze / 2 x 2in. (50mm.) tossaway brushes / 2 x 1in. (25mm.) tossaway brushes / badger blender or dusting brush / fitch / swordliner or fine artists' brush / cloth

INSTRUCTIONS

ALWAYS WORK IN A WELL-VENTILATED AREA

Base coat

1 Pour the oil-based eggshell paint into one of the large containers. Add the neutral gray and stir well.

2 Apply an even coat to the prepared surface (see pp. 24–7) with a 2in. (50mm.) tossaway brush, and allow to dry (24 hours).

First glaze coat

1 Pour the oil-based glazing liquid into a second large container. Add the zinc white and 5 oz. (150ml.) mineral spirits (a little at a time), stirring well.

2 Apply to the base coat in diagonal, random strokes with one of the 1in. (25mm.) tossaway brushes, allowing about a quarter of the base coat to show through.

3 Skim lightly over the glaze with the badger blender (or dusting brush) to soften the brushstrokes.

4 Using the fitch, flick some of the remaining mineral spirits onto the surface. Your aim is to disperse the glaze a little.

Second glaze coat

1 Pour the oil-based glazing liquid into a third large container. Add the neutral gray, zinc white, and 5oz. (150ml.) mineral spirits (a little at a time), and stir well.

2 With the other 1in. (25mm.) brush, apply the second glaze randomly to some of the areas not covered by the first glaze coat. You should still be able to see parts of the base coat.

3 Repeat the softening process, and again flick some of the remaining mineral spirits onto the glaze.

First veining

1 Place the black oil color in one of the small containers. Add the mineral spirits (a little at a time), and stir well.

2 Using the swordliner (or fine artists' brush) to apply the solution, make a series of small, twisting lines on the wet glaze. Work diagonally across the surface, but try to vary the path of each vein. Make some of them travel vertically, add "branches" here and there, and continue them from one side to the other. Avoid producing too uniform an effect.

❶ GRAY MARBLE
The final stage of the basic recipe is about to begin: the veining stages are complete and the effect has been softened with a blender brush.

Sample A shows the first glaze stage: white glaze has been applied to some areas, but parts of the base coat still show through. The glaze has been softened and then dispersed.

Sample B shows the second, darker glaze and first veining. Now black and white blend to produce authentic two-tone veins.

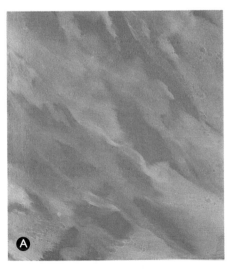

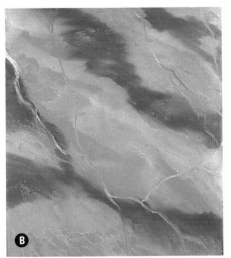

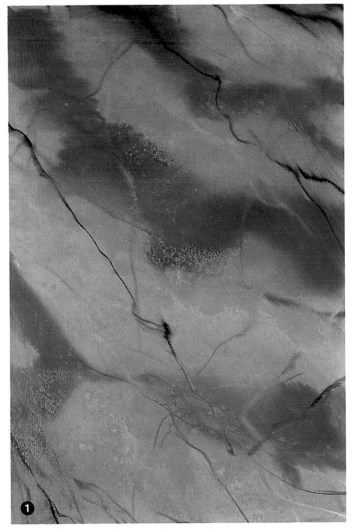

MARBLING

The paneling in this room has been marbled using natural, sandy tones. This is a handsome demonstration of how successful and authentic a marble finish can be.

Second veining

1 Place the yellow ocher in the other small container. Add the mineral spirits (a little at a time), and stir well.

2 Create more veins—these should be smaller and fewer than the black veins of the previous stage.

3 Skim lightly over the yellow ocher veins with the blender or dusting brush. Allow to dry (24 hours).

Sealant coat

1 Apply one coat of varnish with the other 2in. (50mm.) tossaway brush, according to the manufacturers' instructions.

2 Sprinkle the powdered chalk onto the partially dry surface and buff with a cloth—this helps to give the "cloudy" appearance typical of real marble.

VARIATION—BLACK AND GOLD FANTASY MARBLE

INGREDIENTS

To cover approximately 8m² (86ft²)

Base coat ► 1 pint (500ml.) black oil-based eggshell paint

First glaze coat ► 8¹/₂ oz. (250ml.) oil-based glazing liquid (transparent) / 3tbsp. zinc white artists' oil color / 1tbsp. oxide of chromium artists' oil color / 7 oz. (200ml.) mineral spirits

Second glaze coat ► 8¹/₂ oz. (250ml.) oil-based glazing liquid / 2tbsp. zinc white artists' oil color / 1tbsp. yellow ocher artists' oil color / 7 oz. (200ml.) mineral spirits

First veining ► 1tbsp. oil-based glazing liquid / 1tbsp. zinc white artists' oil color / 1tbsp. mineral spirits

Second veining ► 1tbsp. oil-based glazing liquid / ¹/₂tbsp. zinc white artists' oil color / ¹/₂tbsp. yellow ocher artists' oil color / 1tbsp. mineral spirits

Protective coat ► 1 pint (500ml.) clear satin matte or polyurethane varnish

EQUIPMENT

2 x 2in. (50mm.) tossaway brushes / 2 large and 2 small containers for mixing glaze / 2 x 1in. (25mm.) tossaway brushes / badger blender or dusting brush / fitch / swordliner or fine artists' brush / cloth

INSTRUCTIONS

Base coat

ALWAYS WORK IN A WELL-VENTILATED AREA.

Stir the oil-based eggshell paint well, and apply an even coat to your prepared surface (see pp. 24–7) with one of the 2in. (50mm.) tossaway brushes. Allow to dry (24 hours).

First and second glaze coats

Follow the Basic recipe; add 5 oz. (150ml.) mineral spirits to the glazing liquid and reserve 2 oz. (50ml.) to soften the glazes.

First and second veining

Follow the method in Basic recipe, First and Second veining, adding the oil color and mineral spirits to the glazing liquid.

Protective coat

Apply one coat of varnish with the other 2in. (50mm.) tossaway brush, according to the manufacturers' instructions.

❷ BLACK AND GOLD MARBLE Bolder, more fantastic effects are a possibility with this type of finish, and the opportunity for experiment and color variation is enormous. The glazes used here are thinner than those of the basic recipe, and the result is a more translucent finish.

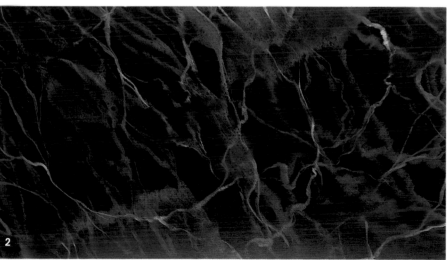

GRANITE

Real granite has traditionally been used on the grand scale—mainly for exterior decoration—but the paint finish can be used successfully on small features inside a modern or period home. This recipe uses sponging and spatter techniques to recreate granite's characteristic granular look. However, like many stones, it comes in different forms, so study the real thing for an authentic effect. Table tops, pillars, and garden ornaments and furniture are all potential projects.

BASIC RECIPE—GRANITE

INGREDIENTS

To cover approximately 6m² (65ft²)

Base coat ▶ 17 oz. (500ml.) white latex flat paint / 2tbsp. neutral gray artists' acrylic color

First glaze coat ▶ 3¹/₂ oz. (100ml.) white latex flat paint / 2tbsp. neutral gray artists' acrylic color / 1tbsp. burnt umber artists' acrylic color / 2tbsp. water / denatured alcohol (see instructions)

Second glaze coat ▶ 3¹/₂ oz. (100ml.) white latex flat paint / 2tbsp. water / denatured alcohol

First spatter coat ▶ 1tbsp. Mars black artists' acrylic color / 1tbsp. water

Second spatter coat ▶ 1tbsp. zinc white artists' acrylic color / 1tbsp. water / denatured alcohol

Protective coat ▶ 1 pint (500ml.) clear satin acrylic varnish

EQUIPMENT

3 large and 2 small containers for mixing paint and glaze / 1 x 2in. (50mm.) paintbrush / 3 natural sponges / water to dampen sponges / spray bottle / 2 fitches / 1 x 2in. (50mm.) varnish brush

INSTRUCTIONS
Base coat

1 Pour the latex paint into one of the large containers. Add the neutral gray and stir well.
2 Apply evenly to the prepared surface (see pp. 24–7), using the 2in. (50mm.) paintbrush. Allow to dry (2–4 hours).

First glaze coat

1 Pour the latex paint into another large container. Add the neutral gray, burnt umber, and water (little by little). Stir well.
2 Immerse one of the sponges in water and wring out. Using the damp sponge, apply glaze to the entire surface in light, dabbing movements.
3 Half fill the spray bottle with denatured alcohol and spray a fine mist over the surface. This causes the glaze to disperse or spread slightly, producing a more interesting texture. Allow to dry (2 hours).

Above left: This tub, made of heavy-duty plastic, was bought cheaply at a garden center and painted as described in the recipe. Its basic shape recalls that of a traditional garden urn, so it makes an ideal subject for a stone effect, and the finish helps to disguise the fussy detail on the lip.

Second glaze coat

1 Pour the latex paint into a third large container. Add the water (a little at a time), stirring well.

2 Apply to the entire surface with a second damp sponge in the same way.

3 Again using the spray bottle, spray denatured alcohol onto the glazed surface.

4 While the glaze is still wet, sponge again, using a third damp sponge, and carefully blend the two colors.

First spatter coat

1 Place the Mars black in one of the small containers. Add the water (a little at a time), and stir well.

2 Load one of the fitches with glaze. Holding a clean fitch in one hand and the loaded fitch in the other, tap the handle of the loaded brush against the handle of the other so that flecks of paint spatter onto the surface. You are aiming for a fine haze of dots, applied more densely in some areas than in others.

Second spatter coat

1 Place the zinc white in the other small container. Add the water (a little at a time), and stir well.

2 Again spatter the surface with fine dots, using the second fitch and aiming for a random, uneven effect.

3 Using the spray bottle, spray a fine mist of denatured alcohol over the surface. Allow to dry (2 hours).

Protective coat

Apply one coat of varnish, using the varnish brush, according to the manufacturers' instructions.

Exterior use Substitute two coats of satin polyurethane varnish for protection, according to the manufacturers' instructions.

❶ GRANITE
The effect of the basic recipe on a flat surface: this finish would work well on paneling or on a table top. You could also try it on a plain, formal mantelpiece.

TERRACOTTA

Terracotta's chalky look is widely used for garden containers. However, some of the largest pots are expensive, and because they have a limited lifespan, the possibility of creating durable reproductions is attractive. Authenticity is achieved with simple dripping and sponging techniques; work the surface hard to enhance the effect. Objects with detail are especially successful because you can add extra aging in the crevices. This finish is perfect for containers but works well on surfaces too.

BASIC RECIPE—TERRACOTTA

INGREDIENTS

To cover approximately 6m² (65ft²)
First base coat ▶ 17 oz. (500ml.) white latex flat paint / 2tbsp. yellow ocher artists' acrylic color / 1tbsp. raw sienna artists' acrylic color
Second base coat ▶ 17 oz. (500ml.) white latex flat paint / 2tbsp. Venetian red artists' acrylic color / 2tbsp. raw umber artists' acrylic color / 1tbsp. bronze ocher artists' acrylic color
Glaze coat ▶ 3½ oz. (100ml.) white latex flat paint / 5 oz. (150ml.) water

EQUIPMENT

3 containers for mixing paint and glaze / 2 x 2in. (50mm.) paintbrushes / stippling or block brush / water to dampen brush and sponge / 1 x 1in. (25mm.) round fitch / natural sponge

INSTRUCTIONS
First base coat

1 Pour the latex paint into one of the containers. Add the yellow ocher and raw sienna, and stir well.
2 Apply evenly to your prepared surface (see pp. 24–7) with a 2in. (50mm.) paintbrush. Leave to dry (2–4 hours).

Second base coat

1 Pour the latex paint into a second container. Add the Venetian red, raw umber, and bronze ocher, and stir well.
2 Apply to the surface, using the other 2in. (50mm.) paintbrush, with random strokes, allowing some of the base coat to show through. Leave to dry (2–4 hours).

❶ TERRACOTTA
Here the terracotta finish is applied to a flat surface and a three-dimensional detail (a plaster shape from a ceiling rosette). Note how aging on the irregular areas adds to the weathered effect. Plaster and plastic are ideal surfaces for the terracotta finish.

Three plastic pots were prepared and painted using the technique described in the basic terracotta recipe. They were finished with two coats of satin polyurethane varnish and sunk into the wet plaster of a roughly textured wall, colorwashed (see p. 48) in a soft pink. Masonry nails driven through the back of the pots into the wall will give extra security.

Glaze coat

1 Pour the latex paint into a third container. Add the water (a little at a time), stirring well.

2 Dip the stippling (or block) brush in water, and, with a light, tapping action, dampen the painted surface.

3 Hold or place the object in an upright position. Using the fitch, drip the glaze vertically down the surface—you are imitating the action of weathering. Repeat to cover the surface.

4 Immerse the sponge in water and wring out. Dab it lightly over the glaze to take up the excess water as the surface begins to dry to a chalky finish. Allow to dry (2 hours).

Exterior use Finish with two coats of satin polyurethane varnish, according to the manufacturer's instructions.

PATINATION ON METAL

When exposed to the elements, metal fittings and architectural details tarnish and corrode over time. The results are often beautiful, evoking a wonderful sense of history, and craftsmen have now developed ways of reproducing patination on new metal. Some methods are complex and use dangerous chemicals, but cold-patination fluids (available for a variety of metals) are less dangerous, easier to use, and able to create natural effects. Try experimenting with inexpensive candlesticks; the results can be effective. The key to success is timing—the process works very quickly—but it is a lot easier than waiting years for an object to age naturally or burying it in the garden. Although these fluids are not as dangerous as some chemicals, they are still toxic, so take care.

BASIC RECIPE—COLD PATINATION ON BRASS

INGREDIENTS

For three candlesticks
10 oz. (300ml.) denatured alcohol / 6$^1/_2$ oz. (200ml.) brown cold-patination fluid (tourmaline) for brass, copper, and bronze
Optional protective coat ▶ 7 oz. (200ml.) clear wax or oil fixative (approx.)

EQUIPMENT

Cotton balls / water for rinsing / rubber gloves / protective mask / steel wool / rags (optional)

INSTRUCTIONS

WEAR GLOVES AND MASK WHEN USING COLD-PATINATION FLUIDS. FOLLOW MANUFACTURERS' INSTRUCTIONS, AND WORK IN A WELL-VENTILATED AREA.

1 Clean the surface with cotton balls soaked in denatured alcohol. Rinse in water and allow to dry (2 hours).

2 Put on the rubber gloves and protective mask. Rub clean cotton balls soaked in cold-patination fluid over the surface. It works very quickly—the metal changes color as the fluid goes on. Rinse the surface in fresh water as soon as you have the color you want. Leave it too long, and it will be very dark. Never leave the fluid on for more than 2 minutes.

❸ ON COPPER
Cupra patination fluid gives an authentic verdigris effect in seconds. Again, follow the basic recipe, applying the fluid with cotton balls or stippling it on with a soft brush. A second coat gives a more "crusty" feel.

❶ ON BRASS
The basic method: only the middle of this sample is worked with steel wool, leaving the softer, aged effect at the edges.

❷ ON STEEL
This shows the use of the black cold-patination fluid for steel and iron. Simply follow the quantities and method given in the basic recipe.

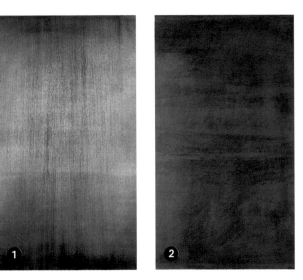

3 As soon as you have rinsed the surface, rub it gently with the steel wool to remove the color until you have the effect you want. Rinse in fresh water and allow to dry (1 hour).

Notes For a more hardwearing finish, rub wax (or oil fixative) over the entire surface with rags and allow to dry (1 hour).
Exterior use Apply one coat of oil fixative to the surface in the method described above.

Instant aging and antiquing: these inexpensive candle-sticks and holders have been patinated with the fluids used in the basic recipe and samples.

RUST

Probably the most extreme of the metal finishes, this look of age and corrosion is very popular. Our recipe, which uses water-based materials, is fast, safe, and simple, and you can vary the technique to enhance the impression of age. For example, you can simply apply both coats more heavily, remembering that for authenticity the effect must be uneven. Or give the rust more texture by adding about 2¹/₂ oz. (70g.) fine sand to the base coat. It works well on metal, but can be applied to other surfaces.

BASIC RECIPE—RUST

INGREDIENTS

To cover approximately 6m² (65ft²)
Base coat ▶ 17 oz. (500ml.) premixed black latex flat paint / 2tbsp. titanium white artists' acrylic color / 2tbsp. ultramarine blue artists' acrylic color
First rust coat ▶ 3¹/₂ oz. (100ml.) raw sienna artists' acrylic color / 3tbsp. Venetian red artists' acrylic color / 1tbsp. burnt umber artists' acrylic color / 1tbsp. red oxide artists' acrylic color
Second rust coat ▶ 3¹/₂ oz. (100ml.) yellow ocher artists' acrylic color / 2tbsp. yellow oxide artists' acrylic color / 1tbsp. raw sienna artists' acrylic color

EQUIPMENT

3 containers for mixing paint / 1 x 2in. (50mm.) paintbrush / 2 x 1in. (25mm.) round fitches

INSTRUCTIONS
Base coat

1 Pour the latex paint into one of the containers. Add the titanium white and ultramarine, and stir well.
2 Apply an even coat to your prepared surface (see pp. 24–7) with the latex brush, and allow to dry (2–4 hours).

First rust coat

1 Place the raw sienna, Venetian red, burnt umber, and red oxide in a second container, and stir well.
2 Using a fitch, stipple the mix onto the surface with a gentle tapping action. Allow a little of the base coat to show through. Leave to dry (1 hour).

Second rust coat

1 Put yellow ocher, yellow oxide, and raw sienna in a third container, and stir.
2 Using the other fitch, again stipple the mix onto the surface. Apply this coat more heavily, although parts of the other coats must remain visible. Build up the color in some areas to avoid a uniform finish. Allow to dry (1 hour).

Exterior use Finish with two coats of matte polyurethane varnish, according to the manufacturers' instructions.

❶ RUST
This inexpensive metal table was an ideal subject. Detail (as in the coat-of-arms, above left) always lends itself to the technique. Aging has been increased with two applications to the top and rim.

VERDIGRIS

Verdigris is perhaps the most stunning of the weathering effects to be seen on metal, occurring naturally on copper and bronze in the characteristic streaks of salty, acidic greens and whites. Simulating this effect originally involved the use of extremely toxic chemicals and intense heat (see also the less hazardous cold-patination technique for verdigris explained on p. 104). However, this recipe uses water-based products, so it is much safer and easier. You can increase the aged effect by working the surface over and over again.

The finish can be applied to many surfaces, so hunt out all sorts of unusual objects to work on. Anything with lots of detail will pick up the look wonderfully well, although the method works on a flat surface just as successfully. Look at the real thing on statues and metalwork that have been exposed to the elements for years.

This decorative weather vane is a good example of the verdigris effect. It has added to the character of the piece, and since the vane would once have been used outdoors, verdigris is an obvious and appropriate choice.

BASIC RECIPE—VERDIGRIS

INGREDIENTS

To cover approximately 6m² (65ft²)
Base coat ► 1 pint (500ml.) latex chalkboard paint or black latex flat paint
First verdigris coat ► 2tbsp. titanium white artists' acrylic color / 2tbsp. viridian green artists' acrylic color / 4tbsp. water / denatured alcohol
Second verdigris coat ► 2tbsp. titanium white acrylic artists' color / 1tbsp. yellow ocher artists' acrylic color / 3¹/₂ oz. (100ml.) water / denatured alcohol
Sealant/finishing coat ► 1 pint (500ml.) clear matte acrylic varnish / 1 oz. (30g.) whiting or powdered chalk

EQUIPMENT

1 x 2in. (50mm.) paintbrush / 2 containers for mixing paint / 3 x 1in. (25mm.) round fitches / spray bottle / 1 x 2in. (50mm.) varnish brush / rags

VERDIGRIS

INSTRUCTIONS
Base coat

Stir the chalkboard or latex flat paint well, and apply an even coat to the prepared surface (see pp. 24–7), using the paintbrush. Allow to dry (2–4 hours).

First verdigris coat

1 Place the titanium white and viridian green in one of the containers. Add the water (a little at a time) and stir well.
2 Load one of the fitches with the solution, and, holding or positioning the object vertically, dribble the liquid onto the surface so it drips downward. Repeat to cover the surface.
3 Half fill the spray bottle with denatured alcohol and spray a fine mist onto the surface to disperse the paint slightly.

Second verdigris coat

1 Place the titanium white and yellow ocher in the other container. Add $1^3/4$ oz. (50ml.) water (a little at a time), and stir well.
2 Using a second fitch, dribble the solution in the same way.
3 Spray a fine mist of denatured alcohol, as described above.
4 Dribble the remaining water onto the vertical surface as before, using a third fitch, until you have the effect you want. Allow to dry (2 hours).

Sealant/finishing coat

1 Brush one coat of varnish onto the entire surface, using the 2in. (50mm.) varnish brush, and leave to become tacky (approx. 20 minutes).
2 Rub in some whiting (or powdered chalk), paying particular attention to any detail. This helps to give an authentic "chalky" finish. Wipe off any loose, excess whiting with rags and allow to dry (2–3 hours).

Exterior use Add two coats of satin polyurethane varnish, according to the manufacturers' instructions.

Opposite: This impressive lion-head fountain is, in fact, made of plastic, transformed by the use of the verdigris effect. It was prepared and primed with two coats of latex chalkboard paint. To protect a surface from regular exposure to water, add two or three coats of marine varnish after the sealant/finishing coat, according to the manufacturers' instructions.

❶ VERDIGRIS
The basic recipe applied to a flat surface and three-dimensional detail. You can, if you prefer, substitute 1 pint (500ml.) premixed rust latex flat paint for chalkboard paint in the base coat. The effect is similar.

LEAD

Aged, weathered lead has a gray-blue, salty, or chalky appearance, the result of chemical changes in the metal. It is a look that is easily created with water-based products—simply by dripping colored glazes onto a vertical surface and then aging with whiting. Plastic flower pots and planters are ideal subjects, but plain, cheap metal items are equally effective and will look wonderfully expensive. As with most of the metal effects, you choose how much to age the finish.

BASIC RECIPE—LEAD

INGREDIENTS

To cover approximately 6m² (65ft²)

Sealant coat ▶ 1 pint (500ml.) white glue / 1 pint (500ml.) water

Base coat ▶ 17 oz. (500ml.) white latex flat paint/ 1tbsp. burnt umber artists' acrylic color / 1tbsp. premixed black latex flat paint

First glaze ▶ 4tbsp. premixed black latex flat paint / 2tbsp. titanium white artists' acrylic color / ¹/₂tbsp. burnt umber artists' acrylic color / 5 oz. (150ml.) water

Second glaze coat ▶ 5tbsp. titanium white artists' acrylic color / 2tbsp. burnt umber artists' acrylic color / 1tbsp. ultramarine blue artists' acrylic color / 5 oz. (150ml.) water

Sealant/finishing coat ▶ 1 pint (500ml.) white glue / 1 pint (500ml.) water / 1³/₄ oz. (50g.) whiting or powdered chalk

EQUIPMENT

5 containers for mixing paint and glaze / 2 x 1in. (25mm.) paintbrushes / 3 x 2in. (50mm.) paintbrushes / 1 x 1in. (25mm.) round fitch / rags

INSTRUCTIONS

Sealant coat

1 Pour the white glue into one of the containers. Add the water (a little at a time) and stir well.

2 Brush the solution onto your prepared surface, using one of the 1in. (25mm.) paintbrushes. Allow to dry (1 hour).

Base coat

1 Pour the white latex flat paint into a second container. Add the burnt umber and black latex paint, and stir well.

2 Apply evenly to the prepared surface (see pp. 24–7) with a 2in. (50mm.) paintbrush, and allow to dry (2–4 hours).

❶ LEAD
The classic effect: highly successful on flat surfaces and relief detailing, so you can, for example, convert cheap plastic into something a great deal more splendid. Success depends partly on finding an appropriate design.

The inexpensive metal sconce on the left of the picture has been changed beyond recognition by the application of the lead effect described in the basic recipe.

First glaze coat

1 Pour the latex paint into a third container. Add the white, burnt umber, and 3 1/2 oz. (100ml.) water gradually; stir well.
2 Apply the glaze to the entire surface with random strokes using a second 2in. (50mm.) paintbrush.
3 Load the fitch with water, and, holding the object vertically, drip the liquid onto the surface so it runs from top to bottom. This helps to disperse the glaze, allowing some of the base to show through. Repeat to cover. Allow to dry (1 hour).

Second glaze coat

1 Put the titanium white, burnt umber, and ultramarine in a fourth container. Add 3 1/2 oz. (100ml.) water gradually; stir.
2 Using a third 2in. (50mm.) brush, apply with random cross-hatched strokes. Parts of the other coats must remain visible.
3 Drip water onto the surface again. Allow to dry (2 hours).

Sealant/finishing coat

1 Put the white glue in a fifth container. Add the water (a little at a time) and stir well.
2 Apply to the entire surface with the other 1in. (25mm.) paintbrush, and leave until it is tacky (5–7 minutes).
3 Rub the whiting (or powdered chalk) into the surface, using rags. Pay special attention to any detail. Remove excess whiting with clean rags. Allow to dry (2–3 hours).

Exterior use Add two coats of matte polyurethane varnish, according to the manufacturers' instructions.

TORTOISESHELL

This effect simulates the appearance of the shell of the sea turtle, which was first used as a decorative veneer in the East. Imitated for centuries, the pattern is created with diagonal strokes on different background colors, such as white, cinnamon, and gold. The latter was once real gold leaf, but imitation metal leaf or gold sprays are just as successful. This recipe reproduces the classic colors. It works well on small, flat surfaces—the shell cannot be carved—but it is striking on screens and table tops.

BASIC RECIPE—UMBER AND OCHER

INGREDIENTS

To cover approximately 6m² (65ft²)

Base coat ▶ 17 oz. (500ml.) white latex flat paint / 3tbsp. raw sienna artists' acrylic color

Glaze coats ▶ 3tbsp. yellow ocher artists' acrylic color / 3tbsp. raw sienna artists' acrylic color / 3tbsp. burnt umber artists' acrylic color / 17 oz. (500ml.) acrylic glazing liquid (transparent) / 5 oz. (150ml.) water

Spatter coat ▶ 1tbsp. burnt umber artists' acrylic color / 3¹/₃tbsp. water

Protective coat ▶ 1 pint (500ml.) clear satin acrylic varnish

EQUIPMENT

Container for mixing paint / 1 x 2in. (50mm.) paintbrush / 4 saucers for mixing glaze / 1 x 2in. (50mm.) paintbrush / 3 x 1in. (25mm.) flat artists' brushes / badger blender or dusting brush / toothbrush / disposable gloves / 1 x 2in. (50mm.) varnish brush

INSTRUCTIONS

Base coat

1 Pour the latex paint into the container. Add the raw sienna and stir well.

2 Apply an even coat to your prepared surface (see pp. 24–7) with the latex brush and allow to dry (2–4 hours).

An interesting example of the use of the tortoiseshell finish, the little lampshade blends delightfully with the surrounding objets d'art and antiques. The effect could easily be reproduced on a simple metal shade.

❶ UMBER AND OCHER
The basic recipe colorway: the sample is painted on an area larger than is normally undertaken, but it illustrates well the potential use of tortoiseshell on flat surfaces, such as small decorative panels or trays.

Glaze coats

1 Place each of the three colors in a separate saucer. Add 1³/₄ oz. (50ml.) acrylic glazing liquid and 1³/₄ oz. (50ml.) water (a little at a time) to each color and stir well. Set aside.

2 Apply the remaining 11³/₄ oz. (350ml.) acrylic glazing liquid in a thin, even coat to the base coat, using the tossaway brush.

3 Using one of the artists' brushes, apply the yellow ocher glaze to the surface in random, diagonal strokes. You are aiming for a rough, "daubed" effect, with much of the base coat still showing through.

4 Repeat the process, using a different brush for each of the remaining, darker colors. Brush glaze onto other random areas until the base coat is completely covered.

5 Skim lightly over the surface with the badger blender (or dusting brush), allowing the hairs of the brush to touch the glaze. Your aim is to remove the brushstrokes and to merge the colors into each other to create the tortoiseshell effect. Allow to dry (24 hours).

These simple boxes illustrate a variation of the basic recipe in colors often found in tortoise-shell. The base coat was a premixed deep red latex paint; in the glaze coats 3tbsp. cadmium red replaced the yellow ocher; the spatter and protective coats were unchanged.

Spatter coat

1 Place the burnt umber in the fourth saucer. Add the water (a little at a time) and stir well.

2 Put on the disposable gloves. Load the toothbrush with paint. Holding it about 8in. (20cm.) from the surface, flick back the bristles with the fingers of your other hand to produce a fine mist of paint dots. You are aiming for little patches of dots, rather than the even coverage typical of spattering. Allow to dry (4–5 hours).

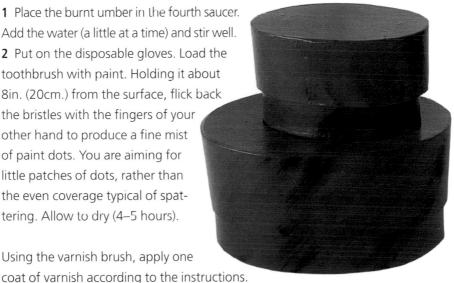

Protective coat

Using the varnish brush, apply one coat of varnish according to the instructions.

113

BRONZING

Bronzing is an ancient technique used as an alternative or supplementary method to gilding (see p. 116). An object or area is sized, and a fine metallic powder, originally real gold, is brushed or blown onto it to produce a subtly bronzed, antique look. The powders are very fine and toxic, so always wear a mask and take care. Try not to use too much at a time to avoid waste and mess. Several colors and tones are available: most tones of gold, bronze, and copper are easily found and other colors, such as purple, green, and red, can be obtained from specialist suppliers.

Bronzing can be used on a variety of surfaces and many objects. The technique produces an opulent look which is great for transforming old or secondhand objects. Metal chairs and garden ornaments are ideal. So, too, are plaster architectural moldings and statues. It is also an excellent way of applying subtle decoration to painted items. Just mask the areas you want to protect, and follow the recipe. The powders tend to spread, so you should allow newly painted or varnished areas to dry overnight.

BASIC RECIPE—DEEP GOLD

INGREDIENTS

To cover approximately 3m² (32ft²)
Base coat ▶ 8¹/₂ oz. (250ml.) red iron oxide primer
Bronzing ▶ 8¹/₂ oz. (250ml.) water-based size / 2¹/₂ oz. (75g.) deep gold bronze powder
Protective coat ▶ 8¹/₂ oz. (250ml.) amber French enamel varnish

EQUIPMENT

2 x 1in. (25mm.) tossaway brushes / protective mask / 1 x 1in. (25mm.) flat artists' brush / small, soft-bristled brush / soft cloths / 1 x 1in. (25mm.) varnish brush

❶ DEEP GOLD
The basic recipe:
a rich, yet subtle
effect.

❷ COPPER
This variation
follows the basic
recipe, simply sub-
stituting copper
bronze powder at
the bronzing stage
and red French
enamel varnish for
the protective coat.

INSTRUCTIONS

ALWAYS WEAR A MASK AND WORK IN A WELL-VENTILATED AREA

Base coat

Stir the red iron oxide primer well and apply an even coat to your prepared surface (see p. 24–7), using one of the tossaway brushes. Allow to dry (24 hours).

Bronzing

1 Shake or stir the size according to the manufacturers' instructions. Apply a thin, even coat to the base coat, using

Bronzing a metal chair, following a variation of the basic recipe.

A rust inhibitor and metal primer were applied first, and then came two coats of premixed black oil-based primer (8¹/₂ oz. [250ml.] each). Light gold bronze powder was stirred into the size at the bronzing stage, and the protective coat was a neutral French enamel varnish.

A final coat of satin polyurethane varnish was added, according to the manufacturers' instructions, for extra protection, as the chair was to be used outside.

the other tossaway brush. Allow to become tacky and transparent (approx. 20–30 minutes).

2 Put on the protective mask. Using the artists' brush, take up a little of the bronze powder at a time and brush it carefully onto the surface until most of the base coat is covered.

3 Gently remove some of the excess powder with the soft-bristled brush.

4 Rub carefully with soft cloths to burnish.

Protective coat   Apply one coat of varnish to the surface, using the varnish brush, and allow to dry (1 hour).

GILDING

Real gold leaf is both costly and time consuming to use, and today there are a variety of alternatives (see p. 18). Imitation metal leaf, also called Dutch metal leaf, is the most convincing, being also cheaper and simpler to apply, and the modern gold sizes—water-based and oil-based—are effective and faster drying than the traditional substances. To give a smooth surface for gilding, a gesso is traditionally applied, tinted red to give a good base color to the leaf. Gesso can be bought ready mixed or a modern version made from whiting and PVA adhesive. But it is simpler and equally effective to substitute, as this recipe does, a coat of red oxide primer or deep red latex paint. Gilding is ideal for plaster moldings, picture and mirror frames, candlesticks, and numerous other ornaments.

❶ CLASSIC AGING
This plaster leaf is gilded using the imitation metal leaf method described in the basic recipe. Here the aging glaze is gray.

❷ OLD GOLD
The aging glaze for this leaf is colored with 2tbsp. yellow ocher mixed with 1tbsp. Acra gold. This tone brings out the richness of the metal leaf and is reminiscent of the Italian gold used on many religious paintings.

❸ PALE GOLD
The base coat is pre-mixed dark green latex flat paint. The aging glaze is tinted with 1tbsp. cerulean blue and 1¹/₂tbsp. titanium white. The green base gives the gold a thinner tone.

❹ MODERN GOLD
This aging glaze is simply colored with 2tbsp. diox-azine purple and is a more contemporary way of treating a gilded object.

BASIC RECIPE—GOLD IMITATION METAL WITH CLASSIC AGING

INGREDIENTS

For one plaster leaf molding

Base coat ▶ 8¹/₂ oz. (250ml.) red oxide primer or deep red latex flat paint

Sizing coat ▶ 8¹/₂ oz. (250ml.) water-based quick-drying gold size

Gilding ▶ 12 gold imitation metal leaves

Optional additional aging ▶ 2tbsp. denatured alcohol

Sealant coat ▶ 8¹/₂ oz. (250ml.) amber shellac

Aging glaze ▶ 2tbsp. white latex flat paint / ¹/₂tbsp. neutral gray artists' acrylic color / ¹/₂tbsp. yellow ocher artists' acrylic color / 2tbsp. water

EQUIPMENT

3 x 1in. (25mm.) paintbrushes / bowl / disposable gloves / 1 x 1in. (25mm.) round, very soft-bristled brush / 2 soft polishing cloths / steel wool (optional) / 1 x 1in. (25mm.) varnish brush / container for mixing glaze / rags

INSTRUCTIONS

Base coat

Stir the primer (or latex paint) well, and, using one of the latex brushes, apply an even coat to your prepared surface (see pp. 24–7). Allow to dry (2–4 hours).

Sizing coat

Shake or stir the size, following the manufacturers' instructions. Using a second latex brush, apply a thin but even coat of size to the entire surface. Never overload the brush, because it is important to leave as few bubbles on the surface as possible. Allow the size to dry a little (20–30 minutes) until it becomes transparent and tacky.

Gilding

1 Place the bowl on your work surface with the metal leaves close at hand.

2 Put on the gloves, and hold the object over the bowl to catch any broken leaf. Lift up each leaf and lay it carefully on the surface. Cover the object completely, or, for an aged effect, allow some of the primer to show through.

3 Use the soft-bristled brush to dust the object lightly, brushing the excess leaf into the bowl. You can use small pieces to cover gaps and keep larger ones for another project.

4 Rub the surface gently with one of the polishing cloths until it is smooth and shiny. Take care not to rub too hard, or too much or the leaf will lift off.

Sealant coat

Using the varnish brush, apply a thin but even coat of shellac to the surface to deepen the color. This is important, as imitation metal can look tinny. Leave to dry (45 minutes).

Aging glaze

1 Pour the latex paint into the container and add the neutral gray and yellow ocher. Stir thoroughly, and then add the water (a little at a time), mixing again.

2 Using a third paintbrush, dab the entire surface with glaze and then quickly rub off with rags so that the glaze remains only in the detailing.

3 Rub the gilding on the raised and highlighted areas with the other soft polishing cloth to buff. Allow the remaining latex paint to dry (30 minutes).

Notes You can increase the aging effect by gently taking back the gilding in places where the object would naturally become worn. Use a little steel wool dipped in denatured alcohol, then apply the sealant coat.

Gilding transforms a galvanized garden planter: a blue metal primer designed for car paintwork substitutes for red iron oxide in the base coat, another variation on the basic recipe (see also p. 45). About 20 gold imitation metal leaves were applied and sealed with amber shellac. The aging glaze was colored simply with 4tbsp. cerulean blue.

VARIATION—GOLD SCRAP LEAF

❺ GOLD SCRAP LEAF
Follow the basic recipe for the base coat, sizing, and gilding stages. You will need 3¹/₂oz. (100g.) scrap leaf. Seal with a diluted amber French enamel varnish (5³/₄oz. [170ml.] varnish to 2³/₄oz. [80ml.] denatured alcohol), using a 2in. (50mm.) tossaway brush. Allow to dry (30 minutes).

As the name suggests, scrap leaf is composed of the fragments that result when making imitation metal leaf. Gold and aluminum (see below) are available. You buy it by weight, and it is cheaper than whole leaf. Scrap leaf takes much longer to apply—to be honest, it takes some patience—but done well it creates a more worn, aged effect because more of the base coat shows through. There is no need to apply an aging glaze.

VARIATION—COPPER LEAF

❻ COPPER LEAF
As basic recipe for base coat, sizing, and gilding, using 12 copper leaves. Seal with 8¹/₂oz. (250ml.) clear satin acrylic varnish, applied with a 2in. (50mm.) brush. Allow to dry (1 hour). Finish with a blue aging coat (2tbsp. white latex semigloss paint, ¹/₂tbsp. neutral gray, scant 1tsp. ultramarine blue, and 2tbsp. water).

Theatricality is really the keynote here, although copper imitation metal leaf gives a less opulent effect than the more traditional gold leaf. We think it works well in contemporary interiors, and in particular with more unusual *objets d'art* and ethnic collections. If you have a taste for the less predictable, you could experiment with colored French enamel varnishes for the sealant coat (see sample 5 for the proportions). We have sometimes used bright red to create an exciting, modern effect.

VARIATION—ALUMINUM LEAF

❼ ALUMINUM LEAF
The process and quantities are as for the basic recipe, but use a premixed blue latex flat paint for the base coat, seal with transparent acrylic glazing liquid instead of shellac, and omit the yellow ocher from the aging ingredients.

Aluminum imitation metal leaf is used to create a silver-leaf finish. Again, like copper leaf, it seems to suit modern interiors best. Premixed blue or green latex flat paint is substituted for red oxide primer (or deep red latex paint) at the base-coat stage because either will complement the silver well. In the sample shown here we used a medium blue, but if you like bold effects try experimenting with the darker tones of either color.

PART THREE

DECORATIVE DESIGNS & FINISHES

An introduction to the techniques you will need for applying both paint and pattern, together with ideas on how to incorporate them into simple and effective designs in a range of colors

An example of what can be achieved using a combination of techniques. The fossil set in granite (see pp. 163–5) is made by combining stone effects, stenciling, and a whiting resist. The result is an elegant and unusual table top.

INTRODUCTION

In Parts Three and Four we set out to show how color, texture, and pattern can come together in designs that have a certain vitality, whether it be radiated out in highly charged contrasts or conveyed in a quiet and stylish manner. Here in over 70 paint recipes are a variety of decorative techniques, designs, and projects that can be followed, like a cookery recipe, teaspoon for teaspoon, or used as a point of departure for you to develop and realize your own ideas.

In Part Three we include the techniques you will need for the project and design ideas in Parts Three and Four. These are simply ways of applying and manipulating paint to create a range of surface textures, from flat matte to highly decorative. To these techniques we have added stamping, stenciling and the use of masking and resists—all methods of producing and/or reproducing a design in a controlled manner.

All the techniques are simple. None requires specialist knowledge or expensive equipment, and they can usually be mastered quickly. In the case of the stencils and stamps, we have kept our designs simple, too, so they are easy to cut and apply. We have aimed to use all our techniques in a way that gives a great deal of freedom, providing a result that looks fresh and contemporary.

Gaining confidence in handling your materials and equipment is all part of the pleasure of decorating. There is no doubt that the best way to do this is to practice. Use an area of wall that can be painted over afterward, or scraps of drywall, which is what was used for many of the examples in this book. These have the extra advantage that you can pick them up and move them around, since colors will change their appearance in different lights and according to their position in a room.

Although we have chosen the equipment and materials to be as simple as possible, there will always remain, for those who want to abandon plain white interiors for decorative paint effects, the difficult question of which colors to choose. Decisions about color are always going to require pause for reflection. There was a time when rules of taste gave guidance, but at the beginning of a new century almost all of these have been rejected. Blue with green, for example, is perfectly acceptable. You may choose colors because of the memories they evoke, for cultural reasons, or because they are soothing. These choices are all personal, and only you can make them. You may seek guidance in color theory, but understanding the spectrum and how to mix paint will not be much help in choosing which colors to use, although it can explain why certain color combinations behave in the way they do. We know of only one artist who derives inspiration from the color wheel. The rest spend more time looking at other painters' work.

We believe a lot can be learned by looking, and this partly explains why we give such a broad range of color combinations. We usually show two or three alternative colorways for each design. Even the basic

techniques are shown in alternative colorways as well as with some additional decorative device—whether it be to manipulate them into stripes or panels, or to add a masked-out motif. Not only does this give you a choice; it will also, we hope, let you see the effect a change of color, be it ever so small, can have. You also have the option of using a recipe from elsewhere in the book if it is more in keeping with your scheme. Whatever you do, always look at other interiors, at textiles, clothing, and painting, and take your lead from those you like.

Interiors, like the colors we wear, are influenced by fashion. This is potentially a problem if you live in a building that was built many decades ago, but don't let this trouble you. With care we can combine the old with the new. You can have respect for the old, even venerate it, but that does not mean you have to live in a time warp. Nevertheless, we personally have been influenced by a lot of what we have seen from the past, not least because the colors of old, derived from natural pigments, have a quality we happen to like.

Apart from the task of choosing and mixing colors, you will have to arrange them into shapes on your surface. In the realm of pattern, fashion again exerts its influence, but the mood is a lot more individual than it was twenty years ago—softer, yet full of vitality. The fleur-de-lis of yesterday has been replaced by the altogether more lively spiral.

Some design classics will always remain, but they can be adapted to suit the current look. One example of this is stripes. These seem to change their personality each season. One year all slim and Regency, they reappear the next as broad and eighteenth-century Swedish. Whatever form they take, you know that stripes will bring a great sense of style to a room. While stripes seem to go naturally on a wall, plaids gravitate readily onto the floor. This is not a hard and fast rule, though, so try applying plaids to walls, window frames or even furniture.

Applying plaids and stripes needs only the skills of planning and layout, and maybe some dexterous use of masking tape. Other designs can be helped onto wall or floor with stencils and stamps. These are an excellent way of controlling where your paint goes, as well as a means of covering a surface quickly. In most cases, we give the motifs for the stencils and stamps we use at the back of this book, because we realize that many readers will lack the confidence to develop a pattern or draw a motif. You can very easily trace and enlarge our motifs to the size you require, then transfer them to your surface.

If you like what you see here, you can incorporate it right away in your own decorating. Otherwise, you could take one technique—say dry brushing—and use it as the background to a stenciled or stamped design. Or, if you like a technique but not our choice of colors, experiment using a color recipe from elsewhere in the book. We hope we have provided you with a starting point. The rest is up to you.

COLORWASHED STRIPES

Colorwashing is probably one of the most useful techniques in decorative painting. We have made much use of it throughout Parts Three and Four, either as a background to the motifs or for the motifs themselves. A single glaze can be an effective treatment for a wall, leaving a broken surface, as opposed to the flat, single-toned finish that results from a roller. If you apply several layers of glaze, the surface becomes richer and multi-toned. Brush marks disappear under each successive glaze coat, leaving a soft, gently textured surface. (For an alternative effect, in which individual brush strokes remain clearer, see Part Two, p. 48.) Here we show how colourwashing can be used by itself to stripe a wall. In two of our samples, the two glazes we use are the same color. This enriches the first glaze and brings it down a tone. In the other two samples, the second glaze is a different but similar color. This creates a more complex and subtle surface. If you opt to use a second color that is from a different part of the spectrum than the first, you will not end up with such subtlety of color; however, you should not let this stop you from experimenting if you wish.

The wall you are to work on should be well prepared and white. High-quality latex flat paints are ideal as a base. Cheaper latex paints may have chalk or whiting as a pigment, which makes them too absorbent, so the glaze cannot be moved around on the surface.

The colorwash dries quickly, so if you are tackling a large surface, it is a good idea for two people to work together. The glazing liquid in the colorwash mix helps to extend slightly the glaze's drying time, making it easier to manipulate. It also gives the glaze a slightly harder finish.

The recipes are for a wall approximately 54ft.^{2} (5m.^{2})

BASIC RECIPE—BLUE ON BLUE COLORWASHED STRIPES

INGREDIENTS

See swatch captions. Colorants: artists' acrylic colors.

EQUIPMENT

Medium-textured paint roller plus tray / 1 or 2 large containers / 2 or 4 x 4in. (100mm.) paintbrushes / rags/ tape measure / straightedge / water-soluble marker or chalk line / safe-release masking tape / cash register tape

INSTRUCTIONS

1 Prepare the surface thoroughly. See pp. 24–7.
2 Use a medium-textured paint roller to apply two coats of white latex flat paint to the wall. You should be aiming to create a surface that is free of brushstrokes but has a slight texture. Leave 4 hours to dry between coats, and 24 hours after the second coat to make a really hard surface ready for the next stage.
3 Mix your glaze or glazes in one or more containers.
4 Load one of the paintbrushes with glaze, and apply to a

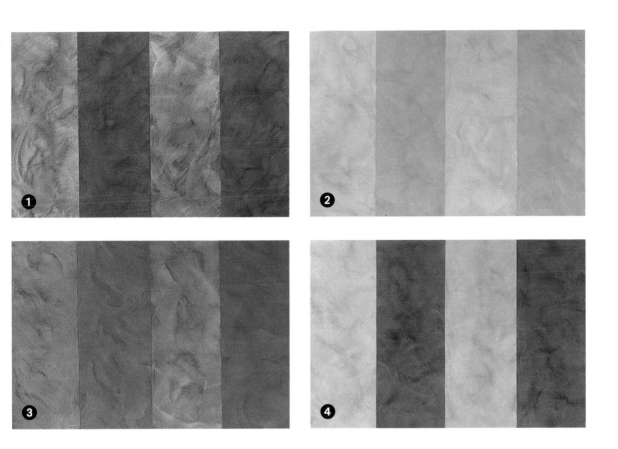

❶ BLUE ON BLUE
On a base of 1qt. (1 liter) white latex flat, a mixture of 3tbsp. white latex flat, 1½tsp. quinacridone violet, 6tbsp. ultramarine plus 5oz. (150ml.) acrylic glazing liquid and 20oz. (600ml.) water will colorwash the wall twice.

❸ DULL TURQUOISE GREEN ON BLUE
On the same base coat, apply a first glaze of swatch 1 colorwash, and a second glaze of 3tbsp. white latex flat, 3tbsp. cobalt blue, 2tsp. yellow ocher, 3½oz. (100ml.) acrylic glazing liquid, and 13½oz. (400ml.) water.

section of the wall. Brush it on in all directions in quick, curving, random strokes. Almost immediately, follow up with the clean, dry paintbrush. Skim the second brush over the paint in all directions until you reach the point where the brush begins to drag and starts to lift the paint off rather than moving it around. Now you should work a little more firmly. Aim to soften all the brushstrokes, but do not worry if some remain stronger than others. That is all part of the desired effect. The paint will be completely dry in only a matter of seconds.

5 Move quickly on to the next section of the wall, and repeat the process. The second brush will become wet as you work, so you will need to dry it off frequently on a rag. Repeat the process until you have completed the wall. Leave to dry at least 4 hours.

6 Use the tape measure, straightedge, and marker to measure and mark out a series of 8in. (20cm.) stripes (see p. 35). Mask out alternate stripes with masking tape and cash register tape (see pp. 40–1). Take care when applying masking tape to the freshly painted areas. If possible, use a safe-release masking tape.

7 Use the paintbrushes to apply the second glaze coat in the same manner as the first. Remove all the masking, and allow to dry (4 hours).

❷ BEIGE ON BEIGE
Again on a base coat of 1qt. (1 liter) white latex flat, a mixture of 7½tbsp. white and 3tbsp. raw sienna mixed with 5oz. (150ml.) acrylic glazing liquid and 20oz. (600ml.) water will colorwash the wall twice.

❹ BROWN ON BEIGE
On the same base coat, apply a first glaze of swatch 2 colorwash, and a second of 2tbsp. white latex flat, 4tbsp. burnt sienna, and 1½tsp. dioxazine purple, 3½oz. (100ml.) acrylic glazing liquid, and 13½oz. (400ml.) water.

DRY-BRUSHED PANELS

Dry brushing is similar in many ways to colorwashing, but the overall effect is softer. Its real practical advantage in decorative contexts is that because the brush is not fully loaded with paint, runs, splashes, dribbles, and seepage beneath masking tape are not usually a problem. The technique of dry brushing, however, requires some vigor, so we normally apply only a single coat, and we also work in small, contained areas. Here we show that dividing a wall into panels of color not only gives you a means to manage the technique but also provides a discreet and easy-to-achieve design for a wall. We have used it on walls of random stripes, too. All of them were multiples of 2in. (50mm.) wide, with three colors applied in an ordered sequence.

As with colorwashing, your base coat should be high-quality white latex flat paint. Our standard recipe for dry brushing in Parts Three and Four is 1 part color : 1 part glazing liquid : 2 parts water, but it can be varied by using less or no water. Dark colors require the most water to lighten them, whereas pale colors work better with less. You should also take into account the quality of your paint. If it is thin and watery to begin with, you will have to reduce the amount of water. Check the consistency by doing a trial run on a scrap of drywall. (See also Part Two, p. 58, where more water is used.)

These recipes are for a wall approximately 65ft.² (6m.²).

BASIC RECIPE—EMERALD GREEN DRY-BRUSHED PANELS

INGREDIENTS

See swatch captions. Colorants: artists' acrylic colors.

EQUIPMENT

Medium-textured paint roller plus tray / tape measure / straightedge / water-soluble marker or chalk line / safe-release masking tape / cash register tape or clean paper / container / 1 x 4in. (100mm.) paintbrush / ceramic tile

INSTRUCTIONS

1 Prepare the surface thoroughly. See pp. 24–7.

2 Use a medium-textured paint roller to apply two coats of white latex flat paint to the wall. You should be aiming to create a surface that is free of brushstrokes but has a slight texture. Allow 4 hours to dry between coats, and 24 hours after the second coat.

3 Using the tape measure, straightedge, and marker, mark the wall into panels measuring 22–43ft.² (2–4m.²). The exact size will be governed by the size of your wall. Using the masking tape, mask off as many alternate panels as possible, extending the width of the masking with cash register tape or clean paper (see pp. 40–1).

4 Mix the glaze coat in the container, then dab the tips of the paintbrush into the glaze. Only a little is needed. Stipple

❶ EMERALD GREEN
Over a base coat of 1qt. (1 liter) white latex flat paint, we applied an emerald green glaze made from 4tbsp. phthalocyanine green and 3tbsp. yellow ocher added to 4oz. (120ml.) white latex flat. The yellow ocher takes some of the sharpness out of the green. The color was mixed with 7½oz. (220ml.) acrylic glazing liquid, and 17oz. (500ml.) water.

the brush on the tile to distribute the paint evenly across the bristles. Starting at the top of a panel, brush the paint out in all directions. You can also use a rubbing action. The paint will spread out into a softly textured layer with many variations in tone. Do not overwork the glaze, or you may start to rub it off.

5 Once you have used up the glaze on your brush, dip it into the glaze again, stipple it on the tile, and continue down the panel. You must work briskly in order to successfully blend one section with the next. As you proceed, you will see the wisdom of dividing the wall up into small, manageable areas.

6 Complete each of the masked-off panels in turn, then remove the masking tape. Leave to dry for 2 hours to ensure that the glaze is not disturbed at the next stage.

7 Mask off another set of panels and repeat. Take care when applying masking tape to the freshly painted areas. If possible, use a tape designed for delicate surfaces. Remove the masking and allow to dry (2 hours).

Continue like this until all the panels have been completed. The soft checkerboard effect will appear as a result of slight variations in the color and texture that are typical of this technique.

❷ TERRACOTTA
With the same base coat as swatch 1, we used a glaze made from 5½oz. (160ml.) pimento red latex flat, to which we added 8tsp. burnt sienna and 4tsp. white. The burnt sienna helps give the color a more antique look. The color was mixed with 7½oz. (220ml.) acrylic glazing liquid and 15oz. (450ml.) water.

❸ DOVE GRAY
The simplest recipe and the most subtle. On the same base coat as described previously, apply a glaze made from 6½oz. (200ml.) white latex flat paint and 1tbsp. black artists' acrylic color, mixed with 7oz. (210ml.) acrylic glazing liquid and 15oz. (450ml.) water.

COMBED BORDERS

This involves dragging a purpose-made comb through wet paint to leave a pattern of ridges similar to the look of a woven fabric. The combs are often sold in sets, giving a choice of three different-sized teeth in four or five widths of comb. You can achieve similar effects with tile-cement spreaders or with homemade combs cut from plastic or cardboard. These recipes will cover approximately 43ft.² (4m.²).

COMBING OVER COLORWASHING

INGREDIENTS

See swatch captions. Colorants: artists' acrylic colors.

EQUIPMENT

Choose from the following:
Screw-top jars / paint roller plus tray / small paint bucket / 2 x 4in. (100mm.) paintbrush / safe-release masking tape / cash register tape / 3–4in. (75–100mm.)-wide graining comb or other broad-toothed comb / rag / sandpaper

INSTRUCTIONS

1 Prepare the surface thoroughly. See pp. 24–7.

2 Mix the first color—the background and combing color—in a screw-top jar. Using the roller, paint on two coats, allowing 2–4 hours for each coat to dry.

3 Mix the colorwash in another screw-top jar, and use the two larger brushes to apply two coats (see pp. 124–5), allowing 2 hours between coats and overnight for the second coat to dry.

4 Using masking tape for delicate surfaces, in conjunction with cash register tape, mask out the border (see pp. 40–1). If the border is going to turn a corner, as here, miter the corner also with masking tape.

5 Using the smaller brush, apply a liberal amount of the first color along a 3–6ft. (1–2m.) section of the border. Don't skimp. It must be thick enough for the comb to leave it standing up in ridges.

6 Without hesitation, drag the comb across the wet paint at

❶ WISTERIA OVER PEA GREEN Here the first color is 17oz. (500ml.) white latex flat mixed with 1tbsp. ultra-marine. The colorwash is 2tbsp. white latex flat, 4tbsp. cadmium yellow, and 2tsp. raw umber, mixed with 3½oz. (100ml.) acrylic glazing liquid and 13½oz. (400ml.) water.

❷ LINEN OVER HYACINTH The first color is 17oz. (500ml.) white latex flat with 5tsp. raw umber. The color-wash is 4tbsp. white latex flat and 2tsp. each ultramarine and dioxazine purple, mixed with 5½tbsp. glazing liquid and 11oz. (320ml.) water.

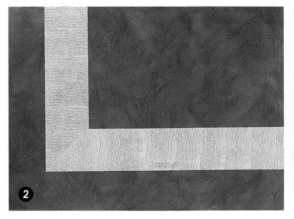

right angles to the masking tape. Do not stop until you reach the opposite edge of the border. As you pull the comb across, vary the pattern by increasing and decreasing the pressure on it or by allowing it to wander in gentle wavy lines. Reposition the comb in the adjacent area of wet paint, slightly overlapping the first, and pull it across the paint once more. You will occasionally need to wipe excess paint from the comb with a damp rag.

7 Repeat along the border until you reach the corner, as it is not easy to join wet combing to dry. Remove any masking tape and leave to dry thoroughly. As the paint is rather thick, this may take longer than the normal recommended drying time of 4 hours.

8 Mask the other sides of the miters, and repeat the combing on the remaining sides.

9 Remove the masking along the edges of the border to reveal a crisply edged border with a ribbed finish.

COMBING UNDER COLORWASHING

This makes the combed band more subtle. It is carried out in basically the same manner as described above, except that the combing is done first and the colorwashing second. After colorwashing, sand the combed ridges very lightly with sandpaper dipped in water.

❶ WISTERIA UNDER DANDELION YELLOW
The background and combing color is 17oz. (500ml.) white latex flat mixed with 1tbsp. ultra-marine. The colorwash is 4tbsp. white latex flat, 4tsp. yellow ocher, and 2tsp. each phthalocyanine green and Payne's gray, mixed with 6tbsp. acrylic glazing liquid and 12oz. (350ml.) water.

❷ LINEN UNDER CLEMATIS
The background and combing color is once again 17oz. (500ml.) white latex flat mixed with 5tsp. raw umber, as in swatch 2 of combing over colorwashing, while the color-wash consists of 2tbsp. each dioxazine purple, quin-acridone red, and white latex flat, mixed with 6tbsp. glazing liquid and 9oz. (270ml.) water.

SPONGED PANELS

More ideas for panels: two-color bands for a border design and simple repeating motifs. Experiment with the range of sponges available: each gives a different finish. Here we use standard cellulose sponges. Try varying the amount of paint applied to achieve anything from an opaque finish to an open texture which allows the color below. (See Part Two, p. 52, for a finish that combines Sponging off and on.)

SPONGING ON

Sponging on is our standard method of applying paint for stenciling. It is also a quick and easy way of giving a texture to a surface—for example, the granular texture on our counter front on pp. 184–7. This recipe will cover an area approximately 54ft². (5m.²).

INGREDIENTS

See swatch captions. Colorants: artists' acrylic colors.

EQUIPMENT

Paint roller plus tray / 3 cellulose sponges / scissors / 3 screw-top jars / 3 large plates / tape measure / safe-release masking tape / cash register tape

INSTRUCTIONS

1 Prepare the surface thoroughly. See pp. 24–7.
2 Use the roller to apply two coats of white latex flat paint, allowing each coat to dry (4 hours).
3 Squared-off sponges can leave lines in the paint, so trim them into a rounded shape with scissors.
4 Mix each of the sponging colors in a screw-top jar, and spoon some of the first color onto a plate. Dip your sponge into it, then pat it up and down for a moment to spread the paint evenly across the surface of the sponge. If you feel you have too much on your sponge, pat it on the plate a little longer. To create the lightly textured effect that is required here, the holes in the sponge should not be filled with paint.
5 Use a light dabbing motion to sponge the paint on. Try to vary the action as you work, or you may find that you are building up a pattern that is too repetitious. Complete the sponging in this manner, reloading your sponge with paint at regular intervals. Allow to dry (2–4 hours).
6 Use masking tape and cash register tape to mask off an 8in. (20cm.) wide band (see pp. 10-1). Sponge in the same way with the second sponging color. Remove the masking and allow to dry (2–4 hours).
7 Mask off the second band in the same way, and sponge in the third color. Remove the masking and allow to dry. The final effect is similar in appearance to a woven fabric such as gingham or madras cotton.

❶ BLUE-GREEN AND DARK GRAY OVER CREAMY YELLOW
Here the base coat is 1qt. (1 liter) white latex flat, with a first sponged coat of 17oz. (500ml.) white latex flat mixed with 2tsp. cadmium yellow, 2tsp. yellow ocher, and 1tsp. neutral gray. The second sponged coat is 8tsp. white latex flat with 6tbsp. black and 2tbsp. burnt umber. The third is 5½tbsp. white latex flat, 5½tbsp. cobalt blue, and 4tsp. yellow ocher.

❷ BLUE-GRAY AND PEACH OVER LILAC
With the same base coat as in swatch 1, the first sponged coat is 15oz. (450ml.) white latex flat mixed with 1tbsp. neutral gray and 2tsp. dioxazine purple. The second sponged coat consists of 5oz. (150ml.) white latex flat mixed with 2tbsp. ultramarine, while the third sponged coat is 5tbsp. white latex flat mixed with 3½oz. (100ml.) yellow ocher and 1tbsp. naphthol red.

SPONGING OFF

This technique is an essential part of the stone finishes on pp. 94–5. It also provided the backgrounds for the tables on pp. 212–15 and gave texture to the stripe on pp. 144–6. On a small scale sponging off will also modify a motif's texture: use a clean, damp sponge on the freshly painted surface.

With sponging off, paint is applied to a surface, then some is lifted off with a wet or damp sponge. If you splash, spray, or sprinkle water onto the paint as it dries, it will soften in those places, and this paint will lift off more readily. Open, more vigorously textured sponging off requires a lot of water, so can successfully be carried out only on a horizontal surface. On walls, use spray bottles and wet sponges.

For an area such as the top of a small table, you will need only about two or three tablespoons of color, depending on the texture you want. This recipe will cover an area approximately 32ft.² (3m.²).

INGREDIENTS **See swatch captions. Colorants: artists' acrylic colors.**

EQUIPMENT **Paint roller plus tray / 2 large plates / 1 x 3in. (75mm.) paintbrush / bowl of water / spray bottle (optional) / 2 or 3 cellulose sponges / paper / scissors / repositionable spray adhesive**

SPONGED PANELS

INSTRUCTIONS

1 Prepare the surface thoroughly. See pp. 24–7.

2 Use the roller to apply two coats of white latex flat paint, allowing each coat 2–4 hours to dry .

3 Now work in sections no larger than 11ft.^{2} (1m.^{2}). Mix the first sponging color on a plate, and apply it loosely with the paintbrush. Alternatively, you can sponge it on, but work quickly and avoid letting the paint dry out, especially at the edges. Maintaining a wet edge is essential if you are to blend one area successfully into another.

4 While the paint is still wet, splash and sprinkle water on its surface, or use a spray bottle. Leave for a moment, then dab at the surface with the sponge to pick up the paint from the wet areas. Rinse your sponge out frequently.

5 Repeat step 4 a number of times, according to how much paint you would like left behind and how much texturing you want. You will discover that differing textures can be created by varying the timing between painting and splashing, and splashing and dabbing. The amount of water you use will also have an influence on the finish.

6 Once you have a surface you are pleased with, leave it to dry for a couple of hours.

7 For the motif, cut a wobbly-edged moon from paper and attach it to the sponged surface with spray adhesive.

8 Spoon some of the second sponging color onto a plate, and dip a barely damp sponge into it. Rub this evenly over the surface until you are left with a thin, transparent layer over the sponging. Remove the paper mask and allow to dry. The magenta gives the sponging a remarkable richness and extravagant coloring.

❶ MAGENTA OVER PRUSSIAN GREEN
With a base coat of 4oz. (120ml.) white latex flat, the first sponged color is 2tbsp. Payne's gray and 2tbsp. phthalo-cyanine green, while the second is 2tbsp. magenta.

❷ MAGENTA OVER CADMIUM YELLOW
The base coat is as swatch 1. Replacing the Prussian green with 4tbsp. cadmium yellow changes the mood completely. The 2tbsp. magenta used again for the second sponging color converts the yellow into intensely rich and varied pinks.

Graining is done with a rubber tool called a rocker. When pulled through wet paint with a smooth, slow, rocking motion, it leaves behind a surprisingly accurate wood-grain pattern. You will probably like to practice a little first on a scrap of plywood or drywall.

These recipes will cover an area approximately 32–43ft.^{2} (3–4m.^{2}).

BASIC RECIPE—VIBRANT PINK OVER ACID YELLOW

INGREDIENTS   **See swatch captions. Colorants: artists' acrylic colors.**

EQUIPMENT   **2 containers / paint roller plus tray / tape measure / straightedge / water-soluble marker / masking tape / cash register tape / screw-top jar / 1 x 3in. (75mm.) paintbrush / graining rocker / rags**

INSTRUCTIONS

1 Prepare the surface thoroughly. See pp. 24–7.

2 Mix the base color in a container. Use the roller to apply two coats, allowing 2–4 hours for each coat to dry.

3 Measure and mark out the surface into 12in. (30cm.) squares, using a tape measure, straightedge, and marker. Divide each square into three equal bands as shown below, and mask out as many alternate bands as possible with masking tape and cash register tape (see pp. 40–1).

4 Mix the graining color and brush it on three or four masked-off bands. Drag the rocker slowly through the paint, pulling it toward you and gradually and smoothly changing its angle. You can vary the graining by altering your speed, as well as by graining with the rocker facing the opposite way. As you work, wipe excess paint from the face of the rocker.

5 Continue in the same way down each band, aiming for variety from band to band, but maintaining a family likeness between them all.

6 Remove the masking and allow to dry (2–4 hours).

7 Mask off another set of bands, and grain these in the same way. Continue until the design is complete.

❶ VIBRANT PINK OVER ACID YELLOW
For the base coat you will need 8½oz. (250ml.) cadmium yellow, 4oz. (120ml.) white, and 4oz. (120ml.) raw umber, while the graining requires 10oz. (300ml.) white, 3½oz. (100ml.) naphthol red, and 3½oz. (100ml.) vermilion.

❷ TURQUOISE OVER ACID GREEN
The base coat is 17oz. (500ml.) Hansa yellow light with 1tbsp. ultramarine. Over this the graining is 8½oz. (250ml.) white, 4oz. (120ml.) phthalocyanine green, and 4oz. (120ml.) phthalocyanine blue.

GRAINED FLOOR DESIGN

This is a development of the graining design illustrated on the previous page, but in it we make use of more subdued color schemes. You will need to start with a smooth floor—one made of thick plywood, for example. We envisioned using the design to cover a floor from wall to wall, although you could easily adapt it to make a border for a floor or even an allover design for a table top.

BASIC RECIPE—TURQUOISE AND EGGPLANT

PREPARATION

Prepare the surface thoroughly. See pp. 24–7.

INGREDIENTS

For a floor approximately 54ft.² (5m.²)
First color ▶ 1¼qt. (1.2 liters) white latex flat paint / 10oz. (300ml.) neutral gray artists' acrylic color / 1tbsp. phthalocyanine green artists' acrylic color
Second color ▶ 1¼pint (600ml.) raw umber artists' acrylic color / 7½oz. (220ml.) neutral gray artists' acrylic color / 7½oz. (220ml.) dioxazine purple artists' acrylic color
Protective coat ▶ 1½qt. (1.5 liters) flat acrylic floor varnish

EQUIPMENT

2 containers / 2 paint rollers plus trays / cardboard / metal ruler / pencil / X-Acto knife / cutting mat / chalk line / water-soluble marker / 2in. (50mm.) masking tape / 2½in. (60mm.) cash register tape / scissors / repositionable spray adhesive / paper / safe-release masking tape / 1 x 2in. (50mm.) paintbrush / graining rocker / 1 x 4in. (100mm.) varnish brush or roller

INSTRUCTIONS
Background

Mix the first color in a container, and paint the floor with two coats, using the roller. Allow 2–4 hours between coats, and leave overnight after the second coat.

Squares

1 Cut a 2½in. (6cm.) square hole at the center of a 12in. (30cm.) square piece of cardboard. Cut another piece of cardboard 3½ x 12in. (9 x 30cm.). With the aid of these templates, the marker, and a chalk line, mark out a grid of 12in. (30cm.) squares separated by 3½in. (9cm.) spaces across the whole floor. Use the 2in. (5cm.) masking tape to mask out the spaces (see pp. 40–1).

2 Mix the second color in another container, and use a roller to paint the squares with two coats of this color, allowing 4 hours for each coat to dry.

3 Cut the cash register tape into as many squares as you have painted. Spray one side of each of these with adhesive, and set them at the center of each painted square, using the square cardboard template as a guide.

❶ TURQUOISE AND EGGPLANT
The basic recipe.

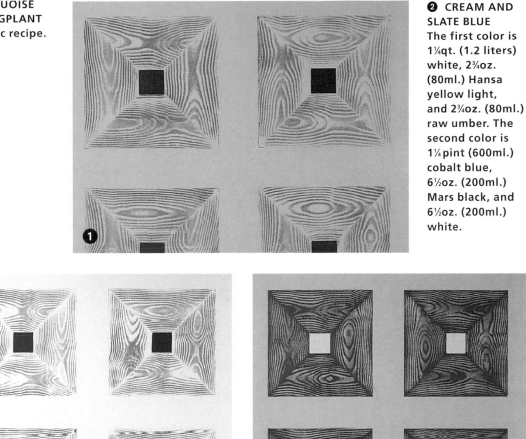

❷ CREAM AND SLATE BLUE
The first color is 1¼qt. (1.2 liters) white, 2¾oz. (80ml.) Hansa yellow light, and 2¾oz. (80ml.) raw umber. The second color is 1¼ pint (600ml.) cobalt blue, 6½oz. (200ml.) Mars black, and 6½oz. (200ml.) white.

4 Cut plenty of 12in. (30cm.) squares of paper each into four triangles.

5 Using the safe-release masking tape, in conjunction with the triangles cut from the paper, mask off opposite sections of each of your squares completely, along the diagonals, leaving the two other sections exposed. Hold down the bottom edge of the paper triangles with another piece of masking tape.

Graining

1 Using the paintbrush and the first color, paint in the two exposed sections fairly thickly. Immediately drag the rocker across the wet paint to create the graining pattern (see p. 133). Remove the paper triangles and the masking tape, and allow to dry (at least 4 hours).

2 Mask out for the remaining two sections of each square and repeat step 1 above, then very carefully remove all the masking. Leave to harden (1–2 days).

Protective coat

Using the varnish brush and following the manufacturers' instructions, apply at least three coats of varnish.

❸ BRONZE AND SLATE BLUE
The first color is a ready-mixed light bronze latex flat paint. The square is painted in a mixture of 30oz. (900ml.) white and 5oz. (150ml.) neutral gray, while the graining color is 1qt. (1 liter) of the second color from swatch 2.

STAMPED MOTIFS

Like stencils, rubber stamps are an effective way of reproducing a motif, but they are much quicker to use, producing a soft, varied texture which suits both contemporary and more traditional interiors. You can buy readymade rubber stamps, but it is not difficult to make your own (see p. 38). Acrylic paint is ideal for stamping. If the stamp is small, press it onto a layer of paint rolled out on a tile. For larger stamps, apply the paint to the stamp with the roller (see p. 39).

Practice stamping on a scrap of paper to discover how much paint you need and how much pressure to apply. The following recipes will cover approximately 43ft.^{2} (4m.^{2}).

INGREDIENTS

See swatch captions. Colorants: artists' acrylic color.

EQUIPMENT

Choose from the following:
Container / paint roller plus tray / tape measure / water-soluble marker / string / cardboard (optional) / 6 x 10in. (15 x 25cm.) foam-rubber mat / 6 x 10in. (15 x 25cm.) foamcore backing board / clear paper cement / 2 screw-top jars / 2 ceramic tiles / small paint roller / bowl of water / 1 or 2 sponges / ordinary marker / tracing paper / pencil / paper / X-Acto knife

A SIMPLE STAMP

This design uses one square stamp twice to produce a motif with a shadow of itself behind. It could be stamped at random, but, as with the stenciling (see pp. 156–7), we prefer a more orderly arrangement.

INSTRUCTIONS

1 Prepare the surface thoroughly (see pp. 24–7), and use the roller to paint on two coats of background color, allowing 2–4 hours for each coat to dry.

2 Measure and mark out the layout, using string as a guide for each of the horizontal lines of squares (see p. 35).

3 Mark out the spacing between each square with the water-soluble marker, or cut a piece of cardboard to the width of the space required and use this as a guide.

4 Make a 1½in. (4cm.)-square stamp of foam rubber, glued

❶ PALE SHADOWS
The background is 6½oz. (200ml.) white latex flat mixed with 10oz. (300ml.) yellow ocher. The first stamp color is ¼tsp. Payne's gray with 1¾oz. (50ml.) white latex flat, and the second is 1¾oz. (50ml.) Payne's gray. These will each print approximately 100 squares.

to a backing board of the same dimensions (see p. 38).

5 Mix the two colors, and spoon some of the first onto a tile. Roll out a generous, even layer and press your stamp into it. Stamp lines of squares along and up the wall. Clean the stamp by patting it up and down in a little water or on a wet sponge, then gently dry it with a cloth.

6 Press the stamp into a little of the second color on a tile. The second motif overlaps the first, a little below and to the left of it. To get it in the right place each time, mark a line on the upper and right-hand edges of the backing board, and align these with the left-hand side and lower edge of the first squares each time you print.

AN ORNATE STAMP

This stamp is in two sections, but there is no reason why any number of sections should not be used, depending on your patience and ingenuity. It has been designed to make a border, but it could be used for an allover pattern.

INSTRUCTIONS

1 Follow the instructions for simple stamping.

2 Measure for the lower edge of the border, and tightly stretch a string along this line.

3 Trace the motif on p. 216, enlarge it to 8½in. (22cm.), and cut out the two sections. Arrange them on the foam rubber and use as templates (see p. 38). The stamp will print as a mirror image, so its two sections must be the right way around. Draw a line on the reverse of the backing board opposite the tip of the motif to help with lining up.

4 Mix the stamping color and spoon some onto a tile. Roll it out with a small roller, then roller over the stamp to deposit an even film of paint on it. Place it in position, lining up its bottom edge with the string, then press firmly.

5 Repeat to complete the border. Because there is no spacing between motifs, when you print, you must place the end of the stamp alongside the end of the previous motif.

❷ **PAYNE'S GRAY ON PALE OCHER** This background is the same as that used for the simple stamp, and the stamp color is again 1¾oz. (50ml.) Payne's gray, but this amount will print only 50 of these larger motifs.

❷

6 You may come up against an obstruction, such as a window, door, or corner, where you will not be able to stamp a complete motif. If the empty spaces are very small and unobtrusive, you can simply leave them as they are. If you have finished the rest of your border and have only one or two more spaces to fill, you can cut the stamp down to make a motif that will fit the spaces. This will be easy to do if you have used a foamcore backing board. If you need a lot more motifs, stamp several prints on paper, and cut them out to make paper stencils which you use only once. Bend the paper stencils into corners or cut them to fit up to doors or windows, then sponge on the paint, mimicking the texture of the design as a whole.

A TWO-STAMP DESIGN

Here we employ the already prepared simple stamp and ornate stamp to make a third, more elaborate design, which we use as a border.

INSTRUCTIONS

1 Follow the instructions for simple stamping.

2 Use a tape measure to measure out two lines spaced 8½in. (22cm.) apart. Tightly stretch strings along these lines.

3 Follow step 5 of A Simple stamp, printing the squares at 4in. (10cm.) intervals inside the two lines. Note how the squares of the lower line are staggered to the right by the width of one square.

4 Spoon a little of the second color onto a tile, roll it out, and roll it over the second stamp. Print this vertically between the squares, using the string and the squares as a guide. Make sure that the top and bottom points of the second stamp fall exactly between two squares. You should not need any complex marking out, provided you have cut the backing board of the second stamp square and its stamp is centered on it.

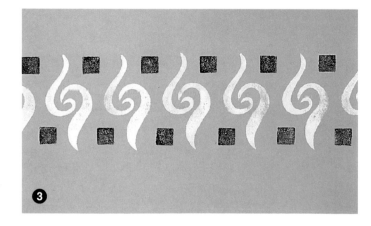

❸ PALE GRAY AND PAYNE'S GRAY
Again, the background color is the same as that already used, and the first and second stamp colors are as before.

MOSAIC BORDER DESIGN

Painting a mosaic might seem a time-consuming business at first glance, but using a set of foam-rubber stamps can speed things up considerably. We have confined this design to a border on a floor, but if you are more ambitious, you could cover the whole floor in a similar way. With careful planning you can make your border go around corners and into alcoves, or you could set it as a rectangle or square, regardless of the shape of your room. You could also, of course, easily run this border along a wall.

If you apply the border to a floor, the smoother and flatter the floor, the easier it will be to print. We have used ¾in. (2cm.)-thick plywood as our base. This takes a water-based wood stain very well, and the stain can subsequently be painted over without any problem using acrylic paints. If you like the idea of the mosaic but have a different floor surface, then alter the background accordingly. Particleboard, for example, could be given a stone finish (as for the *Rose des Vents* on pp. 166–7). Floorboards might seem an unlikely site for a mosaic, but if you have new, featureless boards, a mosaic might prove to be the quirky idea that will bring them to life.

BASIC RECIPE—BLACK AND WHITE ON UMBER

PREPARATION

Prepare the surface thoroughly. See pp. 24–7.

INGREDIENTS

For a border approximately 33ft. (10m.) long
Background ▶ umber water-based floor stain. See manufacturers' instructions for quantity required for your floor.
Base coat ▶ 10oz. (300ml.) white latex flat paint / 2tbsp. raw umber artists' acrylic color
First mosaic color ▶ 5oz. (150ml.) white artists' acrylic color
Second mosaic color ▶ 3tbsp. black artists' acrylic color / 1tbsp. phthalocyanine blue artists' acrylic color / 2tsp. white artists' acrylic color
Protective coat ▶ acrylic floor varnish. See manufacturers' instructions for quantity required for your floor.

EQUIPMENT

1 x 4in. (100mm.) paintbrush / medium-grit sandpaper / tape measure / ruler / graph paper / pencil / chalk line or string / masking tape / cash register tape / container / 3 small paint rollers / 1 paint tray / 3 ceramic tiles / 4 foamcore backing boards: 2 of 7 x 7in. (18 x 18cm.); 1 of 2½ x 2½in. (6 x 6cm.); 1 triangular piece 2½ x 1½ x 1½in. (6 x 4 x 4cm.) / 1 piece foam-rubber mat 5½ x 8in. (14 x 20cm.) / X-Acto knife / cutting mat / tube paper cement / 2 screw-top jars / newspaper / 1 x 4in. (100mm.) varnish brush

MOSAIC BORDER DESIGN

INSTRUCTIONS
Background

Using the paintbrush and following the manufacturers' instructions, give the floor one or two coats of stain as required. Sand lightly after each coat with the sandpaper.

Border

The 7in. (18cm.)-wide border consists of two alternating 7in. (18cm.)-square motifs. Plan the position of your border on the floor. In a perfect world, each length of border would divide exactly into an odd number of squares, but the chances of this are slim. With the aid of graph paper and a little forethought, though, you can plan for the best possible layout. If you are unable to fit in all the squares exactly, it will not be too serious a problem. When printing, you will be starting from a corner and working along a side to its mid-point, which is where the problem will be resolved (see Printing, step 2, below).

Set out the border with a chalk line or string, and mask the surrounding area with tape and cash register tape (see pp. 35 and 40–1).

Base coat

Mix the base coat color in the large container, and apply the paint to the border using a small roller. Some of this base coat will show through between the mosaics as "grout," so ensure a good coverage. Give it two coats if necessary.

Stamps

1 Make the four individual stamps used in the design (see p. 38). The two main stamps—the crosses—are 7in. (18cm.) square. For these, draw a grid of ¾in. (2cm) squares on the first 7 x 7in. (18 x 18cm.) backing board. Draw a similar grid, but this time set out on the diagonal, on the other 7 x 7in. (18 x 18cm.) board. (Note that if you work in inches, you will need to make the squares ever so slightly larger than ¾in. to fill the space.) Cut the foam mat up into ⅝in. (1.7cm.) squares, and glue these with clear paper cement to the backing boards to form the two crosses. You will also need a few small triangular pieces of foam to complete the diagonally placed cross.

2 Using the small square backing board and the triangular piece, make the other two stamps in the same way.

Printing

1 Mix the first and second mosaic colors in the jars. To print the border, begin with the two crosses. Place a spoonful or two of the first color on a tile, then transfer some to the stamp with a roller. Test the stamp before you start. This will let you see if the design is printing well and will allow you to gauge how much paint to roller on and how much pressure

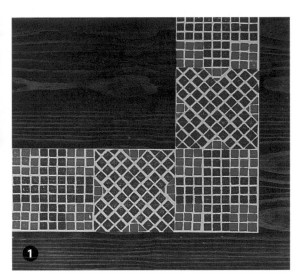

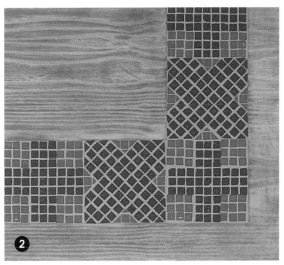

❶ **GREEN AND TERRACOTTA ON MAHOGANY**
Here we used more traditional wood coloring—in this case a mahogany stain —for the background. The base coat is as for the basic recipe. The red mosaic is mixed from 3tbsp. magenta, 3tbsp. Mars red, and 2tbsp. white, while the green mosaic is made using 4tsp. white, 4tsp. phthalocyanine green, and 1tsp. Payne's gray.

to apply. Press the stamp down firmly, but not so hard that paint squeezes out sideways.

Once you are confident that you have the knack, begin at a corner, printing alternate crosses as you go. As you approach the center of the side, switch to the opposite corner and work along from there, starting with the same cross as before.

2 If you are unable to finish the side with a complete cross, make sure that the last prints on each side of the center line are of the same pattern.

You now have to fill the remaining space with a motif that may be larger or smaller than a complete print. To do this, place a sheet of newspaper beyond the center, along a line that gives half the width of a "grout" line. The newspaper will act as a mask and will not allow you to print beyond this center line. Print the next cross butted up to the last, but overlapping the newspaper. Remove the newspaper and allow this print to dry for 5–10 minutes.

3 Place a fresh sheet of paper over this last print and again along a line half a "grout" width beyond the center line. Print the motif in the remaining space. Remove the paper to reveal a symmetrical center motif.

Alternatively, you could design a completely new stamp for this space—for example, a series of vertical stripes or a stamp with your initials.

4 Complete the design in the same way with the second mosaic color and the two remaining stamps.

❷ **BLUE AND OCHER ON PALE BLUE**
The ready-mixed floor stain is in one of the brighter colors that are now available and has been used as a background for a border with a Mediterranean coloring. For the blue, we mixed 4tbsp. cobalt blue with 4tbsp. white and 1tsp. Payne's gray. The contrasting mosaics are in 3–4tbsp. yellow ocher. The base coat is again as for the basic recipe.

Protective coat

Leave to dry for at least 24 hours. Then, using the varnish brush, apply a minimum of three coats of varnish according to the manufacturers' instructions.

OAK-LEAF BORDER DESIGN

Borders are a classic way of dividing up walls. They may be used at chair-height to divide a wall into an upper and a lower section or, as here, around a panel to create a frame. In this project, we have made an oak-leaf stamp from a piece of foam rubber and used it to stamp a border marking the dividing line between an area of colorwashing and one of flat painting.

BASIC RECIPE—LINEN, RASPBERRY, AND SALMON

PREPARATION

Prepare the surface thoroughly. See pp. 24–7.

INGREDIENTS

For a wall 43–54ft.² (4–5m.²) with a 26ft. (8m.) border
Colorwash ▶ 5tsp. naphthol red artists' acrylic color / 5tsp. white artists' acrylic color / 10tsp. acrylic glazing liquid / water in the ratio 1 part color : 1 part glazing liquid : 4 parts water
Flat paint ▶ 13½oz. (400ml.) white latex flat paint / 4oz. (120ml.) yellow ocher artists' acrylic color / 4tsp. Payne's gray artists' acrylic color
Leaf motif ▶ 1tbsp. white artists' acrylic color / 2tsp. Mars red artists' acrylic color

EQUIPMENT

Tape measure / chalk line and/or carpenter's level / water-soluble marker / 2 large containers / 2 x 5in. (120mm.) paintbrushes / safe-release masking tape / paint roller plus tray / tracing paper / pencil / foam-rubber mat / scissors or X-Acto knife / cutting mat / foamcore backing board / small tube clear paper cement / screw-top jar / ceramic tile / small paint roller

INSTRUCTIONS
Layout

Plan the layout of your design (see p. 34), and mark the line between the colorwashed and the flat-painted areas using a water-soluble marker.

Background

1 Mix the colorwash in one of the large containers and brush it on (see pp. 124–5), extending it to just beyond the marker line. Allow to dry thoroughly for at least 4 hours.
2 If the marker line is no longer visible, mark it out again, then mask off the colorwashed area with masking tape (see p. 40).
3 Mix the flat paint color and apply it using the roller. Apply a minimum of two coats in order to achieve an evenly flat matte surface, allowing 4 hours between coats. Remove the masking tape and allow to dry (4 hours).

Stamp

1 Meanwhile, trace the motif on p. 216 and use it to make the stamp (see pp. 38–9).

❶ LINEN, RASPBERRY, AND SALMON
The basic recipe.

❷ MIDNIGHT, ACID YELLOW, AND BLUE-GRAY
Here the color-wash is made from 10tsp. Hansa yellow light mixed with a scant ⅛tsp. Payne's gray, 10tsp. acrylic glazing liquid, and water in the correct ratio. The flat color consists of 13½oz. (400ml.) black latex flat, 4oz. (120ml.) phthalo-cyanine blue, and 16tsp. white latex flat. The motif color is made with 1tbsp. white, with ½tsp. Payne's gray and a scant ¼tsp. each cobalt blue and yellow ocher.

❸ FLAME, SLATE, AND ACID YELLOW
The colorwash here is made from 2tbsp. Payne's gray, 1tbsp. white, 3tbsp. acrylic glazing liquid, and water in the correct ratio. The flat paint is a mixture of 17oz. (500ml.) ready-mixed pimento red latex flat and 4tsp. naphthol red. The motif is stamped with 5tbsp. Hansa yellow light and ⅛tsp. Payne's gray.

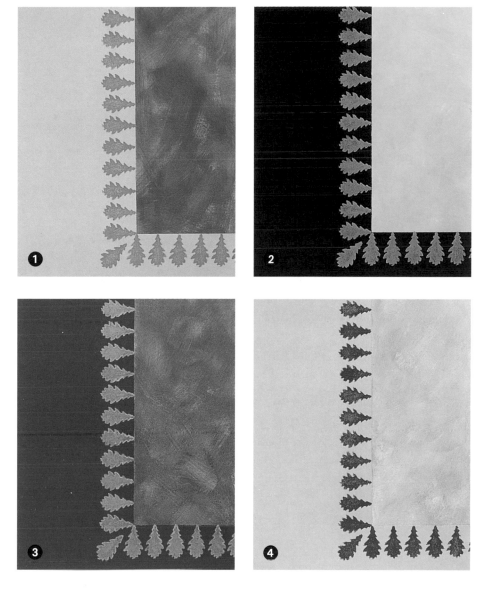

2 Here the leaf is stamped at 2in. (5cm.) intervals around the colorwashing. Mark the positions of the leaf with the marker.

3 Mix the white and Mars red artists' acrylic colors in the screw-top jar to make the leaf color, and spoon a little of it onto the ceramic tile. Spread it out with the small roller, then press the stamp into the paint to coat the stamp with an even layer of the color (see p. 39).

4 Press the stamp down firmly onto the flat-painted section of wall, making sure that the stamp is at right angles to the line and that the stalk of the leaf is on one of your marks.

5 Continue along the line, recharging the stamp with paint to print each motif.

6 If you are working on a panel design, the corners will appear empty, so you must stamp an extra leaf here. For this extra leaf, position the stamp so that the outer tips of its leaf line up to form a right angle at the corner.

❹ ACID YELLOW, EMERALD, AND TERRACOTTA
Here the color-wash is 5tsp. white with 2½tsp. yellow ocher and 2½tsp. phthalocyanine green, together with 10tsp. acrylic glazing liquid and water in the correct ratio. The flat paint is 17oz. (500ml.) ready-mixed jasmine latex flat, and the motif is 1tbsp. Mars red.

SIMPLE BORDER DESIGN

You could paint this border single-handedly, but it would be quicker and more fun to enlist the help of a friend. This will also ensure that, as you proceed along the stripe, you maintain a wet edge while one of you paints and sprays and the other follows up with the sponge to create the texture. If you want to pause, you should do so only at a corner or at a fixture such as a door. If you can foresee that you will have to pause partway along a wall, you should first divide the border into equal lengths using masking tape. You should then complete alternate sections, taking your breaks when a section is painted. When you are ready to start again, mask off the painted sections and fill in the others. The joins between the sections will show, but they will be quite smart and at predetermined intervals.

BASIC RECIPE—BOTTLE GREEN WITH COPPER

PREPARATION

Prepare the surface thoroughly. See pp. 24–7.

INGREDIENTS

For a wall 43–54ft.² (4–5m.²) with a border 16ft. x 4in. (5m. x 10cm.)
Background color ▶ 17oz. (500ml.) white latex flat paint / 1 tsp. Payne's gray artists' acrylic color / 1 tsp. raw umber artists' acrylic color / 1 tsp. ultramarine artists' acrylic color
Stripe ▶ 2tsp. phthalocyanine green artists' acrylic color / 2tsp. black artists' acrylic color / 2 tsp. white latex flat paint
Motif ▶ ⅔oz. (20ml.) iridescent copper artists' acrylic color

EQUIPMENT

Container / paint roller plus tray / tape measure / water-soluble marker / string / safe-release masking tape / newspaper / screw-top jar / 1 x 2in. (50mm.) paintbrush / spray bottle / water / 2 cellulose sponges / tracing paper / pencil / flat, square eraser / X-Acto knife / ceramic tile / small paint roller

INSTRUCTIONS
Background

Mix the background color in the container. Use the roller to apply 2–3 coats to the wall, allowing 4 hours for each coat to dry, then leave the surface to harden off thoroughly—several days, if possible.

Layout

1 Having decided on the height you would like for the top edge of your border, measure up from the floor, in one corner of the room, or down from the ceiling, to this height (see p. 35). Mark lightly on the wall with water-soluble marker. Repeat in the next corner. Stretch a string between these two points, attaching it with masking tape.
2 Stand back and consider this line. Once you are satisfied, stick masking tape both along the string line and 4in.

❶ BOTTLE GREEN WITH COPPER
The basic recipe.

❷ PEWTER WITH FLAX
Here the background color is the same as in the basic recipe, while the stripe is painted with 2oz. (60ml.) iridescent pewter and the motif is stamped with a mixture of 5tsp. white latex flat, 1½tsp. yellow ocher, and ¼tsp. Payne's gray. The iridescent paint used here for the stripe will take longer to dry than the paint used in the basic recipe. You should wait about 5 minutes instead of 2 or 3, before spraying with water.

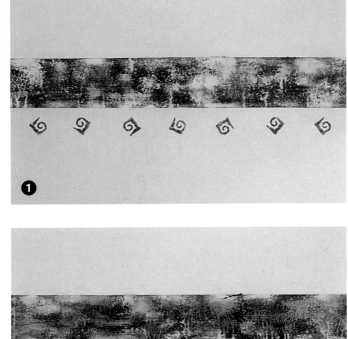

❸ DUSTY MAUVE WITH OLD GOLD
Here the background color is a mixture of 17oz. (500ml.) white latex flat, 5oz. (150ml.) yellow ocher, and 5tsp. Payne's gray. The stripe is painted with 5tsp. white latex flat mixed with ½tsp. dioxazine purple and 2tsp. Payne's gray. The motif is stamped first using ⅔oz. (20ml.) purple, then with ⅔oz. (20ml.) iridescent gold. Leave the purple paint to dry before you overstamp.

❹ COPPER WITH DUSTY MAUVE
The background color is the same as in swatch 3, with the stripe painted in 2oz. (60ml.) iridescent copper. The motif uses the purple of the motif of swatch 3. As in swatch 2, the iridescent paint used here for the stripe will take longer to dry than the paint used in the basic recipe.

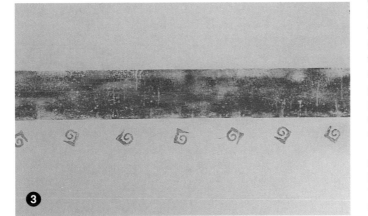

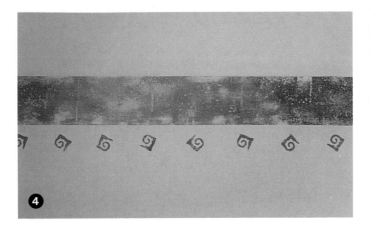

SIMPLE BORDER DESIGN

(10cm.) below it to mark the lower edge of the border. Repeat on each of the walls to be painted. To protect the wall during the next stages, extend the masked-off area with the addition of newspaper above and below the lines of tape.

Stripe

1 Mix the stripe color in the screw-top jar and brush it on to a length of about 1 yard (1 meter) between the lines of tape. Leave to dry for 2–3 minutes.

2 Spray the painted area with water from a spray bottle, and leave again for 2–3 minutes.

3 Use a sponge to dab the wet surface. Where the water has landed on or run down the surface, the paint will be soft and the sponge will start to lift it off, leaving a textured effect (see pp. 131–2).

4 Repeat the spray-wait-dab (and perhaps rub and wipe) procedure until you have achieved the effect you want.

5 Paint the next yard (meter) or so of stripe, joining it gently to the completed section. Repeat the texturing technique with the spray and sponge. This will also allow you to make invisible joins between the sections.

6 As you proceed along the wall, take off the masking tape and remove any color that has seeped behind the tape, using a clean, damp sponge. If any of it has dried, wipe off what you can and touch up with the background color.

Motif

1 Trace the design on p. 216, and use it to make the spiral motif rubber stamp (see p. 38).

2 Stretch a string, as in Layout, step 1, above, 1in. (2.5cm.) below the stripe.

3 Spoon a little of the motif paint onto a large ceramic tile, roll the paint out using the small roller, and press the stamp into it, just as you would a stamp into an ink pad (see p. 39). Stamp the spiral motif along the string line, turning it a little each time as you progress to give the impression that it is spinning along. The spacing between motifs is not critical; you can eyeball it.

STIPPLED PANEL DESIGN

Earlier in Part Three, we showed that techniques such as dry brushing and colorwashing, normally used to create an allover texture, can also be applied in blocks or stripes. Stippling can be similarly organized. This not only makes it more manageable when using water-based paints, which dry quickly, but also visually breaks up the wall with a restrained geometric design. (See Part Two, p. 56, for oil-based stippling.)

BASIC RECIPE—COBALT BLUE ON MARS RED

PREPARATION

Prepare the surface thoroughly. See pp. 24–7.

INGREDIENTS

To cover approximately 43ft.^{2} (4m.^{2})
Base coat ▶ 10oz. (300ml.) white latex flat paint
Stipple coat ▶ 2tsp. Mars red artists' acrylic color / 2tsp. yellow ocher artists' acrylic color / 6½oz. (200ml.) acrylic glazing liquid / water in the ratio 1 part color : 10 parts glazing liquid : 3 parts water
Motif ▶ 1tsp. cobalt blue artists' acrylic color / 1tsp. Mars red artists' acrylic color

EQUIPMENT

1 x 8in. (200mm.) medium-textured paint roller plus tray / tape measure / plumb line and/or spirit level / water-soluble marker / safe-release masking tape / large container / 1 x 6in. (150mm.) paintbrush / stippling brush / sponge / tracing paper / pencil / flat, square eraser / X-Acto knife / ceramic tile / square of paper

INSTRUCTIONS
Base coats

Use the roller to paint the wall with one or two coats of white latex flat paint. This should leave it opaque white with a slight orange-peel texture. Allow 4 hours to dry between coats, and at least 24 hours before the next stage.

Stipple coat

1 Divide the wall into rectangular or square blocks, marking them out using the tape measure, plumb line and/or spirit level, and the water-soluble marker (see p. 35). Each block should be no bigger than 16in. (40 cm.) along each side. Mask off alternate blocks with masking tape.

2 Mix the stipple coat in the large container. Before applying it to the wall, bear in mind the short amount of time you will have when using water-based paint. One way around this difficulty is to work in small sections. The other is for two people to work in unison. The first worker spreads out the paint with the ordinary paintbrush, while the second follows with the stippling brush. The aim is to maintain a wet edge at all times. Once the paint dries it will be impossible to stipple it off and create the distinctive soft texture. So, using the

ordinary paintbrush, apply the glaze in a thin layer to one of the panels. Immediately taking up the dry stippling brush, dab it all over the wet glaze. Continue until all the brush marks are replaced with an even, allover, grainy texture.

3 Once you have stippled alternate squares, remove the masking tape. Allow to dry (3–4 hours).

4 Mask out and stipple the remaining blocks. To achieve the darker tone and a gentle checkerboard pattern, these blocks were stippled twice, with half an hour left between coats.

❶ COBALT BLUE ON MARS RED
The basic recipe. The red is as strong as the blue and, being almost the same tone, begins to resonate with it.

❷ MARS RED ON GREEN
Here the motif is 1tsp. Mars red stamped with phthalocyanine green. The stipple is made from 2tsp. white, 2tsp. raw umber, and 1tsp. phtha-locyanine green mixed with 8½oz. (250ml.) glazing liquid and water in the same ratio as the basic recipe.

❸ YELLOW OCHER ON PALE BLUE
To make the cool stipple color, dilute 4tsp. white, 1tsp. cobalt, and ½tsp. raw umber with glazing liquid and water as before. Here the motif back-ground is 1tsp. yellow ocher stamped with 1tsp. white.

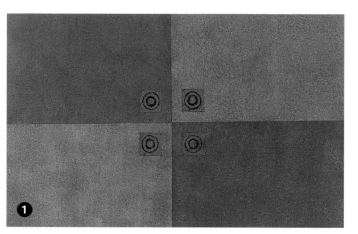

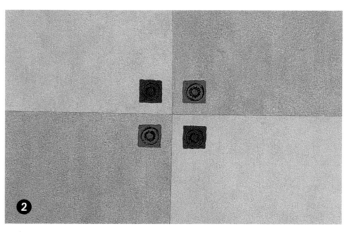

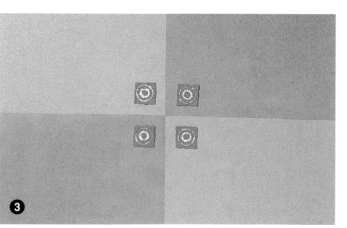

THE MOTIFS
In our swatches we have gone a step further and decorated the corners of the blocks with a simple motif. We would not decorate every set of four squares in this way. In fact, not decorating them all would look far more effective. You could, for example, dot groups of four around a room at random or arrange them at any height along a wall to form a border.
To create the four squares, lay a grid of torn masking tape (see p. 35), sponge on the background color, and leave to dry. Trace the design on p. 216, and make the rubber stamp (see p. 38). Roll out a little of the motif paint on a tile, press the stamp into it, and apply (see p. 39).

The principle of resists is quite simple. Apply a design in a resist to a background, then paint over it and the surrounding area. The resist will prevent this layer of paint from adhering. Once it is dry, remove the resist, together with the paint, to reveal the design in the background color. The following recipes will cover approximately 43ft.² (4m.²).

PAINTED-WAX RESIST

INGREDIENTS — **See swatch captions. Colorants: artists' acrylic colors.**

EQUIPMENT — **2 containers / 2 x 3in. (75mm.) paintbrushes / tracing paper / pencil / paper / chalk / jar or can / saucepan / plate warmer (optional) / small artists' fitch or other small artists' brush / spatula / sandpaper (optional)**

INSTRUCTIONS

1 Prepare the surface thoroughly (see pp. 24–7), and use a paintbrush to give it two generous layers of background color, allowing each coat 2–4 hours to dry.

2 Trace the heart on p. 216, enlarge it on a photocopier, and trace it onto the surface (see introduction, p. 216).

3 To melt the wax, place a tablespoonful in a jar in a pan of freshly boiled water. As it cools, you may have to replenish the water or keep it hot on an electric plate warmer. Never heat the wax over direct heat, as it is highly flammable.

4 Use an artists' fitch to paint the wax into the design. It will harden almost immediately. Do not use your favorite brush, as it will probably be useless for painting afterward.

5 Mix the top coat and brush it on. Leave an hour or so to become touch-dry, then use a spatula to remove the wax, leaving the motif in the background color.

6 To give an aged effect around the heart, sand the top coat slightly with sandpaper dipped in water.

❶ LEMON UNDER SAGE
The background is a mixture of 5tbsp. white latex flat with 8tsp. Hansa yellow light, and the top coat is 4tbsp. white latex flat mixed with 1tbsp. neutral gray and 1¼tsp. phthalo-cyanine green. The resist is 1tbsp. soft wax.

❷ CERULEAN UNDER EGGPLANT
This background is a mixture of 6tbsp. white latex flat with 2tbsp. phthalo-cyanine blue, and the top coat is 2tbsp. neutral gray, 4tsp. raw umber, and 2tsp. dioxazine purple. The resist is the same as for swatch 1.

RESISTS

SPRAY-WAX RESIST

Using aerosol beeswax polish in conjunction with a stencil is easier for decorating large areas than using a painted-wax resist.

INGREDIENTS

See swatch captions. Colorants: artists' acrylic colors.

EQUIPMENT

Paint roller plus tray / stencil board / pencil / X-Acto knife / cutting mat / tape measure / water-soluble marker / repositionable spray adhesive / paper / aerosol beeswax polish (see page 20) / paper towels / container / 2 x 3in. (75mm.) paintbrushes / rags / mineral spirits

INSTRUCTIONS

1 Prepare the surface thoroughly (see pp. 24–7), and use a roller to give it two coats of background color.

2 Cut the simple motif shown below from stencil board, and measure and mark out its positions on the wall.

3 Attach the stencil to the wall with spray adhesive, then protect the surroundings with paper. Spray the wax evenly into the stencil. Remove the stencil and blot excess wax from it using paper towels. To prevent wax from getting on the back of the stencil while you do this, lay it flat on a smooth surface such as a Formica-topped table or sheet of glass.

4 Carefully replace the stencil in the position after next, spray with wax as before, then repeat for all alternate positions. Allow the wax 2–3 hours to harden, then, if some is still wet, blot it up by pressing gently, not rubbing, with paper towels. Stencil the remaining sections.

5 Mix the colorwash, paint this over the wax resist (see pp. 124–5), and allow to dry (15–20 minutes).

6 Soak a rag in mineral spirits, and rub the design very firmly to break through the paint and dissolve the wax below, leaving a slightly tinted, broken-edged design.

❶ **BRONZE**
The background is 1qt. (1 liter) white latex flat, and the top coat is 9oz. (270ml.) ready-mixed pumpkin latex flat, diluted in the ratio 4 parts water : 1 part color.

❷ **DUSKY BLUE**
Here the background is 1qt. (1 liter.) white latex flat, and the top coat is 8½oz. (250ml.) white latex flat, mixed with 2tsp. black and 2tsp. phthalocyanine blue, diluted as for swatch 1.

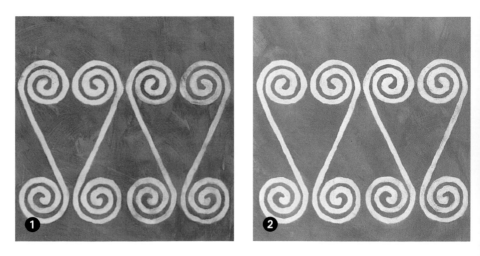

WHITING RESIST

A resist made from whiting, water, and a pinch of wallpaper paste is a cheap and solvent-free alternative to wax, although it does not give quite such a refined finish. It makes a water-soluble paint which can be washed off very easily and leaves no residue. This means that you can wipe it off at any time during the procedure and also paint on more layers of paint or glazes, since no waxy residue will have been left.

INGREDIENTS   **See swatch captions. Colorants: artists' acrylic colors.**

EQUIPMENT   **Paint roller plus tray / paper / 1 small and 1 medium artists' brushes / pencil / tracing paper / screw-top jar / container / 1 x 4in. (100mm.) paintbrush / spatula**

INSTRUCTIONS

1 Prepare the surface thoroughly (see pp. 24–7), and use a roller to give it two coats of background color.

2 Use one of the artists' brushes to paint a flick of a freehand oval on paper, enlarge it on a photocopier, and trace it carefully onto the wall (see p. 216).

3 Combine all the resist ingredients in the jar, put the lid on securely, shake hard for 30 seconds, then let stand for 5 minutes. The resist should be thick and creamy. If it is too thin, add a little whiting; if too thick, add more water.

4 Using the two artists' brushes, fill the motif with a thick layer of resist, following the outline as accurately as you can. Leave to dry for an hour or more.

5 Mix the topcoat and use a soft paintbrush to paint on two coats. The resist will crumble easily, so do not be too robust. Allow each coat to dry (2–4 hours).

6 With a spatula, gently scrape away the resist and its covering of paint. It will come off in a powder which can be swept away and any residue washed off.

❶ SALMON
The background is 1qt. (1 liter) white latex flat, with a topcoat of 10oz. (300ml.) white latex flat, mixed with 5oz. (150ml.) raw sienna and 5tsp. magenta. The resist is 10tbsp. whiting, 5tbsp. water, and 1tsp. wallpaper paste.

❷ BARLEY
Here the background is again 1qt. (1 liter) white latex flat, with a topcoat of 13½oz. (400ml.) white latex flat, mixed with 3½oz. (100ml.) yellow ocher. The resist is as in swatch 1.

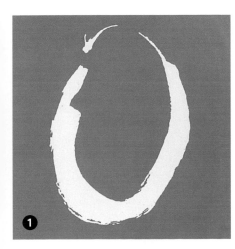

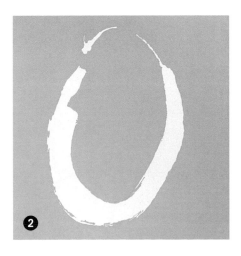

DECORATIVE AGING

Aging is a popular decorative finish, most commonly used on wooden surfaces such as cabinet fronts, paneling, or tables, but also on walls and floors. It works particularly well in an older home, where well-applied fresh paint can look out of place. These, then, are techniques to use for a finish that appears to have been around for a while.

When paint ages, its surface starts to wear away or flakes drop off. In addition, the paint begins to acquire a patina and shine in places where it is frequently handled. For your aging to appear authentic, follow examples of genuinely aged paintwork. The following techniques show how you can achieve a similar look.

RUBBING BACK

You can use steel wool, with or without wax, to give a gently aged look to paintwork. As you rub, you will break through the paint to reveal the surface below. If you use the steel wool with wax, be certain that you do not plan to apply more coats of paint, as few paints will adhere to wax.

Another method of aging paint is to rub it with waterproof sandpaper. Faster than rubbing with steel wool, this is probably the most subtle of our aging techniques. It will leave the paint surface looking gently aged as well as wonderfully smooth. Use only the finest grades of paper, and always use them with plenty of water.

The following recipes are for a panel approximately 43ft.^{2} (4m.^{2}).

See Part Two, p. 79, for rubbing off for a soft, allover effect, and p. 87 for rubbing back with cloth on 'set' paint.

INGREDIENTS

See swatch captions. Colorants: artists' acrylic colors.

EQUIPMENT

3 containers / 2 x 4in. (100mm.) paintbrushes / 1 x 2in. (50mm.) paintbrush / tape measure / straightedge / water-soluble marker or chalk line / fine-grit waterproof sandpaper / large bowl of water / cellulose sponge

INSTRUCTIONS

1 Prepare the surface thoroughly. See pp. 24–7.

2 Mix each color in a container as you need it.

3 Use the two larger paintbrushes to apply two coats each of the base and top color, allowing each coat to dry (2–4 hours).

4 Decide on the position and dimensions of your stripe. Ours is 8in. (20cm.) wide, and 8in. (20cm.) from the top of the panel. Measure and mark it out using the tape measure, straightedge, and marker (see p. 35).

5 Use the smaller brush to paint in the stripe. Allow the paint to dry overnight.

6 Dip a postcard-sized piece of sandpaper in water and use it to begin to rub away at the paneling. As you work, the

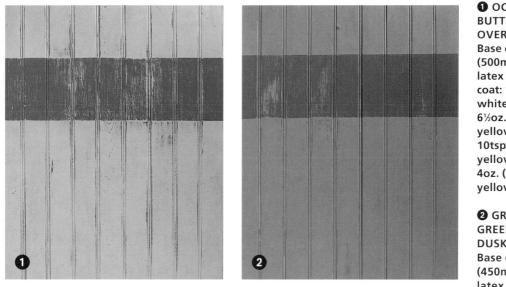

❶ OCHER ON BUTTERMILK OVER BLACK Base coat: 1 pint (500ml.) black latex flat; top coat: 10oz. (300ml.) white latex flat, 6½oz. (200ml.) yellow ocher, 10tsp. cadmium yellow. Stripe: 4oz. (120ml.) yellow ocher.

❷ GRAY ON GRAY GREEN OVER DUSKY PINK Base coat: 15oz. (450ml.) white latex flat, 4tsp. each Mars red and neutral gray. Top coat: 12oz. (350ml.) white latex flat, 4oz. (120ml.) neutral gray. Stripe: 4oz. (120ml.) neutral gray.

paint will come off in a slurry, and the piece of sandpaper will start to get clogged up. Mop up the slurry with the sponge, rinse the paper out, and continue with the rubbing until you are happy with the effect. The paint will rub off more quickly on corners and edges.

MELTED-WAX RESIST

This technique exploits the incompatibility of wax and water-based paint. The following recipes are for a panel approximately 43ft.² (4m.²). (See also pp. 84 and 90 in Part Two, where furniture polish is used for this effect and where wax under the base coat can reveal bare wood.)

INGREDIENTS   **See swatch captions. Colorants: artists' acrylic colors.**

EQUIPMENT   **3 containers / 2 x 4in. (100mm.) paintbrushes / 1 x 2in. (50mm.) paintbrush / small glass jar / old saucepan / plate warmer (optional) / old artists' fitch / tape measure / straightedge / water-soluble marker or chalk line / spatula / fine-grit sandpaper or fine steel wool**

INSTRUCTIONS   **1** Prepare the surface thoroughly. See pp. 24–7.

2 Mix each color as you need it in a container.

3 Using one of the larger paintbrushes, apply two coats of the base color. Allow each coat to dry (2–4 hours).

4 Put the wax in the jar and the jar in a saucepan of boiling water. The wax will melt with the heat from the water. You can keep the water hot by using a plate warmer. Alternatively, replace the water from time to time with freshly boiled water. Do not attempt to melt the wax over a

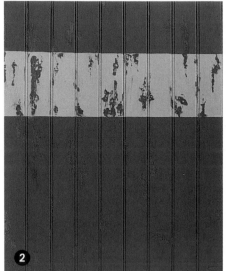

❷ PEACH ON STEEL OVER FLAME
Here the base coat is simply 1 pint (500ml.) ready-mixed pimento red latex flat paint, and the topcoat is 1 pint (500ml.) of another ready-mixed latex flat in cadet blue. The stripe uses 4oz. (120ml.) white latex flat combined with 1tsp. each Mars red and neutral gray. The resist is as for swatch 1.

❶ PALE YELLOW-GREEN ON JADE OVER GREEN
This base coat uses 1 pint (500ml.) ready-mixed emerald green latex flat paint, with a top coat of 13½oz. (400ml.) white latex flat, 4oz. (120ml.) raw umber, 2tsp. phthalocyanine blue, and 4tsp. Payne's gray. The stripe is 5oz. (150ml.) white latex flat, mixed with 2tsp. cobalt blue and 1tsp. yellow ocher. The resist is 3–6tbsp. beeswax.

flame, as there is a danger that it will ignite.

5 Using the artists' fitch, apply the melted wax loosely but thickly to the paneling in random shapes. These will become the areas where the paint will appear to have peeled off.

6 Once the wax is hard, use a large brush to apply two coats of the top color, allowing 2–4 hours for each coat to dry.

7 Measure and mark out the 8in. (20cm.)-wide stripe.

8 Apply more drops of wax within the stripe, mostly over and around the wax that is already there.

9 Once the wax has hardened, use the smaller paintbrush to paint the stripe. Allow to dry (1 hour).

10 Next, use the spatula to scrape off the wax. You will easily be able to locate its thick layers beneath the paint. Of course, as you remove the wax, you will also take the paint with it, and this is what gives the aged effect.

11 You can now use either a piece of sandpaper or steel wool dipped in beeswax to gently rub the whole paint surface back a little, smoothing off the sharp, new edges of paint left by the removal of the wax.

WHITING RESIST

Whiting mixed with water is a type of paint without a binder. When dry, it can easily be scraped off with a spatula, and it is water-soluble. Like wax, it can be used as a resist for an aged effect. It does not produce such refined results, but it has some advantages. One is that you can wipe it off easily at any stage, so if you do not like what you have done, you can simply and cleanly remove it. Second, because the whiting is water-based, it does not leave an oily or waxy residue. This means you can continue adding more coats of paint or glazes (see pp. 163–5). The following recipes cover approximately 43ft.² (4m.²).

INGREDIENTS　See swatch captions. Colorants: artists' acrylic colors.

EQUIPMENT　3 containers / screw-top jar / 2 x 4in. (100mm.) paintbrushes / 1 x 2in. (50mm.) paintbrush / artists' fitch / tape measure / straightedge / water-soluble marker / spatula / sponge / fine-grit sandpaper or fine steel wool / 2tbsp. beeswax

INSTRUCTIONS

1–3 Follow the instructions for Melted-wax resist.

4 To make the resist, put the whiting, water, and wallpaper paste in the screw-top jar. Put the lid on and shake vigorously for 30 seconds, then let the mixture stand for 5 minutes. If you find the mixture too thick or too thin—it should be thick and creamy—you can adjust the consistency by adding either water or whiting as appropriate.

5 Using the fitch, apply the resist in random blobs and shapes. As with the wax resist, these will become the areas where the paint will appear to have peeled off. Leave to dry for 1–2 hours.

6 Next, use another of the larger paintbrushes to apply two coats of the top color, allowing 2–4 hours for each coat to dry completely.

7 Measure and mark out the 8in. (20cm.)-wide stripe.

8 Use the fitch to apply more blobs of resist to the stripe, mainly over and around the resist that is already there.

9 Once the resist has hardened off—about 1–2 hours—use the smaller paintbrush to paint the stripe in the stripe color. Allow to dry (1 hour).

10 Now use the spatula to carefully scrape off the resist and the paint layers with it. When you have finished, you will see that a residue of whiting is left on the surface. Wash this off with a wet sponge.

11 Finish as for the wax resist.

❶ SLATE ON BLUE OVER LILAC This base coat is 15oz. (450ml.) white latex flat mixed with 1tbsp. neutral gray and 1tsp. dioxazine purple. The resist is 10tbsp. whiting, 5tbsp. water, and 1tsp. wallpaper paste. The top coat is 1 pint (500ml.) ready-mixed medium-blue latex flat, while the stripe is in 5tbsp. Payne's gray, 1tbsp. white, 2tsp. burnt umber, and 1tbsp. phthalo-cyanine green.

❷ SALMON ON PALE YELLOW-GREEN OVER GREEN The base coat is 1 pint (500ml.) ready-mixed latex flat paint in light sea green, and the top coat is 15oz. (450ml.) white latex flat mixed with 2tbsp. cobalt blue and 1tbsp. yellow ocher. The resist is as for swatch 1. The stripe is in 5oz. (150ml.) white latex flat, 2tbsp. naphthol red and 4tsp. cadmium yellow.

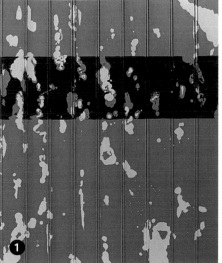

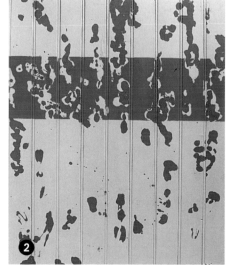

STENCILED DESIGNS

Stencils are common decorators' devices. They are partly a way of controlling where your paint goes and partly a way of making repeat patterns. In these examples we have endeavored to keep our stencils simple. This makes them easy to cut and also gives them a more modern look, which we prefer.

When stenciling, use repositionable spray adhesive, both to hold the stencil in place as you work and to stop paint from seeping under its edges. Spray the back of the stencil lightly, protecting the surrounding surfaces with newspaper. The spray is highly toxic, so always spray in a well-ventilated area and avoid breathing it.

The following recipes are for approximately 17oz. (500ml.) of background color and 7–8tbsp. of stencil color—enough, probably, for an average wall. We have applied all our backgrounds with a roller.

INGREDIENTS

See swatch captions. Colorants: artists' acrylic colors.

EQUIPMENT

Choose from the following:
Large container / large paint roller plus tray / tracing paper / pencil / paper / stencil board / repositionable spray adhesive / cutting mat / X-Acto knife / scissors / tape measure / ruler / compass / carpenter's level / water-soluble marker / string / scraps of cardboard / masking tape / screw-top jars / saucers / sponges

SIMPLE STENCILING

Perhaps the most commonly used design for a simple stencil is the *fleur-de-lis*, a favorite motif of interior decorators and now a classic. Lettering has an equally long history as a decorative motif but also allows you an element of personalization. You could stencil your initials across a wall, floor, window, or any other surface. The stencil is easy to cut and use, but a disciplined layout is essential for a classy look.

INSTRUCTIONS

1 Prepare the surface thoroughly. See pp. 24–7.
2 Trace the motifs from an alphabet in a lettering book or from an old manuscript. Plan the layout and the size of your stencil in unison. Our motif is 7 x 4in. (18 x 10cm.), cut from a piece of stencil board 12 x 8in. (30 x 20cm.). To assist in top-to-bottom positioning, rule light lines 3in. (8cm.) below the required positions of the letters, using a spirit level and water-soluble marker (use string on large areas; see p. 144). Then cut the stencil motif with its lowest part 3in. (8cm.) up from the lower edge of the stencil board. By placing this edge of the stencil board on your marked line each time you stencil, you will always be assured of a correct position.
3 Spray the back of the stencil with adhesive, and, starting

❶ GRAY-BLUE BACKGROUND AND DEEP MAGENTA For this background, mix 10tsp. cobalt blue and 10tsp. Payne's gray into 17oz. (500ml.) white latex flat. For the stencil color—a surprisingly intense contrast against the background —add 4tsp. white and 2tsp. yellow ocher to 3½oz. (100ml.) magenta.

from the left, place it in its first position on one of the lines. Sponge in the color and remove the stencil.

4 Use a spacing bar to determine side-to-side placements. This is a scrap of cardboard attached to the side of the stencil with masking tape. Attach the spacing bar to the left of the stencil. Reposition your stencil to the right for the second print, aligning the left-hand end of the bar with the right-hand edge of the first motif. If you want a 10in. (25cm.) space between motifs, the left-hand end of the bar should be 10in. (25cm.) from the left edge of the cutout motif in the stencil. Sponge in as before.

To stencil to the left of your first image, you will have to attach the spacing bar to the right-hand edge of the stencil.

5 Repeat along the marked lines until you have completed your design. Note how, in our example, each stenciled image is set half a space along from the one above.

OVERLAPPING STENCILS

Simple stencils can be designed to link up to create flowing borders. On p. 158 a tendril and a flower have been stenciled together along a line.

INSTRUCTIONS

1 Prepare the surface thoroughly. See pp. 24–7.

2 Trace each motif on p. 216 separately, together with their registration holes. Enlarge them on a photocopier and use to make the stencils (see p. 36). The registration holes should be carefully positioned on each stencil.

3 Rule a line along the wall at the height you would like your border, and place one of the stencils on it with its holes over the line. Lightly mark the wall through the registration holes, using a water-soluble marker.

STENCILED DESIGNS

❶ PALE YELLOW BACKGROUND WITH FUCHSIA PINK
The background is 1tbsp. each Hansa yellow light and raw umber with 19oz. (560ml.) white latex flat. The tendrils are in 4tbsp. white, 2tbsp. raw umber, 1½tbsp. Payne's gray, and 1tbsp. phthalo-cyanine green. The flower is 3½oz. (100ml.) magenta with 4tsp. white and 2tsp. yellow ocher.

❷ LABURNUM BACKGROUND WITH BLUE-GRAY
The background is 1 pint. (500ml.) laburnum yellow latex flat with tendrils in 3½oz. (100ml.) magenta with 5tsp. burnt sienna. The flowers are 6tbsp. white and 1tbsp. Payne's gray.

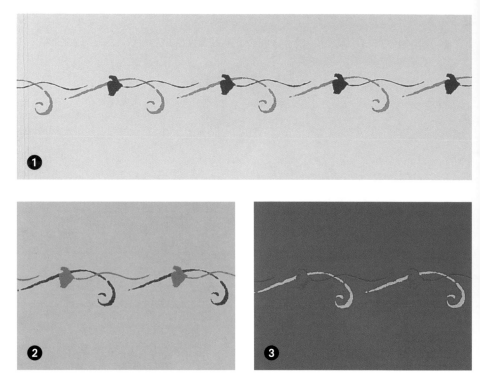

4 Move the stencil along the line toward the right until the right-hand mark shows through the stencil's left-hand hole. Mark the wall again through the right-hand hole. Continue in this way until you have set all the registration marks along the ruled line.

5 Beginning with the tendril, lightly spray the back of the stencil and place it in its first position, lining it up so that its holes are over the first two marks. Sponge in the color.

6 Move the tendril stencil to the position after next, and sponge this in the same way, and so on along the line. By the time you reach the end, the first stenciled tendrils will have dried enough for you to stencil those in between.

7 The flower stencil is sponged in over the top of the tendril, using exactly the same registration marks.

❸ BRONZE BACKGROUND WITH BLUE
The base coat is 1 pint (500ml.) light bronze latex flat with tendrils in 6tbsp. white, 2tbsp. Hansa yellow light, and ¼tsp. raw umber. The flowers are 4tbsp. white, 4tbsp. cobalt blue, and 1tsp. dioxazine purple.

SHADED STENCILING

A second color sponged over the first can give a simple, flat stencil a three-dimensional look. The shaded circles and squares opposite have soft edges, as their stencils have been torn into shape rather than cut.

INSTRUCTIONS

1 Prepare the surface thoroughly. See pp. 24–7.

2 To make the stencils, draw a 2in. (5cm.)-diameter circle and a 4in. (10cm.) square on separate pieces of stencil board. Begin by making a hole in the center of each board, then delicately tear out the shapes as close as possible to the line.

3 Tear two strips of cardboard, each about 6 x 1½ in. (15 x 4cm.), down their long edge.

4 Plan the spacing of your motifs, and use a washable marker to mark out the surface to be decorated. The squares here are spaced at 4in. (10cm.) intervals and the circles at 2in. (5cm.). When positioning the motifs, use the spacing bar method (see p. 157).

5 To stencil a circle, attach the circle stencil with spray adhesive, and sponge quite densely using the first color. With the stencil still in place, take a sponge sparsely loaded with the second color and dab it on, starting on one side of the circle and gradually moving inward. Aim to create a gentle gradation of tone that follows the form of the circle, transforming it into a ball.

6 For a square, place the stencil in position and lightly sponge in the first color. With the stencil still in place, position one of the strips of cardboard across the diagonal, leaving the lower, triangular half of the square exposed. Sponge this in densely with the same color.

7 Reposition the strip across the other diagonal, leaving the opposite lower half exposed, and sponge this in lightly with the second color.

8 Place the second strip across the first, leaving a small triangle exposed on the bottom edge of the square. Sponge this in densely with the second color. Remove all the strips of cardboard to reveal a pyramid with each face in a different color made up of the various layers and densities of paint.

❶ JORDAN ALMOND BACKGROUND
The background is 1 pint (500ml.) palest dusty pink latex flat, and the first stencil color is 4tbsp. white, 2tbsp. cobalt blue, and 1tbsp. yellow ocher. The second requires 6tbsp. Hansa yellow light, 2tbsp. white, 2tsp. yellow ocher, and ½tsp. raw umber.

❷ SHELL PINK BACKGROUND
This background is 1 pint (500ml.) light shell pink latex flat, and the first color is 6tbsp. white, 1tbsp. ultra-marine, 2tbsp. dioxazine purple, and 1½tsp. black. The second color is 4tbsp. white, 4tbsp. Mars red, and 2tbsp. cad-mium yellow medium.

❸ HEATHER GRAY BACKGROUND
The background is 1 pint (500ml.) heather gray latex flat, and the blue is 6tbsp. ultramarine, 3tbsp. white, and 1¼tsp. quin-acridone violet. The acid yellow uses a mixture of 4tbsp. white, 4tsp. Hansa yellow light, and ¼tsp. raw umber.

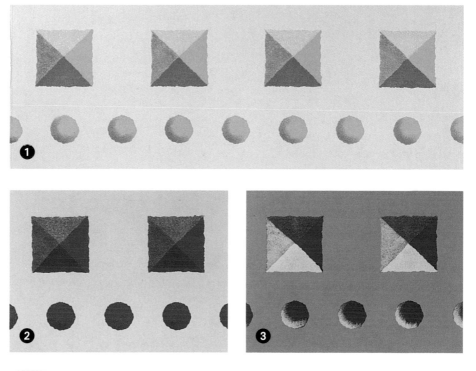

SEASIDE DOOR DESIGN

Even if you live far from the coast, this treatment for doors will give you an appetite for long summer days on the beach. More California than New England, more Mediterranean than British, the colors have been chosen to bring a sunny atmosphere into any interior. If you are anxious to create the look of real weatherbeaten beach-house doors, you will need thick base coats of latex flat to give you plenty of leeway when you are rubbing back. Over these we have stenciled a distant view of a boat in full sail and a close-up of its striped flag. Keep the painting loose. It should look as if it had to be painted quickly. Vacations are not for work.

BASIC RECIPE—SAND ON SKY BLUE

PREPARATION

Prepare the surface thoroughly. See pp. 24–7.

INGREDIENTS

For 2 standard cabinet doors
First base coat ▶ 10oz. (300ml.) white latex flat paint / 3tbsp. ultramarine artists' acrylic color
Second base coat ▶ 10oz. (300ml.) white latex flat paint / 3tbsp. yellow ocher artists' acrylic color
Sails, hull, and flag (colors not mixed together) ▶ 1tbsp. white artists' acrylic color / 1tbsp. ultramarine artists' acrylic color / scant ¼tsp. naphthol red artists' acrylic color

EQUIPMENT

2 screw-top jars / 2 x 3in. (75mm.) paintbrushes / fine-grit waterproof sandpaper / 1 cellulose sponge and 3 pieces / rag / tracing paper / pencil / paper / repositionable spray adhesive / stencil board / X-Acto knife / cutting mat / ruler / water-soluble marker / 3 saucers / small artists' brush / masking tape

INSTRUCTIONS
Base coats

1 Since you will be applying thick coats of paint which are likely to run, remove your cabinet doors and work on them on a horizontal surface.
2 Mix each of the base-coat colors in the screw-top jars. You should have sufficient to apply two good thick coats of each color.
3 Fully load one of the paintbrushes with paint, and apply a generous layer of the first color. Do not worry about brush marks, but in fact aim to leave them showing. However, be organized in the order in which you paint. Start with the door panels, followed by the rails (horizontal), then the stiles (vertical). Finally, paint the edges. Always finish by brushing

out the paint in the same direction as the grain of the wood. Leave to dry. Latex flat paint can normally be re-coated after 4 hours, but the thicker coats used here may need to be left a little longer.

4 The doors will need a second coat of blue, applied in the same way, followed by two coats of yellow. After the final coat, leave to harden for a day.

5 To create the desired weatherbeaten look, sand the final yellow coat with the sandpaper dipped in water (see pp. 152–3). This not only leaves a flat, matte finish but also breaks through the yellow to reveal the blue brush marks below. You can rub off extra yellow in those places where paint would have worn more quickly—for example, around handles and along edges. As you do this, a slurry of paint and water will form, which you should wipe off with a wet sponge as you proceed.

6 Once you are happy with the look of the doors, dry them off with a rag.

Boat motif

1 Trace the designs for the boat and the flag (see p. 217), enlarge them on a photocopier, and use them to make the stencils (see p. 36).

2 Using the ruler and the water-soluble marker, measure and mark the position of the boat in the center of the door panel. Position the boat stencil 1¼in. (3cm.) below and to the right of it as required for the shadow, then sponge the shadow in lightly, using 1tbsp. of the base coat yellow mixed on a saucer with a tiny amount of yellow ocher—just enough to take it down a tone.

3 The shadow will dry quickly, so within a few minutes you can reposition the stencil to paint in the boat itself. Sponge in the hull using the ultramarine blue spooned into a saucer.

4 Sponge the sails in white in the same way, then use the small artists' brush to add their red stripes.

Flag motif

1 For the striped flag, apply masking tape to leave a central rectangle. Its size will be governed by the size of your door panel. Sponge the rectangle in white.

2 Position the flag stencil—the wavy lines—over the white sponged rectangle, and sponge in the ultramarine. Remove the stencil and the masking tape and allow the paint to dry (1 hour).

3 For the shadow, apply masking tape inside the bottom and right-hand edges of the flag, with another line of tape about 1¼in. (3cm.) from the first, to create an L-shaped area.

SEASIDE DOOR DESIGN

❶ SAND ON SKY BLUE
The basic recipe.

❷ SKY BLUE ON SAND
If you prefer sky blues to golden sands, simply reverse the base coats. Everything else remains the same, except, of course, for the shadows, which you make by adding a smidgen of ultramarine to a tablespoon of the blue top coat.

Sponge this in, using the same yellow as you used for the boat's shadow. Both this shadow and that of the boat should give the impression of the boat and flag floating in front of the door on a sunny day.

4 If the boat and flag look a little too freshly painted, you can use the sandpaper, again with water, to give them a worn and weatherbeaten look. But gently does it—the paint here is much thinner than the paint of the base coats, and if you are too vigorous as you sand, you will remove the boat and flag completely.

FOSSIL TABLE DESIGN

This design idea takes the stone-finish technique of pp. 94–5 a step further, by setting an authentic-looking fossil ammonite into a stone-finished table top. Fossils are most commonly found in limestones. The limestones vary so much in color and texture that there is bound to be one that you like. We mimic one that leans toward pink and another that leans toward yellow. The third is more granite than limestone, but you can be more fanciful with your coloring if you wish.

Fossils are beautiful but delicate and fragile. The use of thick paint over a whiting resist can readily create an effect that mimics their appearance. Be confident in the handling of your brush and in the application of the paint, and do not worry about drips or splashes, or misplaced resist. Anything can have happened to the fossil during the last 250 million years. And if you want to make your fossil bigger, then go ahead. They could grow to over 6 ½ft. (2 m.) across.

BASIC RECIPE—PINK-TINTED LIMESTONE

PREPARATION **Prepare the surface thoroughly. See pp. 24–7.**

INGREDIENTS *For a small table*
Base coat ▶ 6tbsp. white latex flat paint / 1tsp. raw sienna artists' acrylic color
Resist ▶ 10tsp. whiting / 5tsp. water / ½tsp. wallpaper paste
First color ▶ 6tbsp. white latex flat paint / 5tsp. raw sienna artists' acrylic color / denatured alcohol
Second color ▶ 6tbsp. white latex flat paint / 2tsp. raw sienna artists' acrylic color / 2tsp. raw umber artists' acrylic color / denatured alcohol
Dabs ▶ scant ¼tsp. each Mars red, yellow ocher, and raw umber artists' acrylic colors
Protective coat ▶ 1tbsp. wax polish

EQUIPMENT **3 containers / coarse-textured paint roller plus tray / tracing paper / paper / hard pencil / chalk / screw-top jar / 1 x ¼in. (6mm.) artists' brush / repositionable spray adhesive / stencil board / X-Acto knife / cutting mat / 1 x 1in. (25mm.) old, stiff paintbrush / spatula / 3 cellulose sponges and 6 pieces / bowl of water / spray bottle / fine-grit waterproof sandpaper / soft cloth**

INSTRUCTIONS
Base coats
1 Mix the base color in one of the containers. Use the roller to apply two coats to the table top and its edges, allowing 2–4 hours for each coat to dry.
2 Trace the ammonite design from p. 217, enlarge it on a photocopier to fit your table, then trace it onto the table top, using tracing paper, a hard pencil, and chalk (see p. 216).

FOSSIL TABLE DESIGN

➊ PINK-TINTED LIMESTONE
The basic recipe gives a pinkish limestone. We have been quite free with the addition of the dabs of color, especially the Mars red. The position of the ammonite on the table top is, of course, a matter of personal preference. Here, we have placed it in one corner.

➋ YELLOW-TINTED LIMESTONE
Here we positioned the ammonite in the middle of the table and used a base coat of 6tbsp. white latex flat mixed with ½tsp. yellow ocher and ½tsp. raw umber; a first color of 6tbsp. white latex flat with 1tsp. raw. umber and 2tsp. yellow ocher, and dabs of yellow ocher, white, and medium gray. The second color was made from 6tbsp. white latex flat with 2tsp. neutral gray and ½tsp. yellow ocher, and colored dabs as before.

➌ GRAY LIMESTONE
This swatch is based on swatch 2 on p. 94 but uses stronger colors and a more vigorous method to create this textured, decorative finish. The base coat is made of 6tbsp. white latex flat with 2tsp. neutral gray. The first color is 2tbsp. white latex flat with 4tbsp. Payne's gray and 4tsp. burnt umber. The second color consists of 1tbsp. white artists' acrylic color, dabbed and spread to create a misty effect.

Resist

Mix the whiting, water, and wallpaper paste in a screw-top jar to make the resist (see pp. 151). Use the round artists' brush to loosely paint the resist onto the sections left white on the design you have copied. Apply it quite thickly, and do not worry about being neat. Leave to dry for a few hours.

Stencil

1 Meanwhile, use your traced design to make a stencil of the ammonite outline (see p. 36). Position the stencil on the table top over the ammonite, holding it in place with spray adhesive.

2 Using the old paintbrush, apply a thick layer of the base coat into the stencil and over the resist. In order to mimic the texture and pattern of the ammonite, brush the paint out so that it makes curved ridges running from the inner edge of the spiral to the outer edge. An old, stiff brush is better for applying this layer than a new one, as an old one leaves good brush marks. If the brush marks disappear, allow to dry for a few moments, then repeat the process. Remove the stencil with care.

3 Spatter a few flicks of the base coat across the table top at random if you want more texture. Allow to harden for at least 4 hours, though it may take longer than usual since the paint has been applied so thickly.

4 Use the spatula and a damp sponge to gently remove the dried whiting resist, together with its covering of paint. This will reveal the ammonite, convincingly textured, but as yet without color.

Stone finish

1 Mix the latex paint and raw sienna in a container to make the first color, and the latex paint, raw sienna, and raw umber in another container to make the second color. Complete the stone finish with these two colors, following the instructions on pp. 94–5 and 132. Apply each color with a sponge across the whole of the table top, including the ammonite, as well as over the edges of the table. Sponge or splash with water, spray with denatured alcohol, and apply sponged-on dabs of Mars red, yellow ocher, and raw umber as desired. Aim for an open texture with plenty of variation. Take care not be too heavy-handed. You should try to achieve a subtle effect.

2 The ammonite will by now be almost camouflaged. To reveal it, very carefully sand away some of the two colors from the ridges, using the sandpaper dipped in water. This will give a worn look. You can accentuate the three-dimensional qualities by rubbing away a little more from one side of the spiral than from the other. However, care is called for, as the coats are quite thin. You should also guard against rubbing away at other parts of the table top.

Protective coat

Leave aside for 24 hours, then buff the whole of the table top with wax polish applied on a soft cloth.

ROSE DES VENTS DESIGN

This design, with its stone-finish background, is particularly suited to chipboard. Sometimes laid in panels as a base for other flooring, chipboard is functional but not attractive. You could resist the urge to cover it up, and instead apply our *Rose des Vents* ("rose of the winds"—the poetic French term for a compass rose). The rough, granular texture of the board lends itself to the stone effect, while each panel becomes a "slab" of stone. The same design could also be applied to a wall or a table top.

BASIC RECIPE—VENETIAN RED, BLUE, AND GREEN ON SANDSTONE

PREPARATION	**Prepare the surface thoroughly. See pp. 24–7.**
INGREDIENTS	*To cover approximately 43–54ft.² (4–5m.²)* **Base coat ▶ 17oz. (500ml.) white latex flat paint / 5tsp. raw sienna artists' acrylic color** **First color ▶ 6½oz. (200ml.) white latex flat paint / 4tsp. raw sienna artists' acrylic color / denatured alcohol** **Second colour ▶ 6½oz. (200ml.) white latex flat paint / 4tsp. raw sienna artists' acrylic color / 10tsp. raw umber artists' acrylic color / denatured alcohol** **Dabs ▶ 1tsp. raw umber artists' acrylic color / 1tsp. raw sienna artists' acrylic color / 1tsp. Mars red artists' acrylic color** **Medium star ▶ 2tbsp. phthalocyanine green artists' acrylic color / 1tbsp. black artists' acrylic color / 2tsp. yellow ocher artists' acrylic color / 2tsp. white artists' acrylic color** **Circle and small star ▶ 1tbsp. magenta artists' acrylic color / 1tbsp. Mars red artists' acrylic color / 2tsp. white artists' acrylic color** **Large star ▶ 1tbsp. white artists' acrylic color / 1tbsp. cobalt blue artists' acrylic color / ¼tsp. dioxazine purple artists' acrylic color** **Protective coat ▶ 1qt. (1 liter) acrylic floor varnish**
EQUIPMENT	**3 containers / coarse-textured paint roller plus tray / 2 cellulose sponges plus 6 pieces / bowl of water / spray bottle / plate / tracing paper / paper / chalk / hard pencil / 3 screw-top jars / 3 medium flat artists' brushes / 3 small round artists' brushes / fine-grit waterproof sandpaper / 1 x 100mm. (4in) varnish brush**
INSTRUCTIONS **Base coats**	Mix the base color in a container and use the roller to apply two coats, allowing 4 hours for each coat to dry.
Stone finish	**1** Mix the first color in another container. Following the instructions for stone finishes on pp. 94–5, apply it to the floor using a sponge, adding water, spraying on denatured alcohol, and dabbing on the raw umber, raw sienna, and Mars red from the plate. We have sponged the texture in

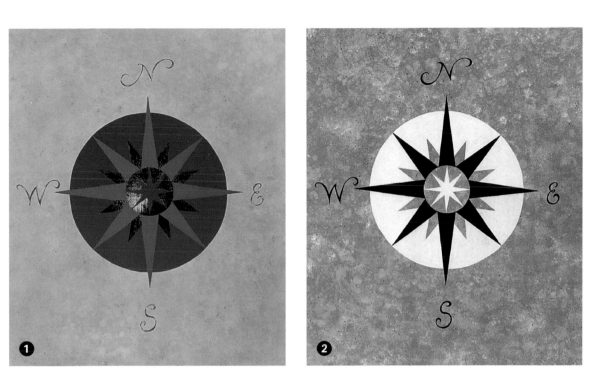

quite evenly, but if you prefer a rugged look to your stone, be a bit freer with the sponge and water.

2 Mix the second color in the third container and apply it in the same way, again adding in the sponged dabs. Take care not to be too heavy-handed. You should aim for a subtle effect. Allow to dry (4 hours).

Motifs

1 Trace the compass design (see p. 217), and enlarge it as required on a photocopier. Trace the compass-point initials you require from a book of lettering. The outer circle in our example measures 12½in. (32cm.) in diameter. Transfer the design to the floor using tracing paper, chalk, and a hard pencil (see p. 216), making sure that it is correctly oriented.

2 Mix the stars and circle colors in the screw-top jars. Use the artists' brushes to paint in the center and points of the medium star, then allow to dry (1 hour).

3 Using the sandpaper, rub the paint back lightly to reveal parts of the base color as highlights.

4 Now you may well have lost some of your tracing. Retrace as necessary, then paint in the other parts of the design using the appropriate colors and brushes.

5 Finally, use a small round artists' brush to paint the initials of the compass points in the same color as the circle.

Protective coat

Use the varnish brush and follow the manufacturers' instructions to apply a minimum of three coats of varnish.

❶ VENETIAN RED, BLUE, AND GREEN ON SANDSTONE The basic recipe. Here, the small touch of aging on the green star helps push the color back, leaving the red and blue stars looking as if they are floating above it. The colors are in keeping with the period look of the design and lettering.

❷ BLACK AND WHITE ON LIMESTONE For a limestone effect, follow the recipe on p. 94. The coloring of the motif is simple: all you will need is 2tbsp. black to paint the large star and 4tbsp. white for the circle and small star.

PAINTING ON GLASS

To judge by the tenacity with which splashes of paint cling to windows, one would imagine that you could decorate glass with almost any type of paint. But special glass paints—opaque, transparent, and frosting varnish for an etched-glass look—are available. It is these last two that we have used for the designs here. As an alternative, you could etch the glass with etching cream, which can then be painted, if desired.

You can apply the paint with a brush or with a sponge or squeegee. It is very liquid, so any masking must be really well stuck down to prevent the paint from seeping underneath. Once the painting is complete, objects such as leaves or postage stamps can be put between this sheet and a second one, the two held together with binder clips.

The recipes will decorate a sheet of glass 12in.^{2} (30cm.^{2}).

PAINTED GLASS FRAMES

INGREDIENTS

See swatch captions.

EQUIPMENT

Ruler / pencil / paper / 2 sheets of glass, 12in.^{2} (30cm.^{2}) / masking tape / small piece of cellulose sponge, its corners trimmed off / saucer / small, round artists' brush / solvent for glass paint / 4 binder clips with removable wire levers

INSTRUCTIONS

1 Prepare the surface thoroughly. See pp. 24–7.

2 Draw a 12in. (30cm.) square on a sheet of paper and within this square rule a tic-tac-toe grid of four lines at 4in. (10cm.) intervals. Rule another four lines, ⅜in. (1cm.) out from the first.

3 Copy the motif on p. 217. Either trace it onto the corners of the grid you have drawn (see p. 216) or glue photocopies in the corners.

4 Attach the drawing to the back of one of the pieces of glass, and hold it in place with tape at the center of each edge. Place the glass face up on a level surface.

5 Tear masking tape along its length, and stick it firmly on the glass along the first set of grid lines, leaving the four corners exposed.

6 Pour a little of the first color into a saucer, and use a small piece of cellulose sponge to apply it to each of the corners. You must paint the color on all at once. Any attempts to apply a second coat will only result in the first coat being disturbed or removed. Leave to harden off (1 hour), then remove the masking tape.

7 Using the artists' brush and the second color, paint in lines of dots at approximately ⅜in. (1cm.) intervals along the second set of lines. Fully load the brush and just dab it onto

❶ GOLDEN OLIVE CORNERS
All the colors are ready-mixed glass paints. The first color is olive green, the second violet, and the third turquoise.

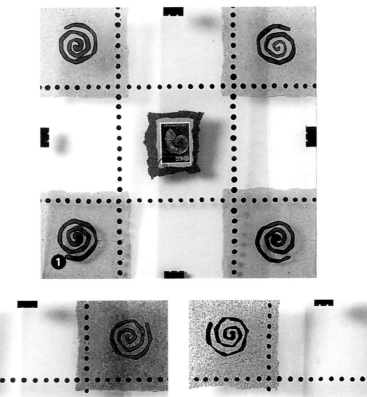

❷ SLATE GRAY CORNERS
Again, the colors are ready-mixed glass paints. The first is gray, the second magenta, and the third golden brown.

the surface to make the dot. Allow to dry (2 hours). As soon as you have completed the dots, clean the brush in solvent; otherwise, the paint will harden in the bristles and the brush will be of no further use.

8 With the artists' brush and the third color, paint in each of the spirals. Again, fully load the brush and let the paint flow off it as you follow the line of the design seen through the glass. Allow to dry (2 hours). Immediately clean the brush with solvent as before.

9 You can now assemble the frame, but since the paint will not be fully cured for a number of days, you should handle it with care. We have used the frames to trap small decorative items—postage stamps and leaves in these examples. These have been stuck in place on the second piece of glass. Hold the two pieces of glass together with the binder clips, then remove their levers.

❸ BRONZE METALLIC CORNERS
Here the first color is 1oz. (30ml.) frosting varnish mixed with a scant ¼tsp. bronze powder, and the second and third colors are both gray glass paint.

PART FOUR

PROJECTS

An inspiring array of ideas for decorating every surface in the home—walls, floors, doors, windows, furniture, and accessories —each in a choice of colorways to show what can be achieved

To paint this seedhead frieze (see pp. 180–3), we used a large stencil in a rather unusual way. Instead of stenciling on paint, as you might expect, we filled the stencil area with sprayed-on beeswax resist, then followed it with paint. For a smaller design you could apply ordinary wax with a spatula.

CHECKERBOARD
WALL

Don't let anyone persuade you that papering a wall is quicker and easier than stamping a design on it. Even if it were true, papering will never match the pleasure to be had from making your own stamp and using it across a wall. The end result will always have a quality that cannot be matched by any wallpaper. It will never be as perfect as, or have the complexity of, a wallpaper pattern, but if that is what you like, the chances are that you are reading this book by accident.

This simple stamp needs few registration marks. Once you have drawn the horizontals and a vertical on your wall, you can proceed, stopping only to change to the smaller stamps to negotiate awkward corners, electric outlets, and such.

BASIC RECIPE—STRAW ON OPAL

PREPARATION

Prepare the surface thoroughly. See pp. 24–7.

INGREDIENTS

For a wall up to 43ft.^{2} (4m.^{2})
Base coats ▶ 1¼ pints (600ml.) white latex flat paint / 1tbsp. cobalt blue artists' acrylic color / 2tbsp. yellow ocher artists' acrylic color / 2tbsp. Payne's gray artists' acrylic color
Motif ▶ 7½oz. (220ml.) white latex flat paint / 1tbsp. Hansa yellow light artists' acrylic color / 1tbsp. raw umber artists' acrylic color
Optional protective coat ▶ 10oz. (300ml.) matte acrylic varnish

EQUIPMENT

2 large containers / 1 large paint roller plus tray / 1 x 2in. (50mm.) paintbrush / plumb line / carpenter's level / water-soluble marker / 8 x 8in. (20 x 20cm.) foam-rubber mat / scissors or X-Acto knife / cutting mat / foamcore backing board / small tube clear paper cement / small paint roller / paper / masking tape / 1 x 2in. (50mm.) varnish brush (optional)

CHECKERBOARD WALL

INSTRUCTIONS

Base coats

1 Mix the color for the base coat in one of the containers, and stir well.

2 Apply two even coats to the wall with the large roller. Use the paintbrush to apply paint around any fixtures and into corners. Allow 4 hours for each coat to dry.

Design

1 Plan the layout of the pattern on the wall (see p. 35), using the plumb line to set a vertical guide and the spirit level and a water-soluble marker to mark the horizontals.

2 Use the foam-rubber mat to make three stamps: one with four stripes, 6 x 6in. (15 x 15cm.), one with one stripe, 6 x ¾in. (15 x 2.1cm.), and one with half a stripe, 3 x ¾in. (75 x 2.1cm.). Attach them to backing boards of foamcore with clear paper cement (see p. 38).

3 Mix the motif color in the other container and stir well. Apply paint to the square stamp, using the small paint roller (see p. 39).

4 Following the vertical guide, stamp a line of motifs on your wall, reapplying paint to the stamp for each motif. Turn the stamp through 90° for alternate motifs in order to create the checkerboard effect. Repeat until most of the wall is covered. The square stamp will cover large areas of wall, but as you come up against corners or fixtures such as light switches, you will need to use the smaller stamps to complete the design, perhaps in conjunction with paper to mask off areas you have already completed.

Notes To prevent the paint from drying on your stamps if you decide to take a break while you are working, you should first gently clean them by dabbing them up and down in a bowl of water, then pat them dry on paper towels.

If your wall is likely to be knocked, kicked, or scuffed, use the varnish brush to give it a coat of varnish for protection.

❶ STRAW ON OPAL
The basic recipe.

❷ OPAL ON STRAW
Here the emphasis has been subtly shifted by reversing the basic color combination, printing the blue onto the yellow. Not only does the balance between the colors alter, making the blue more dominant, but the texture also shifts to the blue.

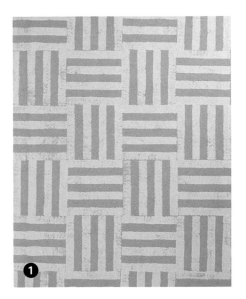

❸ STONE ON BRICK RED
These are the more robust colors of building materials—stone and red bricks. The strong contrast will make a splash in any room, so may need to be confined to a small area, or used to animate a dead corner. The red consists of 10oz. (300ml.) ready-mixed pimento red latex flat, mixed with 5tbsp. burnt sienna and 8tsp.

white. The stone color is made from 10oz. (300ml.) white latex flat colored with 1tbsp. raw umber.

❹ WHITE ON STONE
This combination results in far less contrast. Pale colors such as these are more suited to large areas, while the subdued pattern will not clash with pictures on the wall. The base color is the stone used in swatch 3, overprinted with white latex flat. It couldn't be much simpler than that.

WHIMSICAL WINDOW FRAME

The design for this window frame has four unequal sections, each one wrapped around the corner of the window opening. The overlapping shapes are created by masking with torn paper and masking tape. Where the overlaps occur, a darker area results, which we have stenciled with a diamond motif. The outer edge of the design is masked entirely using torn paper, but where sections overlapped, we masked one of the edges with masking tape to give a straight edge.

You can, of course, adapt a project like this to suit any size or shape of window, and we recommend that if you are decorating more than one window in a room, you should vary the masking from window to window to avoid a regimented appearance.

BASIC RECIPE—RASPBERRY, SALMON, AND PEA GREEN

PREPARATION

Prepare the surface thoroughly. See pp. 24–7.

INGREDIENTS

For an average window and the area surrounding it
Background ▶ 1 pint (500ml.) ready-mixed pale dusty pink latex flat paint
First color ▶ 6tbsp. white latex flat paint / 2tbsp. cadmium yellow artists' acrylic color / 1½tsp. cobalt blue artists' acrylic color / 1½tsp. raw umber artists' acrylic color / acrylic glazing liquid and water (see instructions)
Second color ▶ 3½oz. (100ml.) white latex flat paint / 2tsp. raw umber artists' acrylic color / 2tsp. Mars red artists' acrylic color / acrylic glazing liquid and water (see instructions)
Third color ▶ 4tbsp. white latex flat paint / 4tbsp. magenta artists' acrylic color / 2tsp. raw umber artists' acrylic color / 2tsp. raw sienna artists' acrylic color / acrylic glazing liquid and water (see instructions)

EQUIPMENT

Masking tape / medium-textured paint roller plus tray / 1 x 2in. (50mm.) paintbrush / paper / tape measure / repositionable spray adhesive / 3 screw-top jars / small, fine-textured paint roller plus tray / 3 x 1in. (25mm.) paintbrushes / 3 large, deep plates / 6 x 3in. (75mm.) paint-brushes

INSTRUCTIONS
Background

1 Mask off the window frame with masking tape.
2 Using the medium paint roller and the medium paintbrush for the corners, paint the surrounding wall and the window opening with the background color.

Masking

1 Begin at the bottom right-hand corner by masking with a

WHIMSICAL WINDOW FRAME

vertical strip of torn paper on the face of the wall, 4–6in. (10–15cm.) away from the window opening (see pp. 40–1). Attach with a light spray of adhesive. Run a horizontal line of masking tape across the face of the wall and into the window opening to finish this area of masking with a straight line.

2 Mask beneath the window with a band of torn paper running across the sill and down the face of the wall below the window. Take it down to the baseboard if you wish.

3 Mask off the top left-hand section in a similar manner, again using a torn-paper mask, its lower edge finished with a straight, horizontal line of masking tape.

Painting

1 Mix the first color in a screw-top jar, and use the small roller in conjunction with a 1in. (25mm.) paintbrush to paint the bottom right-hand section. Apply two coats, allowing 2–4 hours for each coat to dry.

2 Dilute 1tbsp. first color with an equal amount of glazing liquid plus 4tbsp. water on a deep plate. Use a 3in. (75mm.) brush to colorwash the masked-off upper left-hand section, and brush off with a clean, soft 3in. (75mm.) brush and a 1in. (25mm.) brush for the corners (see pp. 124–5). Apply a second coat of colorwash, allowing 2 hours between coats. Remove all the masking, but leave it in place at the top left-hand corner, as more coats of paint are to be applied here.

❶ LILAC, SIENNA, AND CREAM OVER GARNET
The background is 1 pint (500ml.) ready-mixed terracotta red latex flat. The first color is 5tbsp. white latex flat, plus 1¼tsp. raw umber and 2½tsp. each raw and burnt sienna. The second color is 4oz. (120ml.) white latex flat, with ½tsp. each dioxazine purple and Payne's gray, while the third color is 4oz. (120ml.) white latex flat with 2tsp. raw umber.

Allow the second coat of colorwash to dry (4 hours).

3 Mask off the two remaining sections in a similar way, allowing the new masking to overlap the adjoining sections, and not omitting the masking tape for the straight edge.

4 Mix the second and third colors in screw-top jars. Dilute a few tablespoons of each color with equal parts of glazing liquid and 4 parts water on plates. Using the same technique as in step 2, give two coats of colorwash to the top right-hand section with the diluted second color, and two to the bottom left-hand section with the diluted third color.

5 The top corners of the window are painted in the undiluted version of their colorwash. The torn-paper masks that are still in place will create soft edges. For their straight edges, use masking tape placed horizontally and vertically in line with the window opening. Use a small paintbrush to paint each corner. Remove all the masking.

6 At each place where the colors overlap at the sides and at the top, use four pieces of torn paper to mask off a loose diamond motif. Attach the pieces of torn paper to the wall with spray adhesive, and paint each of the diamonds in one of the three colors using a small paintbrush.

❷ GRAY, CAFÉ AU LAIT, AND AQUA OVER OFF-WHITE
This background is 17oz. (500ml.) white latex flat lightly tinted with 4tsp. neutral gray. The first color is 4oz. (120ml.) white latex flat with 1tsp. ultramarine and ½tsp. yellow ocher. The second color is 4oz. (120ml.) white latex flat mixed with 2tsp. each burnt sienna and Payne's gray, and the third color is 6tbsp. white latex flat, plus 2tbsp. ultramarine and 1tbsp. yellow ocher.

Window frame
Remove the masking from the window frame and use one of the 1in. (25mm.) paintbrushes to give the frame two coats of the second color, allowing 2–4 hours for each coat to dry.

LATE-SUMMER
SEEDHEAD FRIEZE

For many of us, this design is reminiscent of the autumn nature collections we made as children and displayed in jars in the school art room. There may be fewer wildflowers around now, but the memory of them can become a permanent installation, thanks to this delicate frieze of painted seedheads.

BASIC RECIPE—GOLDEN HAY

PREPARATION

Prepare the surface thoroughly (see pp. 24–7). Apply two coats of paint to the wall in a color that will complement the frieze.

INGREDIENTS

To cover approximately 43ft.² (4m.²)
Base coat ▶ 1 pint (500ml.) thick, white, non-drip latex flat paint
Resist ▶ aerosol beeswax polish (see p. 20)
Colorwash and shadows ▶ 10tsp. Hansa yellow light artists' acrylic color / 1tsp. raw umber artists' acrylic color
Protective coat ▶ 8½oz. (250ml.) clear polish or beeswax

EQUIPMENT

Paper / tape measure / repositionable spray adhesive / 2 x 4in. (100mm.) paintbrushes / plasterers' float / tracing paper / paper / X-Acto knife / stencil board / cutting mat / water-soluble marker / paper towels / screw-top jar / large container / saucer / cellulose sponge / soft rags / mineral spirits / lint-free cloth

INSTRUCTIONS
Base coat

1 Use torn paper to mask off the area above the frieze. This will create a soft, natural edge in keeping with the design. Do not be tempted to use old newspaper, as the spray adhesive may dissolve the ink and transfer yesterday's news onto your clean wall. Instead, use the clean side of old photocopies. Set the torn edge of the paper about 24in. (60cm.) up from the baseboard, and attach it to the wall with the spray adhesive.
2 Use a paintbrush to apply a thick layer of the latex flat to the wall beneath the paper, and spread it out using the plasterers' float. The aim is to create a patchy texture with vertical marks running up and down the design. Leave the paint to dry overnight.

Stencil

1 Trace the seedhead design (see p. 218), enlarge it on a photocopier, and make it into a stencil (see p. 36). Do not forget to cut the notches on the left of the stencil.
2 Set out the spacing for the design on the wall by positioning the stencil at the left-hand side of the frieze. Use

LATE-SUMMER SEEDHEAD FRIEZE

the water-soluble marker to mark the position of the right-hand side of the stencil on the baseboard and on the paper masking. Move the stencil along until its notches are lined up with these registration marks. Make two more marks where the right-hand edge of the stencil is now. Continue in this way along the wall.

Resist

1 Spray the back of the stencil with adhesive, and place it in its first position.

2 Cover the area all around with paper for protection, then spray the beeswax into the stencil (see p. 150).

3 Remove the stencil from the wall and clean off excess wax

from the front of the stencil using paper towels. To do this, lay the stencil down on a smooth surface—a Formica-topped kitchen table would be ideal—and dab the wax off, making sure that none goes on the back of the stencil.

4 Reposition the stencil in the position after next, using the marker registration marks and the notches as a guide. Spray with wax again. Continue along the wall in this way, cleaning up the stencil each time you use it, until you have completed every alternate position on your frieze. Leave to dry (2–3 hours). If there is any wax on the wall that is still wet at this point,

blot it off carefully with paper towels, but do not rub it, or the wax will spread where you do not want it to go.

5 Repeat steps 1–4 on the remaining alternate sections.

Shadows

1 Mix the shadow color in the screw-top jar. Place half the mixture in the large container and put to one side.

2 Clean the stencil thoroughly, then reposition it on the wall half the width of the stencil to the right of its original position. Set out the registration marks in the new position.

3 Pour a little of the shadow color into a saucer, then lightly sponge and rub in the paint. Move the stencil along the wall as before and repeat the sponging. This will create the shadows of the seedheads that appear behind and to one side of the resist images. Allow to dry (30 minutes).

❷ DUSKY MAUVES
The colors in this swatch have been made from 2tbsp. white, 2tsp. dioxazine purple, 1tsp. ultramarine, and ½tsp. black, applied as in the basic recipe over troweled-on white latex flat. This is a some-what more subdued solution for a subtler interior.

❶ GOLDEN HAY
The basic recipe gives a warm, sunny design that will brighten a room even when the sun is not shining.

❸ SAGE AND LEMON
Here, a wash of 10tsp. Hansa yellow light, diluted with water as in the basic recipe, was applied before the wax resist. The shadow color—also the base for a second wash—is 10tsp. white, ¼tsp. phthalocyanine blue,1tbsp. raw umber, and ½tsp. Payne's gray.

Colorwash

1 Use the remaining shadow color to make a colorwash in the ratio 4 parts water : 1 part paint. Use the two paint-brushes to colorwash the whole of the frieze (see pp. 124–5), then leave to dry (15–20 minutes).

2 Soak a soft rag in mineral spirits and rub the motifs fairly firmly to remove the wax. As you do so, you will reveal the background color which the beeswax will have tinted a warm, amber white. Don't overdo the rubbing if, like us, you prefer to leave a little texture on your motifs.

Protective coat

To protect your work, you should wax it by applying polish with a lint-free cloth. Finally, remove all the masking, and you will have completed your field of seedheads casting their shadows on your wall.

SLOT-MACHINE COUNTER FRONT

Generally, allover designs on walls must not be too busy or they will dominate a room, but in many homes there are small areas that can be given more adventurous treatment. This design, inspired by a slot machine, was chosen partly because of the ease with which the motifs could be applied using large, simple stencils. We were quite playful with the design, but aimed for a degree of sophistication because of the counter's location in a dining area. Hence we rejected garish colors in favor of a more subdued palette. The effect was enhanced by sponging the colors on, leaving some of the background showing through.

BASIC RECIPE—MULTICOLORED

PREPARATION

Prepare the surface thoroughly. See pp. 24–7.

INGREDIENTS

For a counter front up to 32ft.^{2} (3m.^{2})
Base coats ▶ 13½oz. (400ml.) white latex flat paint / 1tsp. each yellow ocher and cadmium yellow artists' acrylic color
Motifs ▶ (artists' acrylic colors used throughout)
Stripes ▶ 4 tbsp. white
Plums ▶ 2tbsp. white / 1tsp. dioxazine purple / 1tsp. ultramarine blue
Lemons ▶ 2tbsp. white / 4tsp. yellow ocher / 1tsp. cadmium yellow
Cherries and stars ▶ 1tbsp. white / 4tsp. yellow ocher / ½tsp. naphthol red
Lucky sevens ▶ 2tbsp. white / 2tsp. yellow ocher / 1tsp. phthalocyanine blue / 1tsp. Payne's gray
Bells ▶ 2tbsp. white / ¼tsp. black / ¼tsp. phthalocyanine blue

EQUIPMENT

1 x 8in. (200mm.) medium-textured paint roller plus tray / container / 7 saucers / 1 large and 6 smaller pieces cellulose sponge / tape measure / spirit level / water-soluble marker / masking tape / tracing paper / pencil / paper / stencil board / repositionable spray adhesive / X-Acto knife / cutting mat / string / 5 screw-top jars

SLOT-MACHINE COUNTER FRONT

1 Use the roller to apply half the white latex flat to the front of the counter. Allow to dry (2–4 hours).

2 Pour the remaining latex flat into the container, and add the yellow ocher and cadmium yellow. Stir well. Spoon some of this mixture into a saucer, and, using the large sponge, apply evenly to the counter front, leaving little flecks of the white base coat showing through (see p. 130). Allow to dry (2–4 hours).

Layout

1 Divide the counter front into groups of three bands, as you would see on a slot machine. On our counter, the three 16½in. (42cm.)-wide bands for the motifs are separated by 2in. (5cm.)-wide white stripes. There is a 2¾in. (7cm.)-wide white stripe at each end of both sets of three bands, and a 2in. (5cm.)-wide gap at the center. Mark out all the lines with a water-soluble marker, and use a spirit level to check that they are completely vertical.

2 Mask out for the white stripes (see pp. 40–1). Spoon the white stripe color, a little at a time, into a saucer, and apply it using a small sponge.

Stencils

1 Cut your stencil board to the width of the widest bands. Trace the images on p. 218, enlarge on a photocopier, and use to make the stencils (see p. 36), making sure that the images are centered before cutting. Include the notches from the images. These will act as registration marks, enabling you to line up the stencils correctly.

2 The stenciled motifs are positioned along horizontal lines 12in. (30cm.) apart. To mark for these, stretch a piece of string from one side of the counter to the other, making sure it is the same distance from the floor at each end. Place masking tape at the points where the strings cross the white lines. Repeat for all the horizontal lines.

3 Lightly spray the back of the first fruit stencil with adhesive, and position it between the white lines, with its notches lined up with the masking-tape horizontals.

4 Mix each of the motif colors in a screw-top jar. Matching the paint to the stencil, spoon some of the color you are going to use into a saucer. With a small sponge, stencil the motif on as evenly as possible (see p. 37), but allow the base

186

coat to show through a little. Remove the stencil, then repeat using each of the other fruit stencils.

5 Repeat using the bells, lucky sevens, and stars stencils in the same way and with their respective paints.

6 To achieve the shadows on the fruits, reposition each stencil, then lightly sponge on the second color, taking care not to overload the sponge with paint. Beginning at the bottom edge of each fruit, dab the color on lightly. Keep your sponge on the move, and as it dries out, move it in toward the center so that the color fades out gradually. Reload your sponge as necessary, but take care not to overdo the shading or it will look too heavy. The plum is shaded using the blue of the bells, the cherries in the plum color, and the lemon with the cherry color.

7 The bells, lucky sevens, and stars do not have shadows. Instead, frame them, using the final stencil, which is, in fact, a half-frame. First position the stencil to make the upper half of the frame, and then the lower half. The sponging leaves no seams. The sevens are framed in the cherry red, the stars in the plum color, and the bells in the yellow of the lemons.

❶ CHERRIES AND BELLS
The cherries use a mixture of white, yellow ocher, and naphthol red, and are shaded with the plum color. The bells are sponged in a mixture of white, black, and phthalo-cyanine blue, and are framed in the lemon yellow.

❷ STARS AND LEMON
The lemon is sponged in a mixture of white, yellow ocher, and cadmium yellow, and is shaded with the cherry color. The stars use the cherry red and are framed in the plum color.

❸ PLUM AND SEVENS
The plum is made of white, dioxazine purple, and ultra-marine blue, and is shaded with the blue of the bells. The lucky sevens are a mixture of yellow ocher, white, phthalocyanine blue, and Payne's gray, and are framed in the cherry red.

DAISY-STREWN
FLOORBOARDS

We wanted this floor to look as if it had been strewn with giant flowers. It may look like a difficult project, but there is no need to be discouraged. Thanks to the use of sponging and large, easy-to-use stencils, you could complete it in a day. The arrangement of the flowers is very casual and can be made to fit any shape or size of room. Our flowers are set within a border, which gives the look of a carpet, but one or two small groups of flowers would also be effective. The design is best suited to old floorboards, but it could be used on any floor. A concrete floor, for example, could well benefit from a gentle carpet of flowers, to add a layer of softness to an otherwise austere surface.

BASIC RECIPE—DAISY WHITES ON GREEN

PREPARATION

Prepare the surface thoroughly. See pp. 24–7.

INGREDIENTS

For a floor approximately 97ft.² (9m.²)
Basic green ▶ 4oz. (120ml.) white latex flat paint / 1tsp. phthalocyanine green artists' acrylic color / ½tsp. Payne's gray artists' acrylic color / ½tsp. raw umber artists' acrylic color / water in the ratio 2 parts water : 1 part color
Basic gray ▶ 8½oz. (250ml.) white latex flat paint / ¼tsp. Payne's gray artists' acrylic color
Petals ▶ 8tbsp. white artists' acrylic color
Yellow tinge ▶ 4tbsp. basic gray / ½tsp. cadmium yellow medium artists' acrylic color / ½tsp. yellow ocher artists' acrylic color
Mauve tinge ▶ 4tbsp. basic gray / scant ¼tsp. dioxazine purple artists' acrylic color
Blue tinge ▶ 4tbsp. basic gray / scant ¼tsp. ultramarine artists' acrylic color
Flower centers ▶ 5tbsp. Hansa yellow light artists' acrylic color / ¼tsp. Payne's gray artists' acrylic color
Stalks ▶ 8tsp. basic green / ½tsp. Payne's gray artists' acrylic color / ½tsp. phthalocyanine green artists' acrylic color
Border ▶ 8tsp. basic green
Protective coat ▶ 2qt. (2 liters) acrylic/polyurethane floor varnish

EQUIPMENT

Tape measure / straightedge / right-angled triangle / masking tape / newspaper / container / 7 screw-top jars / 1 x 6in. (150mm.) paintbrush / tracing paper / pencil / paper / water-soluble marker / repositionable spray adhesive / stencil board / X-Acto knife / cutting mat / 7 saucers / 4 cellulose sponges and 3 smaller pieces / artists' hog-hair fitch / 1 x 6in. (150mm.) varnish brush

DAISY-STREWN FLOORBOARDS

1 Mark out the perimeter of your design with masking tape. Protect any areas that are not to be painted with newspaper, also taped down.

2 Mix the basic green color in the large container and set aside 16tsp. of it in one of the screw-top jars. Make a colorwash with the remainder in the ratio 1 part water : 2 parts color. Use the ordinary paintbrush to lightly wash color onto the unmasked area. Do not attempt to cover all the wood in one coat—keep it loose and leave some gaps. A second coat will cover any bare wood, but for the best effect, you should deliberately aim for an uneven finish. Allow to dry (2–4 hours).

Layout

1 Trace the designs for the flowers on p. 219, and enlarge them as necessary on a photocopier to suit the dimensions of your own floor.

2 Plan your design by scattering the photocopies across the floor until you have a layout you find pleasing, then mark their positions with the marker.

Flowers

1 Use the photocopies to cut your stencils (see p. 36), but do not discard the "positives," as you will need them later to act as masks.

2 Spray the back of each flower stencil lightly with adhesive, then place them in position and mask out the centers with their positives.

3 Spoon some of the petal color into one of the saucers and use it to sponge in the flower stencils. You should aim for a soft, misty effect.

4 Round off the ends of three pieces of sponge, to make dabbers about ¾in. (2cm.) across.

❶ DAISY WHITES ON GREEN
The basic recipe. Here the design has been stenciled in the same colors as on page 188, but onto new floorboards, so the colors do not sink in so readily. It has also been varnished with acrylic varnish, which does not darken the wood as much as polyurethane varnish. It also dries very quickly and, being water-based, is safer and more pleasant to use.

❷ MOODY MAUVES ON GREEN This swatch is more robust in its coloring. For the background colorwash you will need 4oz. (120ml.) white latex flat, 4tbsp. raw umber, 3 tbsp. Payne's gray, and 2tbsp. phthalocyanine green, diluted with water as in the basic recipe. Each flower's petals are sponged in one of three colors: (i) 2tbsp. dioxazine purple, 2tbsp. white, and 1tbsp. raw sienna; (ii) 2tbsp. purple,1tbsp. ultramarine, and 2tbsp. white; or (iii) 2tbsp. each purple, white, and quinacridone red. These petals have all been tinged with the same color—Mars red—freely dabbed on. The flower centers and stalks use the same color as the basic recipe, and the flicks are in quinacridone red.

5 Mix the basic gray in another screw-top jar and use it as the base for each of the petal tinges. Mix all the remaining colors and store each in its own jar. When you need to use a color, spoon some into a saucer and dab your sponge in it.

6 With the flower stencils still in place and the centers masked out, use the dabbers to apply patches of tinge color (one color per flower) at the inner ends of the petals. Continue across the floor, varying the colors as you go. They do not have to be exactly the same since these are wildflowers. Leave to dry (30–60 minutes).

7 Now position the stencils for the flower centers, masking off the petals with their positives. Sponge the centers in with their color. Do this quite loosely and coarsely. Leave to dry (30–60 minutes).

8 Position the stalk stencil for each flower, placing it at varying angles to create the scattered-flower look, and sponge in with its color.

9 Use the same color to add random flicks of green around the flower centers, applying them with the artists' fitch.

Border

Finally, create the border. To do this, add a line of masking tape 1in. (2.5cm.) in from the tape marking the perimeter. Sponge this border in with the remaining basic green.

Protective coat

Remove all masking and leave to dry for two or three days. Using the varnish brush, apply two or three coats of flat acrylic or polyurethane floor varnish according to the manufacturers' instructions. If you opt for a varnish that requires two chemicals to be mixed together, check that it is compatible with water-based paints.

MACKINTOSH-STYLE
STAIRCASE

For this project, we took the set of nine squares so often found in the work of the early twentieth-century Scottish architect and designer Charles Rennie Mackintosh and repeated it up a flight of stairs and around a landing. The strong rectilinear structure of the design makes for an effect that is crisp and contemporary. We also wish to acknowledge our indebtedness to the inventor of masking tape, since this project, along with many others we have carried out for this book, would have taken a whole lot longer to accomplish if masking tape had not been available.

BASIC RECIPE—DARK GRAY AND STONE

PREPARATION

Prepare the surface thoroughly. Since the risers on a staircase often get kicked, they will benefit from a coat of primer. See pp. 24–7.

INGREDIENTS

For a 10-step staircase plus a half-landing
Risers ▶ 10oz. (300ml.) ready-mixed off-white latex flat paint
Border ▶ 6oz. (180ml.) white artists' acrylic color / 3tbsp. raw umber artists' acrylic color / 1tbsp. yellow ocher artists' acrylic color
First square color ▶ 4tbsp. black artists' acrylic color / 2tbsp. white artists' acrylic color / 4tsp. burnt umber artists' acrylic color
Second square color ▶ 2tbsp. white artists' acrylic color / scant ¼tsp. raw umber artists' acrylic color
Protective coat ▶ 1qt. (1 liter) acrylic varnish

EQUIPMENT

1in. (25mm.) safe-release masking tape / paper / X-Acto knife or scissors / 2 x 2in. (50mm.) paintbrushes / 3 screw-top jars / fine-grit sandpaper / tape measure / thin cardboard / pencil / 2 saucers / 2 pieces cellulose sponge / 1 x ¼in. (5mm.) paintbrush / 1 x 3in. (75mm.) varnish brush

INSTRUCTIONS
Risers

Protect the treads with masking tape and paper, then apply two coats of color to the risers using a paintbrush. Allow 4 hours for the first coat to dry, then leave the second coat to dry overnight. Remove the tape and paper.

Border

Using more masking tape, mask off a border, 4½in. (11cm.) wide, down each side of the stairway and around the edge of the half-landing. Mix the border color in a screw-top jar, and, again using a paintbrush, apply two coats of paint to the border, allowing 4 hours between coats. Sand down

each coat after it has dried, but extend the drying time of the final coat as long as possible. The next stage requires you to use a substantial amount of masking tape, and the harder the paint, the less chance there is of its being lifted off when you remove the tape. We were quite firm with our final sanding, as we wished to create a flat and slightly worn look to this paint layer in order for it to blend in well with the wood of the stairs.

Squares

1 In this design, each riser is decorated with six squares and each tread with nine, all in rows of three. The pattern continues around the landing. Each of the squares is 1¾ x 1¾in. (4.5 x 4.5cm.) and is separated by the width of the masking tape. You may need to adjust the size of your squares to fit the dimensions of the stairway you are working on. Mark out the design using masking tape to create the squares (see p. 41). You will need plenty of tape and a lot of time for the masking, but it will be worth the investment of both. You can speed things up by making a "ruler" or template from a strip of thin cardboard, the width of a square. Mark the "ruler" with a row of three squares, spaced and positioned as they will be on the stairs. Use this to mark out the treads and risers for the masking tape. You can make a longer "ruler" to suit the dimensions of your landing.

2 Mix the two colors for all the squares in the remaining screw-top jars. To use each color, place a little of it on a saucer and dab the sponge into it (see p. 130). Begin by sponging the first square color on each tread and riser, but leave one square unpainted on each. You should vary the position of these unpainted squares from riser to riser, and from tread to tread. Similarly, as you sponge in the squares around the landing, leave one square unpainted in every block of nine.

3 Once you have finished sponging on the first color, sponge in the unpainted squares using the second square color. This creates a little nonconformity in the otherwise symmetrical design.

4 Remove all the masking tape with care. If any paint has bled beneath the tape, scratch it off with an X-Acto knife and touch it up with a small paintbrush.

5 Allow to dry for two days, protecting the stairway with clean paper if it is in use.

Protective coat

Apply a minimum of three coats of varnish according to the manufacturers' instructions.

❶ DARK GRAY AND STONE
The basic recipe

❷ STONE AND POWDER BLUE
The risers are as in the basic recipe. The border is 7½oz. (220ml.) white latex flat, 1tbsp. cobalt blue, and 1½tsp. yellow ocher. The first square color is half the border color from the basic recipe, and the second square color is 2tbsp. white, ¼tsp. cobalt blue, ¼tsp. yellow ocher, and ¼tsp. Payne's gray.

❸ DEEP RED AND DARK SLATE
The risers are as in the basic recipe. The border is 4½oz. (130ml.) black, 4tbsp. white, and 3tbsp. burnt umber. The first square color is 3½oz. (100ml.) naphthol red and 1tsp. Payne's gray. The second square color is 2tbsp. of the border color from the basic recipe.

SEAWEED AND SHELL CLOSET

Milk paints would be attractive for these closet doors, and if you have an old house and wish to use traditional paints, they would be the ideal choice. Also called casein paints, they are not widely available, but many manufacturers make an acrylic-based, matte-finish paint that could be used in their place. We have chosen ours from a line developed to look like milk paint in finish and color, and we found it a successful alternative. Whether it will be as durable as the real thing remains to be seen.

BASIC RECIPE—ANTIQUE WHITE WITH SAGE

PREPARATION

Prepare the surface thoroughly. See pp. 24–7.

INGREDIENTS

For 3 large closet doors
First color ▶ 10oz. (300ml.) sage "milk" paint
Second color ▶ 10oz. (300ml.) antique white "milk" paint
Third color ▶ 1tsp. dioxazine purple artists' acrylic color / 1tsp. neutral gray artists' acrylic color
Border squares ▶ ¾tsp. phthalocyanine green artists' acrylic color / 1½tsp. neutral gray artists' acrylic color / 1tsp. white artists' acrylic color

EQUIPMENT

2 x 2in. (50mm.) paintbrushes / 2 x 4in. (100mm.) paintbrushes / tracing paper / pencil / paper / 3 pieces stencil board / repositionable spray adhesive / X-Acto knife / cutting mat / tape measure / water-soluble marker / 3 saucers / 2 cellulose sponges plus 2 rounded-off pieces / fine-grit waterproof sandpaper / bucket of water / 1 x ¼in. (6mm.) square-ended artists' brush / tiny, fine natural sponge

INSTRUCTIONS
Background

1 Using the paintbrushes, apply two coats of the first color to the doors. Begin with the panels, then follow up by painting first the cross rails, then the stiles (verticals). Finish each section by brushing out the paint in the same direction as the grain. We have also painted the paneling surrounding the doors. Allow 1–2 hours for each coat to dry.
2 Apply two coats of the second color in the same way.

SEAWEED AND SHELL CLOSET

Stencils

1 Trace the designs on p. 219, enlarge as necessary, and use to make the first stencil—the wavy rectangles with the seaweed—and the second stencil—the registration marks and the shell motifs (see p. 36).

2 Position the first stencil in the center of the door panel, holding it in place with the spray adhesive. Sponge on some of the first color using a trimmed cellulose sponge (see p. 37). Remove the stencil and repeat the process on the other doors. Leave the paint to dry overnight.

3 Using very fine sandpaper with water, lightly sand the doors, including the stenciled areas and the moldings. Avoid removing too much paint from the stenciled areas, and do not sand the paint back beyond the first color (see pp. 152–3). Rinse the sandpaper frequently in a bucket of water, and use a sponge to mop up the slurry of paint. Clean up well with a fresh sponge and plenty of clean water.

4 Position the second stencil on one of the doors, using the registration marks to line it up with the first stenciled motifs. Sponge on the second color, again using a trimmed cellulose sponge and applying the color a little unevenly to create highlights. Remove the stencil and allow to dry (2 hours). Repeat on the other doors.

5 Cut out from the third piece of stencil board the registration marks and the line details of the shells (see p. 217). Do not cut the lines for the border for the moment. Position this stencil over the already-stenciled motifs, lining it up with the registration marks on each corner.

6 Mix the third color on a saucer, using an artists' brush to blend the paints together. Using a tiny natural sponge (synthetic ones are too coarse), stencil in the details—not too evenly—with this color. Remove the stencil and allow to dry (30 minutes). Repeat on the other doors.

❶ ANTIQUE WHITE WITH SAGE

The basic recipe. The antique white and pale sage green showing through suit this room beautifully, giving it a Scandinavian air.

❷ SKY BLUE WITH ANTIQUE WHITE

Here we have painted two coats of sky blue "milk" paint— a total of 10oz. (300ml.)—over two coats of antique white— also 10oz. (300ml.) The third color, for the stencil details, is a mixture of 1½tsp. white and ¼tsp. each burnt sienna and burnt umber. The border squares are in 4tsp. white plus ¼tsp. phthalocyanine green.

❸ PRIMROSE YELLOW WITH EGGPLANT

We began with 10oz. (300ml.) eggplant "milk" paint, followed by 10oz. (300ml.) primrose yellow. The third color is a mixture of 1½tsp. white and ¼tsp. each phthalocyanine blue and neutral gray. The border squares are a lighter version of these colors, made by doubling the quantity of white.

Border

1 Cut the lines for the border out of the third stencil. Reposition this, and use as a template to draw in the border.

2 Mix the border squares color on a saucer, and use a square-ended artists' brush to paint in the small squares between the marked border lines. Make sure that you end up with a square in each corner.

PAINTED PANES ON A PART-GLAZED DOOR

If you are looking for an alternative to glass curtains or Venetian blinds, painting a window may be the answer. It can be more than just a device to distract your eye when there is a less-than-pretty view on the other side. Painting a window is also a lovely way to filter the light that passes through it, and on bright sunny days the colors of the paint will be projected into the room, which can be uplifting, summer or winter. A painted interior glass door will also give a room color that changes as the daylight fades and lamps are turned on.

The windows on these pages were decorated with a paint designed to give the appearance of colored or stained glass. It was bought from an artists' supplier. Once it has hardened, you can clean the glass with a soft cloth, but use only the mildest of detergents.

We wanted to stencil the design and found the best material to make the stencil was self-adhesive plastic film attached to the glass before the motifs were cut out from it. It sticks firmly to the glass, but can be removed easily. We had first tried using acetate and met with some success, but even though the acetate was attached with spray adhesive, the very liquid paint seeped underneath, leaving us with a very messy clean-up operation.

After painting the glass, we chose a harmonizing yellow color to paint the door frame.

BASIC RECIPE—SKY BLUE AND OLIVE

PREPARATION

Prepare the surfaces thoroughly. See pp. 24–7.

INGREDIENTS

For an average window
First color ▶ 1¾oz. (50ml.) sky blue opaque glass paint
Second color ▶ 1¾oz. (50ml.) olive green opaque glass paint
Door frame ▶ 5tbsp. white latex flat paint / 2tbsp. yellow ocher artists' acrylic color / 3tbsp. Hansa yellow light artists' acrylic color / 2tsp. raw umber artists' acrylic color

EQUIPMENT

Tracing paper / pencil / paper / clear acetate (optional) / glue stick / repositionable spray adhesive / transparent self-adhesive plastic film / X-Acto knife / masking tape / 2 saucers / 2 small, rounded-off pieces cellulose sponge / container / 1 x 2in. (50mm.) paintbrush / 1 x 1in. (25mm.) paintbrush

INSTRUCTIONS
Layout

1 Trace the spiral and leaf motifs on p. 219 and enlarge them on a photocopier, making several copies. Arrange them into a design that will fit your door. On our door, we decorated a top and bottom row of panes. Each pane was

divided into three equal bands, with the motifs in each reversed from pane to pane. To make the reversed motifs, photocopy them onto acetate and turn the copies over. If acetate is not available, tape photocopied motifs back to front on a window, and pencil over the image seen. On our door, the upper panes had leaves in the top two bands and spirals in the lower band. The lower panes had spirals in the top band and leaves in the lower two bands. The instructions that follow are for panes with spirals in the top band.

2 Once you have planned your design, glue the individual motifs in position on a sheet of paper that fits your panes, and attach to the glass with a light spray of adhesive.

Stencil

1 Cut pieces of transparent self-adhesive plastic film to the exact size of your window panes, and attach them to the front of the glass. This plastic film is to become your stencil.

2 Using an X-Acto knife, cut carefully along the lines of the design as seen through the glass. (A word of caution: The point of the knife will leave lines scratched on most types of glass. These will not be visible after the painting, as the edges of the paint will coincide with them, but if you decide subsequently to remove the paint, they will show. To prevent this, you can cut the stencils from the plastic film before you stick it down, but be warned that this is a much more tricky procedure.)

3 Peel away the following sections of the stencils: from the lower band, peel off the background, leaving the leaf shapes in place; from the middle band, peel away the leaves, leaving the background in place; from the top band, peel away the background, leaving the spirals in place. You will now be left with a stencil attached to your glass, which the glass paint cannot get behind.

4 Protect the door frame around the glass with masking tape, then, starting with the middle band, also mask off below the leaf stems to prevent the color from seeping into the lower band.

5 Pour a little of the first color into a saucer. Use a small piece of sponge to apply it to the leaves in the middle band. Sponge the color out, working continuously until you have an even texture (see pp. 168–9). Allow to dry (4 hours).

6 Remove the masking from below the stems, and protect the work you have just completed with masking tape laid

❶ SKY BLUE AND OLIVE
The basic recipe. This rather Mediterranean color combination would bring a warm glow to any room.

❷ GRAY AND TURQUOISE
Here the central leaves have been stenciled in gray glass paint, and the two outer bands in turquoise. To make the color for the door frame, mix ½tsp. each phthalo-cyanine green and burnt umber into 6oz. (180ml.) white latex flat.

delicately across stems and leaf tips, where they touch the top and bottom bands.

7 Pour a little of the second color into a saucer, and with a fresh piece of sponge apply it to the top and bottom bands, sponging out as before. Allow to dry (4 hours).

8 Remove the plastic-film stencils and masking tape from the door frame to reveal your design crisply painted on the glass. At this stage it will still be a little delicate, but it becomes harder after a few days.

Door frame

Mix the paint for the door frame in the container, and use the paintbrushes to apply two coats, allowing 2–4 hours for each coat of paint to dry.

JAPANESE FABRIC
SCREEN

This project combines rugged builders' props with a light, translucent fabric. It would be an excellent way of screening off an area of a room for those of you who do not wish to use more traditional screens. When choosing a site for your screen, make sure that the ceiling is solid enough to take the upward force of the props. If possible, locate the screen below a beam. There will be no need to over-tighten the props, as they will be supporting only the fabric, not the building.

BASIC RECIPE—RAW SIENNA AND NEUTRAL GRAY ON CREAM

PREPARATION

Prepare the surface thoroughly. See pp. 24–7.

INGREDIENTS

For a screen 6½ x 4½ft. (2 x 1.4m.)
Screen ▶ 6½ x 5ft. (2 x 1.5m) dark cream firmly woven fabric / 13ft. (4m.) double-sided transparent tape / 7ft. x ½in. (2.2m. x 12mm.)-diameter metal rod / 6½ft. x ½in. (2m. x 12mm.)-diameter metal rod / 2 adjustable builders' props to suit your room size
First color ▶ 2tbsp. raw sienna artists' acrylic color
Second color ▶ 2tbsp. neutral gray artists' acrylic color
Lines ▶ 2tbsp. white artists' acrylic color
Optional ▶ aerosol can silver paint

EQUIPMENT

2 large pieces stencil board / 1in. (25mm.)-wide (minimum) masking tape / straightedge / pencil / 20in. (50cm.) string plus pin / scissors / tape measure / repositionable spray adhesive / 3 large pieces cellulose sponge / 3 saucers / paper / scraps of padding (see Notes)

INSTRUCTIONS
Stencil

1 The design is made up of three large motifs, each stenciled using the same 24in. (60cm.)-diameter stencil. Since stencil board rarely comes this big, you will have to join two pieces of board together. To do this, lay the two pieces flat on a table or on the floor with their edges butting up to one another, then stick masking tape down the joining on both faces of the board.
2 Use the straightedge and a pencil to mark the diagonals of the board; to draw the circle, pin the end of the string at the center of the board where the diagonals cross. Pull the string

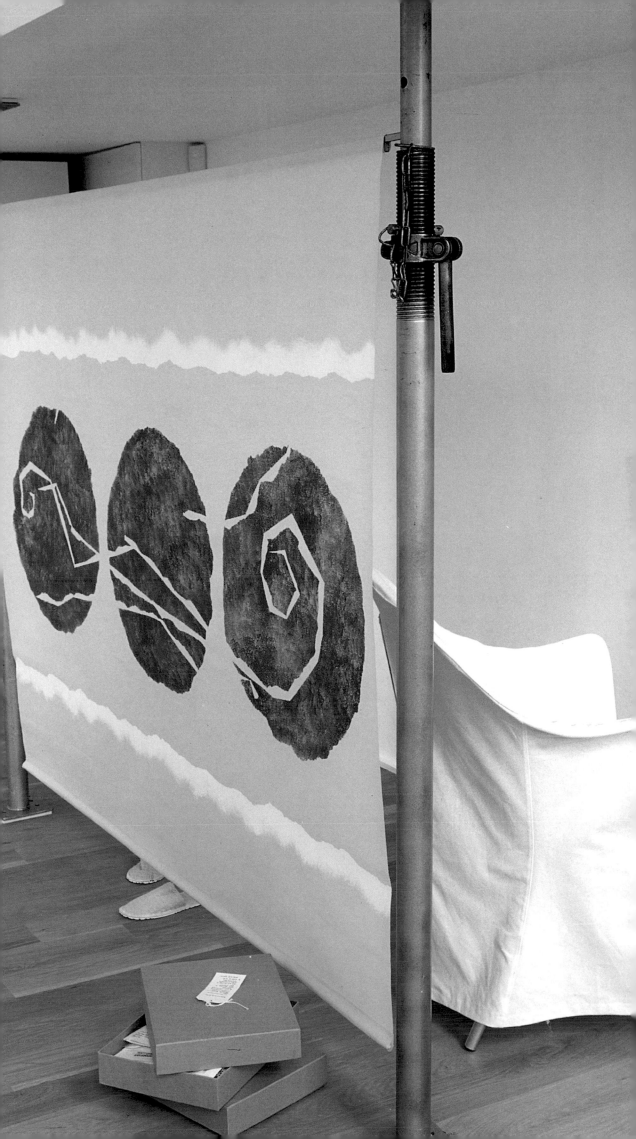

JAPANESE FABRIC SCREEN

tight, and attach the pencil 12in. (30cm.) from the pin using masking tape. Place the pencil point on the board and sweep it around the pin, keeping the string taut. Do not worry if the circle you end up with is less than perfect.

3 Make a hole in the stencil board with the scissors, then carefully tear the board along the line you have drawn to remove the circle.

Motifs

1 Lay the fabric out on a flat surface. Use the floor if you do not have a table large enough. The motifs are stenciled horizontally across the center of the material, with 2in. (5cm.) spaces between. Measure out and mark for the positioning of the motifs using small pieces of masking tape. Do not use pencil or marker, as these marks will be difficult to remove from the fabric.

2 Spray the back of the stencil with adhesive and place it in its first position.

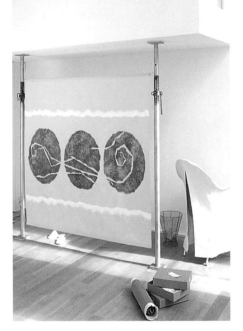

3 To make the lines that run through the circles, firmly stick small strips of masking tape, torn along their length, to the fabric framed by the stencil. Build up the design following the examples shown here.

4 Trim two of the pieces of cellulose sponge into balls, using scissors. Spoon a little of each of the first and second colors into separate saucers, and use the rounded pieces of sponge to apply them to the fabric. The textured effect is created by sponging on the two colors at the same time and letting them overlap in places. There is no need to blend them into one another.

5 Remove the masking tape and the stencil, and allow to dry (20 minutes).

6 Repeat, placing the stencil in its second and third positions. For each new motif, use fresh masking tape positioned so as to continue the linear element of the design.

Lines

1 A sponged white line runs 6in. (15cm) above and below the row of circles. The inner edge of each of these lines is masked off with segments of torn paper (see p. 42). The outer edge is faded off with the sponge. Use a long straightedge laid on the fabric as a guide to positioning the first torn-paper mask. Spoon some of the white paint into

JAPANESE FABRIC SCREEN

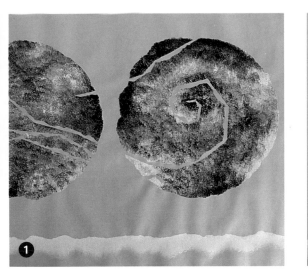

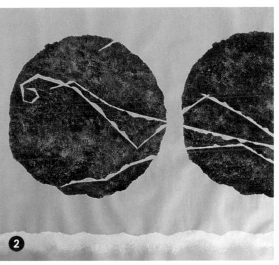

another saucer, and use a sponge to apply it along this edge, fading the color away to make a line approximately 2in. (5cm.) wide. You are not aiming for a line of a perfectly constant width. Remove the masking paper and allow to dry (20 minutes).

2 Repeat for the second line, allowing 1 hour to dry.

Making the screen

1 Turn the stenciled fabric over and stick half the double-sided tape to the top edge. Lay the longer rod on the tape, leaving 4in. (10cm.) protruding at each end. Roll the fabric over and around the rod, fixing it in place with the tape.

2 Repeat, using the shorter rod for the lower edge of the stenciled fabric.

3 If you feel, as we did, that the adjustable props need smartening up, spray them with the spray paint, following the manufacturers' instructions.

4 Now you will need some help. Adjust the props to the height of your room, and set one prop in position, making sure that the holes in its inner sliding section face inward. Slot the longer rod of the screen into one of these holes at the desired height, making sure that the screen is facing the right way around.

5 Move the second prop into place, pushing it along the floor until the rod slides into the corresponding hole on this prop. Fix the second prop in position, and your screen is finished and in place.

Notes Builders' props are not the most delicate of objects and can leave marks on your floor and ceiling. Prevent this by using padding. Scraps of foam rubber, cork, or carpet would all be suitable.

❶ ACHROMATIC The first color uses 2tbsp. Payne's gray and the second 2tbsp. white, in addition to the 2tbsp. white for the two lines.

❷ COBALT BLUE AND TERRACOTTA The first color is 2tbsp. cobalt blue, and the second is 2tbsp. Mars red. The white lines are as in the basic recipe. This recipe gives a more colorful version.

MOCK SLATE
COFFEE TABLE

Slate slabs look wonderful but would be too heavy for a table that is sometimes moved around. They are also expensive. Our alternative—mock slate produced with artists' acrylic color which is burnished as it dries—overcomes both these problems. We took the opportunity to combine it with a painted design. For our basic recipe, we applied it in a deep sea blue to a wooden surface, but there is no reason why it could not be applied in other colors to other surfaces—garden pots, for example, or stenciled motifs on a sunroom wall.

BASIC RECIPE—DEEP SEA BLUE AND SLATE GRAY

PREPARATION

Prepare the surface thoroughly. See pp. 24–7.

INGREDIENTS

For a coffee table
Base coat ▶ 3½oz. (100ml.) white latex flat paint
First color ▶ 2tbsp. Payne's gray artists' acrylic color
Second color ▶ 1tsp. phthalocyanine blue artists' acrylic color / 1tsp. phthalocyanine green artists' acrylic color
Slate undercoat ▶ 3½oz. (100ml.) black latex flat paint
Slate top coat ▶ 5tbsp. Payne's gray artists' acrylic color / 1tbsp. white artists' acrylic color / 1tbsp. phthalocyanine green artists' acrylic color / 2tsp. burnt umber artists' acrylic color
Lines ▶ 1tsp. neutral gray artists' acrylic color / ½tsp. Mars black artists' acrylic color
Burnishing ▶ small can of furniture wax or beeswax
Protective coat ▶ 1–2tbsp. furniture wax

EQUIPMENT

Small, smooth paint roller plus tray / fine-grit sandpaper / tape measure / water-soluble marker / 2 saucers / 3 cellulose sponges / bowl of water / 3 screw-top jars / paper / repositionable spray adhesive / 1 x 2in. (50mm.) paintbrush / flexible spatula / medium flat artists' brush / lint-free cloth

INSTRUCTIONS
Base coat

Use the smooth roller to paint the whole table top with the latex flat paint. This will leave a fine, smooth texture. Allow to dry (4 hours), then sand lightly.

Cross

Our table measures 48 x 18in. (120 x 45cm.). The long arm of the cross on it is 2½in. (6cm.) wide, and the short arm is 5½in. (14cm.) wide. The dimensions of yours will depend on the size of your table. Using a tape measure and the water-soluble marker, roughly sketch out the cross, drawing it 2in. (5cm.) larger all around than the finished design. Do not forget to extend the arms of the cross over the edges of the table as we did.

First and second colors

1 Spoon a little of the first color into a saucer, and sponge it loosely into the cross. There is no need to attempt to sponge a neat edge, as this will be created at a later stage. Before the paint dries, splash and flick water onto it, then sponge off with a clean, damp sponge to leave a variegated texture (see pp. 131–2). Allow to dry (1 hour).

2 Mix the second color in a small screw-top jar, and spoon a little into a saucer. With a clean, barely damp sponge, rub a transparent layer of this color over the first. Allow to harden (1 hour).

Masking

1 Again using the water-soluble marker, lightly redraw the cross, this time to the exact dimensions. Mask off the cross using torn paper held in place with spray adhesive (see p. 41). If you tear the paper along its grain, it will give the cross its straight, soft edges. Again, remember to extend the arms of the cross over the edges of the table.

2 With the paintbrush and the slate undercoat, paint in the four exposed rectangles of the table top. Allow the paint to dry (4 hours).

Burnishing

1 Mix together the colors for the slate top coat in another screw-top jar. Use the spatula to apply this mixture to a small area of a painted rectangle. Create the polished-slate look by

burnishing the paint. To achieve this, use small, circular movements of the spatula while the paint dries. As the paint becomes tacky, add a little wax to the surface and continue burnishing. The wax makes it easier to manipulate the spatula and also forms part of the hard, polished, slate-like finish as it is driven into the paint. Add more wax as and when you need it.

With practice, you will be able to judge when the paint is dry enough for burnishing, as well as what slight changes can be achieved in the patina by variations in the timing, waxing, and burnishing.

Work across the surface of the table in this way, and don't stop until

❶ DEEP SEA BLUE AND SLATE GRAY The basic recipe.

❷ VENETIAN RED AND SLATE GRAY Here, the base coat, the first color, and the slate undercoat and top coat are as in the basic recipe. The second color is 2tsp. magenta and 1tsp. burnt sienna, while the lines are painted using 1½tsp. neutral gray.

❸ DARK YELLOW AND SLATE GRAY Again, the base coat, the first color, and the slate undercoat and top coat re as in the basic recipe. The second color uses 2tsp. Hansa yellow light and ¼tsp. neutral gray, and the lines are painted using a mixture of 1tsp. neutral gray and ¾tsp. white.

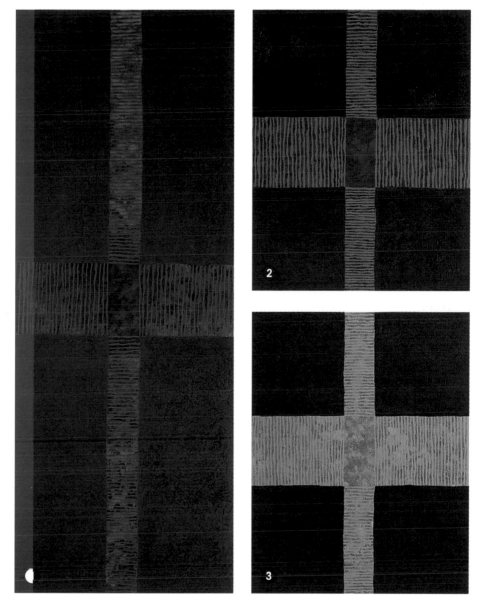

you have completed a whole rectangle. Treat the edges of the table in the same way. The whole procedure will take some time, but it is not arduous, and there is great satisfaction to be gained from watching the texture surface form beneath the spatula as you work.

2 Remove all the paper masking and leave the paint to harden thoroughly overnight.

Lines

Mix the color for the lines in another screw-top jar, and use the artists' brush to paint them across the arms of the cross. Twist the brush a little as you paint in order to create variations in width. Note that the central section of the table does not have any lines. Allow to dry for a day.

Protective coat

Use a soft, lint-free cloth to wax the whole table.

CHECKERBOARD
TABLE TOPS

Table tops—provided they are finished with a protective coat to stop them from getting damaged during use—are the ideal surface for many of the decorative paint techniques we use in this book. These checkerboard table tops are another example of what can be achieved. If we had painted a regular checkerboard pattern on them, they could have been used for playing checkers, but we decided to throw in an asymmetric section, which varies from table to table. You will find that the squares-within-squares are easy to mark out and apply. You will also be able to adapt them to suit any size table. And if you do not have a table, then just paint a board of the size you want, and set it on the biggest wheels you can find.

BASIC RECIPE—SAGE ON RED

PREPARATION

Prepare the surface thoroughly. See pp. 24–7.

INGREDIENTS

For a small side table
Base coat ▶ 6tbsp. white latex flat paint
First color ▶ 2tbsp. Payne's gray artists' acrylic color
Second color ▶ 1tbsp. magenta artists' acrylic color / ½tbsp. alizarin crimson artists' acrylic color
Green checks ▶ 4tsp. white artists' acrylic color / 1tsp. phthalocyanine green artists' acrylic color / 1½tsp. Payne's gray artists' acrylic color / 2tsp. raw umber artists' acrylic color
Beige checks ▶ 2tsp. white artists' acrylic color / ¼tsp. raw umber artists' acrylic color
Gray checks ▶ 2tsp. Payne's gray artists' acrylic color
Protective coat ▶ 3tbsp. matte or satin acrylic varnish

EQUIPMENT

1 x 3in. (75mm.) paintbrush / fine-grit sand-paper / 4 saucers / 4 cellulose sponges / bowl of water / 2 screw-top jars / ruler / water-soluble marker / 2 x ⅜in. (10mm.) flat artists' brushes / 1 x 2in. (50mm.) varnish brush

CHECKERBOARD TABLE TOPS

INSTRUCTIONS
Base coats

Using the paintbrush, apply two coats of white latex flat, allowing 4 hours for each coat to dry. Sand down lightly between coats and after the last coat has dried, to remove any bits of hardened paint or dust; otherwise they may show up later as white spots in the finished surface.

First and second colors

1 Spoon the Payne's gray into a saucer and sponge it loosely onto the table top and sides (see p. 130).

2 Immediately splash the surface with water, then use a clean sponge to sponge off some of the gray paint, leaving a heavily variegated texture (see pp. 131–2). Allow the paint to dry (1 hour).

3 Mix together the magenta and alizarin crimson in a saucer. Dip a clean, damp sponge into this mix and rub it into the surface, leaving a transparent coating over the gray. Your table top should now look like an exotic piece of polished marble. Allow to dry (1 hour).

Painting the checks

1 Meanwhile, mix the colors for the checks.

2 Mark a checkerboard grid on the table top, using the marker. Aim for squares with sides of approximately 2in. (5cm.). Each of our designs is different, although all are based on a common grid. In this example, a group of twenty-one squares has been subdivided into smaller squares.

3 Using the artists' brushes, paint the squares, the alternate larger ones in green and the smaller ones in beige and

Payne's gray. Spoon a small amount of each color into a saucer, and load your brushes from there. If the paint does not flow smoothly, you may need to add a little water.

4 As you complete every two or three squares and before they dry, flick or splash a little water over them, as you did earlier. Leave for a moment, then press a clean, damp sponge onto the squares to create the texture seen in the example. Don't forget to paint the edges.

5 Set your table aside for a couple of days after finishing it to allow the paint to really harden off. Using the varnish brush, apply a minimum of two coats of varnish according to the manufacturers' instructions.

❶ SAGE ON RED
The basic recipe.

❷ DUSTY MAUVE ON EMERALD
Our second table top, which is predominantly green, is started in the same manner as the first. The first color is 2tbsp. Payne's gray. Two coats of phthalocyanine green, a total of 2tbsp., are rubbed into it to make quite a dark tone. The larger checks are painted in a mixture of 4tsp. white, 2tsp. ultramarine, 1tsp. Payne's gray, and ½tsp. magenta. The subdivided checks are painted with 2tsp. Mars red and 2tsp. Payne's gray.

❸ DUSTY MAUVE ON LIME
The third table top begins again with a sponged-on base coat of white latex flat, followed by a coat of 2tbsp. Payne's gray as the first color. A thin coat of 1tbsp. Hansa yellow light is rubbed into that. This gives a lovely depth to the painted surface, remin iscent of marble, though it must be said it is not a marble you are likely to find in a quarry. In this design, a line of larger checks has been added, crossing from one side to the other. The blue checks are in the same blue as the checks in recipe 2, while the green checks are in 2tsp. green from the basic recipe, and the red checks are painted using 2tsp. Mars red.

MOTIFS & TEMPLATES

Most of the motifs we have used in our designs have been drawn here for you to trace. Many of them will have to be enlarged or reduced; this can be done on a photocopier. Any registration marks must be included, as they are essential to the correct placement of the motif in a design. To transfer the full-size design to the surface being decorated, cover the wrong side of the paper with chalk, position the design, and go over the lines firmly with a hard pencil.

Pages 137–8: An ornate stamp

Pages 142–3: Oak-leaf border

Pages 144–5: A simple border

Pages 147–8: Stippled panels

Page 149: Painted wax resist

Pages 157–8: Overlapping stencils

Pages 160–2: Seaside doors

Pages163–5: Fossil table design

Pages 166–7: *Rose des vents*

Pages 168–9: Painting on glass

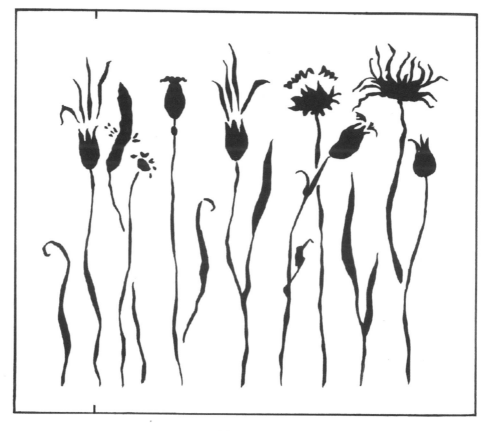

Pages 180–1: Late-summer seedhead frieze

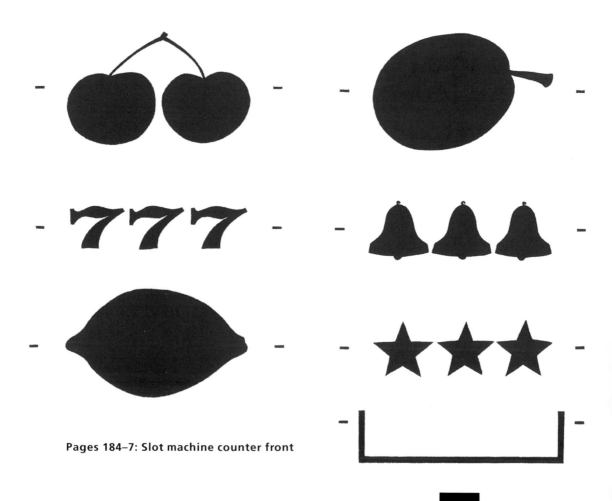

Pages 184–7: Slot machine counter front

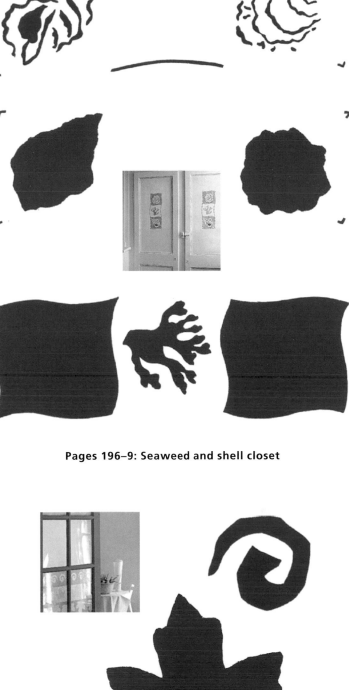

Pages 196–9: Seaweed and shell closet

Pages 189–91: Daisy-strewn floorboards

Pages 200–3: Painted panes on a part-glazed door

LIST OF SUPPLIERS

Most of the tools and material used in this book are available from DIY stores or artists' suppliers. Should you find difficulty obtaining any item, consult the following list of specialist stockists, suppliers and manufacturers. Many manufacturers will give advice on their products, supply catalogues, and may send goods by mail order.

✉ indicates that a mail-order service is available.

3M
ph: 800 722 5463
Call this number for your local supplier of Fineline tape.

Arch ✉
99 Missouri St.
San Francisco
CA 94107
ph: 415 433 2724

The Art Store
(locations nationwide)
www.artstore.com

Carter Sexton ✉
5308 Laurel Canyon Blvd.
North Hollywood
CA 91607
ph: 818 763 5050
fx: 818 763 1034
www.cartersexton.com

Charrette Favor Ruhl ✉
(main location)
31 Olympia Ave.
Woburn
MA 01888
ph: 800 367 3729
fx: 800 626 7889

Curry's Art Supplies ✉
755 The Queensway E
Mississauga,
Ontario
L4Y 4C5
P.O. Box 8696560
ph: 905 272 4460

Dean & Berry Paint & Wallcovering ✉
1380 East 5th Ave.
Columbus
OH 43219
ph: 614 257 7420

Easy Leaf Products ✉
6001 Santa Monica Blvd.
Los Angeles
CA 90038
ph: 213 469 0856
fx: 213 469 0940
www.easyleaf.com

Flax Art Supplies
(locations nationwide)
www.flaxart.com

Gurly's Inc. ✉
2468 South Colorado Blvd.
Denver
CO 80222
ph: 3003 758 8244
fx: 718 361 7288

Janovic/Plaza Inc. ✉
30-35 Thomson Ave.
Long Island City
NY 11101
ph: 718 392 3999
fx: 718 361 7288
www.janovic.com

Jean Hansen Publications ✉
14 Long Sands Rd.
Center Ossipee
NH 03814
ph: 800 399 4276
fx: 603 539 5060

Johnson Paint Co., Inc. ✉
355 Newbury St.
Boston
MA 02115
ph: 617 536 4065/4244
   800 404 8114
fx: 617 536 8832
www.johnsonpaint.com

Liberon/Star Supplies ✉
18701 N. Highway One
Fort Bragg
CA 95437
ph: 800 245 5611
fx: 800 877 3696
www.liberonsupply.com

Pearl Paint Co., Inc. ✉
58 Lispenard St.
New York
NY 10013
ph: 212 334 4530
www.pearlpaint.com

Progress Paint, KCI ✉
201 East Market St.
Louisville
KY 40202
ph: 502 584 0151

Reed's Gold Leaf ✉
216 Douglas St.
Madison
TN 37115
ph: 615 865 2666
fx: 615 865 1903

Rex Art ✉
2263 SW 37 Ave.
Miami
FL 33145
ph: 305 445 1413
   800 REX ART2
fx: 305 445 1412

Seattle Art Supply ✉
2108 Western Ave.
Seattle
WA 98121
ph: 206 625 0711
fx: 206 624 1785
www.seattleartsupply.com

Sepp Leaf Products, Inc. ✉
381 Park Avenue South
New York
NY 10016
ph: 212 683 2840
orders: 800 971 SEPP
fx: 212 725 0308
www.seppleaf.com

Spectrum Paint Co., Inc. ✉
9401 Pole Rd.
Oklahoma City
OK 73160
ph:405 632 6226
fx: 405 632 1181

Texas Art Supply ✉
2001 Montrose Blvd.
Houston
TX 77006
ph: 713 526 5221
   800 888 9278
fx: 713 526 4062
www.texasart.com

Zim's Inc. ✉
Box 57620
Salt Lake City
UT 84107
ph: 801 268 2505
   800 453 6420
fx: 801 268 9859

Standard–metric equivalents
Equivalents given in this book vary occasionally, depending on the context: precise equivalents are given where proportions would be altered by rounding up or down; rough equivalents may be given elsewhere for convenience. It is important therefore to choose either one system or the other and stick to it throughout the recipe.

INDEX

INDEX

INDEX

ACKNOWLEDGMENTS

TEXT ACKNOWLEDGMENTS
Text on the following pages by Lynne Robinson and Richard Lowther: 9–11, 20–22, 24–7, 30–43, 94–5, 122–215. Text on the following pages by Liz Wagstaff: 12–19, 46–93, 96–119.

PICTURE ACKNOWLEDGMENTS
The publisher wishes to thank the following photographers and organizations for their kind permission to reproduce the photographs in this book:

48 Elizabeth Whiting & Associates; 51 Mick Hales; 58 The Interior Archive/Christopher Simon-Sykes (artist: Celia Lyttleton); 60 The Interior Archive/Simon Brown (designer: Christopher Gollut); 68 Arcaid/Richard Bryant (Costa Careyes Villa, between Puerto Vallarta and Nanzamillo on the Mexican Pacific Ocean); 76 © Trevor Richards/Homes & Gardens/IPC Syndication; 83 The Interior Archive/Simon Brown (designer: François Gilles); 87 Elizabeth Whiting & Associates/David George; 89 Elizabeth Whiting & Associates/David George; 90 Paul Ryan/International Interiors (designer: Shinbach); 98 Arcaid/Ken Kirkwood (Penhow Castle, Gwent); 107 Paul Ryan/International Interiors; 112 Elizabeth Whiting & Associates/Andreas von Einsiedel.

All the special photography was by Debbie Patterson, with the exception of the verdigris garden fountain on page 109, which was photographed by Linda Burgess. Studio photography of paint samples, materials, and equipment was by Nicki Dowey (pages 9–11, 20–2, 24–5, 30–32, 34–43, 94–5, 125, 127–9, 131–3, 135–9, 141, 143, 145, 147–51, 153–5, 157–60, 162, 164, 167, 169, 175, 179, 183, 187, 190–1, 195, 199, 203, 207, 211, 215) and Patrick McLeavey (pages 12–19, 28, 49, 53, 55, 57, 59, 61–5, 67, 69, 71–5, 77–8, 81–2, 86, 88, 91, 93, 97, 99–102, 104, 106, 108, 113–4, 116, 119). The paint roller illustrations are by Clive Goodyer.

PUBLISHER'S ACKNOWLEDGMENTS
Special thanks to Fred Johnston and Robert Kramer of ACE Hardware in Williamsburg, Virginia, for their help in preparing this book.